Things Just Haven't Been the Same

Things Just Haven't Been the Same

MAKING THE TRANSITION FROM MARRIAGE TO PARENTHOOD

BRAD E. SACHS, PH.D.

WILLIAM MORROW AND COMPANY, INC.

NEW YORK

It is the policy of William Morrow and Company, Inc., and its imprints and affiliates, recognizing the importance of preserving what has been written, to print the books we publish on acid-free paper, and we exert our best efforts to that end.

Library of Congress Cataloging-in-Publication Data

Sachs, Brad E., 1956-
    Things just haven't been the same: making the transition from marriage to parenthood/
    Brad E. Sachs.
        p. cm.
    Includes bibliographical references.
    ISBN 0-688-10183-6
    1. Parenthood—United States. 2. Marriage—United States.
I.–Title.
HQ755.8.S23 1992   92-13322
306.87—dc20   CIP

Printed in the United States of America

First Edition

1 2 3 4 5 6 7 8 9 10

BOOK DESIGN BY BARBARA COHEN ARONICA

This book is dedicated with love and respect to my wife and best friend, Karen, and our exhilarating seventeen-year ride down Thunder Road,

to the memory of my grandmother, Fannie Glynn (1906–1992), who has finally been reunited with my grandfather, Willie Glynn (1903–1987), and is back to making sure he isn't being taken advantage of,

and

to the memory of my grandfather, Jack Sachs (1905–1992), who smiles down upon me from Cloud Nine every day and every night.

ACKNOWLEDGMENTS

A first book is literally a lifetime in the making, so my gratitude extends in many different directions.

I would like to begin by thanking Saul Rogolsky, Ph.D., and Laura Dittmann, Ph.D., of the Institute for Child Study at the University of Maryland, College Park, Frank Pedersen, Ph.D., of NIMH, and Ruth Lebovitz, Ph.D, for encouraging and stimulating me in my early desire to study the processes of parenthood while I was in graduate school.

Few therapists ripen and develop the capacity to heal others without having a chance to walk through their own wounds and experience healing themselves. My own therapist, Barry Sternfeld, Ph.D., and the therapy group he leads with Fred Klein, Ph.D., hung in there with me during some of my most turbulent times, and honored and celebrated my efforts to change and grow beyond my bewildering past.

I am deeply indebted to Phyllis Stern, M.A., with whom I have been studying individual, marital, and family therapy for seven years, and who also agreed to work with Karen and me during our own transition into parenthood, and became the midwife of our marriage's rebirth. This book is a direct reflection of what I have learned and am learning from her, and from my on-going six-year tutorial in psychotherapy with Elena Manzanera, M.S., which remains a profoundly instructive and inspiring experience.

I joined the consultation group led by Halcy Bohen, Ph.D., when I had already finished the bulk of this manuscript, but it continues to be a wonderfully enlightening process, and what I have learned there has certainly insinuated itself into what I have to say.

My dear colleagues Joanne Irving, Ph.D., John Rhead, Ph.D., Andre Papantonio, M.A., and Lois Chester, L.C.S.W., have taught me a tremendous amount both about therapy and friendship. Special thanks to Tom Burns, Ph.D., and Martha Rubenstein, Ph.D., for their warmth and understanding, and for their thoughtful readings of this book at its various stages of development. I continue to cherish *mio fratello* Steve Rosch's faith in my abilities, and am beholden to Scott Strahlman, M.D., for our weekly conferences on family life that were held on the racquetball court.

My oldest friends, David Gilberg and Norman Gross, and my newest friend, Roberta Israeloff, have always been there with a shoulder to cry on, valuable perspective, and a willingness to talk baseball. It would have been enough if our obstetrician, David Nagy, M.D., Ph.D., had simply helped to bring our children into the world, but I am also appreciative of his backing my efforts to address the needs and concerns of new fathers everywhere.

My agent, Madeleine Morel, has been irredeemably patient and optimistic, and I am so grateful that she stuck with me during "the lean years." My editor at William Morrow, Harriet Bell, good-naturedly tolerated my early thousand-page manuscripts and hundred-page chapters without getting discouraged, and was always available with a helpful comment or a sympathetic ear during the many times I was feeling stuck and confused. I can't imagine having a more astute and sensitive mentor.

I am also especially appreciative of the tireless editorial efforts of Beth Rashbaum, who discovered the "book within the book" and gently but firmly helped me to lure it to the surface.

I owe a lot to Anne Winthrop and *American Baby* magazine for publishing my first attempts at writing for the general public, and for inviting me to contribute the Dad's Corner column for the past several years. I have also appreciated the forum that Bruce Raskin and *Parenting* magazine have provided for my research and viewpoints to be articulated.

I, of course, cannot thank my patients individually, but I would like all of them to know that I greatly value my relationship with them, and feel fortunate to have witnessed, learned from, and participated in their courageous voyages of self-discovery.

My extended family has sustained me in many different ways during the turmoil of early parenthood and the writing of this book. My brothers and sisters-in-law, Paul Sachs, Ph.D., and Janet Sachs, Ph.D., and Lee and Deborah Sachs, and my parents, Herbert and Claire Sachs, all have infused me with hope and confidence during the times when I was feeling depleted. From day one I have been the delighted beneficiary of the special love of my grandmother Anne, my Aunt Karen and Uncle Ken Sachs, Ph.D., my Aunt Diane and Uncle Marty Glynn, and my Aunt Dasia Cherson.

My in-laws, Al and Selma Meckler, graciously accepted this shy and tentative young man into their family from the start, and have consistently been a tremendous support. I will always be indebted to them for their generosity, and for creating the daughter who became my wife.

My sons, Josh and Matthew, have already taught me so much about life and how to live it, and are a boundless source of joy, humor, and passion. I am a very lucky man, indeed, to have sons like these, and cannot imagine my world without them (although I wouldn't mind a little extra sleep now and then).

To suggest that I could not have written this book without my wife, Karen, would be a conventional gesture in a situation in which convention cannot measure debt. There is not one person whom I love more deeply, care for more intensely, and laugh with as easily. Thank goodness I was dumb enough to miss the flight that allowed me to meet her on that spring day seventeen years ago, and that she was willing to share her fudge cookies with me.

CONTENTS

	Introduction	13
1	A Bi-cycle Built by Two	25
2	The Reverberating Journey	45
3	Change and How It Happens: Differentiation and Selfhood	67
4	Dia-logic: The Art of Self-Focused Communication	89
5	Hugs of War: The Fights That Need to Be Fought	111
6	What Mothers Should Know About Fathers	133
7	What Fathers Should Know About Mothers	162
8	The Way In Is the Way Out: Dealing with the Parents from Our Past	184
9	Grandparents and In-laws: Dealing with the Parents in Our Present	211
10	The Marriage of Sex and Parenthood	235
	The Continuing Journey	257
	Index	267

INTRODUCTION

The tremulous crush that I had on Sherri Fishbein at the beginning of third grade was a brief but sweetly impassioned affair. My attempts at wooing her consisted mostly of awkwardly trying to duplicate the ways in which my dad demonstrated affection toward my mom, with understandably comical results.

As I've since come to understand, in both my personal life and my professional life as a psychotherapist specializing in marital and family relationships, we all continue throughout our lives to reverberate to the patterns established for us by our parents, and to demonstrate our loyalties to our first family by either imitating or rebelling against them. And it is always in our closest, most meaningfully intimate relationships that this reverberation is strongest.

Most vivid of my recollections of that early stab at intimacy is the taunting rhyme that echoed over our heads as we romantically ate our lunches side by side:

> Sherri and Brad, sitting in a tree
> K-I-S-S-I-N-G.
> First comes love, then comes marriage,
> Then comes baby in the baby carriage.

The progression from love to marriage to parenthood is etched into our developing psyches from the very beginnings of our lives. We grow up eagerly anticipating this orderly sequence of events. The image of a direct march from solitude to engagement to expansion of the family system is reassuring to us as we grow into and move through the turbulence of childhood and adolescence, and take on the conflicts and struggles inherent in early adulthood.

Real life, however, cruelly interrupts the soothing rhythms of the childhood verse. More than half of the couples who go from "love" to "marriage" end their marriages. Many of these marriages end after baby has come but while baby is still in the carriage. And even if a couple doesn't divorce, their perception of the quality of their marriage drops most precipitously during the first three years of parenthood.

Why do even the strongest of marital bonds suffer such severe jolts and shocks as a consequence of the urge to start a family, and how can it be that affirming and expressing our love in this most natural of ways sometimes results in the breakup of that family?

The decision to become a parent is the most universally dramatic, important, and irrevocable decision any of us will ever make. No experience in our lives will so tax our stamina, influence our feelings, change our relationships, and necessitate with such demanding insistence that we redefine ourselves as men and women as parenthood does.

Our children will make us feel alternately invaluable and worthless, competent and bumbling, tender and furious, optimistic and despairing, usually in the course of a single day.

The fact is that the prevailing cultural mythology notwithstanding, parenthood is a bafflingly difficult experience. No matter how much we *want* them, and how hard we worked to *get* them, children create an enormous strain in our lives as individuals and couples. The conversion from husband and wife to father and mother is one that, particularly at first, has more negative than positive changes associated with it. Children are the vehicles through which we as spouses experience and express a host of often contradictory feelings toward each other. We are prey to a frighteningly powerful disequilibrium that upends our sense of order and stability, and casts us into a disorienting tumult.

There are the obvious disadvantages of having children, which start with the loss of freedom, increased financial responsibilities, less time, more worries, new, and sometimes unpleasant, skills to learn, and go on from there. But all of this upheaval in our outer lives is only a signal of the more profound crisis occurring internally and interpersonally, one that we will respond to in different ways.

Our mode of accommodation will depend on what things were like before this transition occurred, how we interpret the transition, and how resourceful we are at contending with it. Whatever happens, though, it is unlikely that the strategies we previously relied on to maintain our personal homeostases will, on their own, suffice anymore. As Margaret Mead wrote, "The disruption caused by change can only be solved by more change. . . . "

The birth of a child requires an extraordinary shift in how a husband and wife "do" their relationship. Even the most cursory understanding of what the experts tell us about marriage will give us some insight into why this must be so.

Psychologist Kurt Lewin describes the general state of tension in a marriage as a result of four basic conditions:

1. The extent to which our personal needs (such as sex, security, companionship, and so forth) are met

2. The amount of space each of us is allowed for free movement

3. The amount of freedom we have to leave a situation

4. The extent to which our goals as a couple cohere or contradict each other

It is impossible to avoid noting that each one of these is intimately affected by becoming a parent: Our needs are less fulfilled as we attempt to meet those of our child, we have less room to operate in as additional family members join us, we're more dependent on, and thus less free to leave, each other, and our marital, parental, and career goals are inevitably called into question.

Marital therapist Philip Guerin has observed that almost all marital conflict can be confined to four domains:

1. Sex

2. Money, issues of power and control

3. Parenting

4. In-laws, issues of influence

Again, it is impossible to avoid realizing that conflicts in *all* of these areas will be directly provoked, in one way or another, by having a child.

Marital therapist Judith Coche has written that the three "tough" spots in a marriage occur when:

1. Hope gives way to disillusionment.

2. Overextension gives way to burnout.

3. Romance gives way to routine.

It seems that any way you look at it, the time when we most desperately need to work together to assist each other can paradoxically become the time we're least likely to be able to do so. In fact, we may just be too upset to be able to reach out to one another.

There is a wealth of data to back this up. Numerous studies have concluded that the child-rearing years are apt to be one of the least satisfying stages in our marital journeys. We experience a decline in the quality of our union characterized by increased conflict, diminished psychological well-being, less frequent displays of physical affection, more frequent feelings of sadness, doubt, and anxiety, ineffective communication, reduced opportunities for companionship, and more intense disagreements around a range of related, and seemingly unrelated, issues.

Even though there is some evidence that couples are less likely to divorce once they have had children, this does not mean that marriages get better, but simply that parents may feel trapped by having children and weigh the risks of separating more carefully than they might have otherwise. In fact, there is plenty of evidence that suggests that during the early years of parenting, couples become *more* ambivalent about their marriages, and doubt at some level whether they should have become partners, or parents, in the first place. The incidence of "baby blues" attests and contributes to these difficulties. Psychologist Frank Pedersen has estimated that 10–30 percent of women experience mild depression at some point during the first three months postpartum, and more than 50 percent experience "maternity blues" at some point during the first six months. The blues are not limited to mothers, however. His research, as well as my own, includes longitudinal studies of men, and demonstrates that many fathers also experience a depression after the birth of their child. But because most studies until recently only followed new parents up until six months postpartum, and men's low points tend to occur sometime between six and eighteen months postpartum, "Daddy blues" were often invisible and neglected.

In my graduate and postgraduate research and through my practice, I have had the opportunity to hear how hundreds of couples have made their transition into parenthood, and have found results similar to those described above. Yet it was my *own* transition into parenthood that shed the most clarifying light on this subject, and forced me to examine, from the inside out, exactly what is so challenging about this stage of marital development.

When I found out that I was going to become a father, I felt I was at the peak of parental readiness. My wife, Karen, and I had been married for almost seven years, and after some stormy periods early on in our relationship, our bond with one another now felt rich, solid, and strong.

I had years of experience with children behind me, as a camp counselor, a teacher, and a psychologist, and felt both well schooled and instinctively talented when it came to connecting with kids and knowing how to support them in their growth and development.

I was finally free of graduate school, training, and licensure commitments, and capable of making an excellent living doing something that challenged and stimulated me without having to travel or work extraordinarily long hours.

I had good friends, new and old, wise and seasoned clinical mentors whom I regularly met with and learned from, and was in the midst of a very rewarding and growth-enhancing therapy experience myself. I was beginning to find my own "voice" as a clinician, integrating my formal education with my intuition and acumen. I was surely learning as much from my patients as they were learning from me, and was creating my own understanding of what a healthy family should be and how to guide the families who came to me in search of this health. My work seemed to sustain both my patients and myself.

So when our first son, Josh, was born, I was startled to discover that fatherhood was not the delicious sequence of tender and delightful moments that I had anticipated, but a confusing, at times overwhelming, experience, suffused with sadness and despair, darkened by a miasma of contradictory feelings and impulses.

My first fatherly feelings were as often ones of anger, frustration, and incompetence as they were of warmth, engagement, and love. The confidence that I had built up over the years in my abilities to nurture and understand children was quickly eroded in the face of my own squirmy, stubborn son, and I constantly had to confront feelings of rage and intolerance that I wanted to believe were not a part of me.

More alarmingly, though, our marriage was shaken to its depths as we struggled to adjust to the presence of this new person in our lives and balance our roles as husband and wife with those of father and mother. From feeling that we had come very far in our relationship, and mastered many significant obstacles and transitions, we found ourselves once again as bewildered and upset as we'd been in the early years, in turmoil over what we wanted and needed from each other.

We went back to old, unhelpful ways of interacting, found ourselves increasingly unable to share the intensity of our experience with any insight into or respect for one another, and could only watch helplessly and in disbelief as our fantasy of what family life would be like began to disintegrate before our eyes.

For example, I had not been particularly perturbed by the thought that we might regularly have our sleep disrupted by a crying infant for a number of weeks. My preparenthood awakenings in the middle of the night had often been wondrously creative times for me, filled with productive hours at the piano or notepad, or interesting discussions with Karen during which we came to important discoveries about ourselves and our relationship.

Part of me actually looked forward to this aspect of parenthood. I had an image of the weary but good-natured changing-of-the-guards that we would coordinate as we sleepily took our midnight shifts, and the sense of importance and mastery that I would experience as I expertly cradled my fretful baby and strolled peacefully along the silent sidewalks of my neighborhood or blearily watched late night movies on TV. Everything that had hitherto been so important to me, such as making money, developing clinical expertise, and getting published as a writer, would suddenly recede, and I would be blissfully swept up in the ancient cadence of this most profound of human experiences.

This was, in fact, how things went during those enraptured first weeks. I remember one night when Josh wasn't even a month old that he awakened crying, and Karen nursed him and put him back to sleep, and then we passionately made love. "So much for waiting six weeks," we chuckled in self-congratulatory pride.

Gradually, however, the tone began to shift. Some of our friends were excitedly reporting that their infants were beginning to sleep through the night, while ours continued popping up several times to remind us of his presence.

As chronic fatigue began setting in at the three-month mark, the point at which we had been "promised" that a full night's sleep would be ours to cherish, we became convinced we were doing something wrong. Karen wondered whether she should continue nursing him, since the parents of the babies who were sleeping so well seemed to be using bottles or formula. She began to obsess about the best regimen to adhere to, constantly debating whether Josh should be fed and put down to sleep on a schedule or on demand. Of course, for every book, article, friend, or expert that advocated one approach, we would find another that would just as convincingly propose its opposite.

I began to feel neglected, and therefore irritated with Karen's obsessiveness, and to wish (silently) that she would just choose one approach and stick with it. On the other hand, I was too tired, confused, and uncertain to take a stand on any of this myself, or to reassure her that this was one of many minor choices that, in the long run, would matter very little. After all, being a new parent myself, I couldn't be absolutely sure that this was the case.

So, thoughts that maybe she really was nursing him "too much," or that letting him cry at night might cause "long-term damage," began to surface with troubling regularity. But instead of addressing these fears and uncertainties of mine, I dealt with them by blaming her for being "too anxious," while absolving myself of any responsibility.

This made *her* feel neglected and irritated, and she dealt with this by intensifying her focus on the baby's schedule, demanding that we determine "why" he was unable to sleep for more than a few hours at a time. The good-natured changing-of-the-guards that I had anticipated turned dark and ugly, Karen insisting that it was my obligation to help her, and that the "problem" was Josh's sleep pattern and my ineffectiveness at helping her alter it, while I was insisting that it was her obligation to stop making such a federal case out of this, and that the "problem" was her own anxiety. The nightly struggle to hash this out meant, of course, that *nobody* was getting *any* sleep, and our beloved son was being tossed miserably back and forth between us like a beanbag, as we all grew more tense and exhausted.

The problem for us, and for every set of new parents, was *not* that having a baby was "hard," which we were perfectly willing to accept and live with, but that it was hard in ways that we had never before had to encounter and wrestle with. And it was how we were thinking about and reacting to the problems presented, rather than the problems themselves, that had become the major source of our distress. It was really not Josh's irregular sleep itself, but the ways in which we understood it, saw ourselves as deficient, and blamed each other for this state of affairs, that was tearing us apart.

I have learned from my own experience, and from many of my patients, that much of the advice dispensed to new parents is not very helpful precisely because it assumes that the locus of the problem is in the *child* rather than in how the parents are responding to the child.

"Make sure you get some breaks from the baby" implies that the baby is the source of your distress, when in fact what many couples really need is a break from the cycle of feelings of incompetence, disappointment, and rage that they find themselves constantly engaged in.

"You've got to take care of yourselves first" assumes that parents know how to do this and feel no conflicts around doing so, when in fact so much of new parents' turmoil erupts because caring for a baby leaves them temporarily unable and unwilling to take care of themselves.

"Don't worry . . . it'll get easier" promises that as the baby grows more self-sufficient and communicative, s/he'll be less of a drain on the marriage. But unless parents learn to resolve their parenting conflicts, the reverse is often true, since as children become more assertive and sure of themselves, they can be harder, rather than easier, to raise (the parents of any adolescent will confirm this), and the conflicts within and between the parents may become ever more profound.

"Always communicate" suggests that we always know what we are feeling and how to articulate this, and it's just a matter of taking the time to do so. In fact, the emotions stirred up in us by the birth of a child are so complex and inchoate that it seems impossible to understand them ourselves, let alone explain them to each other in a satisfying and meaningful way.

What seems clear to me now, based on my own experience as well as on my research and clinical work, is that the entry of a child into the marital system always has and always will rock the marital boat. But this rocking can either dissolve or strengthen the connubial bond. The direction a marriage takes depends not just on how much a couple loves each other or on how much or little rocking they experience, but on how skillfully they adapt to the ordinary and extraordinary problems that are an inherent part of family life. New levels of understanding, of themselves, of the impact they have on each other, and most of all of the impact their own childhoods have had and continue to have on all of their relationships, will be necessary.

Karen and I were astute enough to understand that at some level we were exacerbating Josh's sleeping problem by blaming each other, but this knowledge by itself didn't ease our troublesome interaction. It was equally important to understand more about why our feelings could be raised to such a pitch by this problem, what it was about this issue that caused us to cease to be able to collaborate in a very sane or civil fashion.

Slowly and painfully, night after sleepless night, we talked and cried our frustrations out, and began to see the outline of the more fundamental issues that provided the underpinning of our anguish.

In Karen's case, a male relative whom she had been extremely close to since childhood has suffered from severe mental illness throughout most of his life. Almost from the day we brought Josh home from the hospital, various members of Karen's family began remarking on the similarity between him and this relative, with respect not only to his looks, but also to his sleeping and eating patterns. The explicit and implicit linkage that was being forged between our son and this unfortunate relative stirred in Karen the impossible-to-avoid fear that Josh might be headed down the same dark pathways.

So every night of disrupted sleep was for Karen not simply an annoyance, a source of physical depletion to be coped with or laughed at, but a waking and heartbreaking nightmare that forced her to relive her relative's lifelong descent into psychosis and to worriedly imagine a similar future for Josh.

I, too, was troubled by the similarities between our son and Karen's relative, and also had concerns about how my own family's genetic endowment might be contributing to Josh's problems, given the debilitating strain of alcoholism and depression that ran ominously through it. However, since nobody was busy pointing out all of the similarities between Josh and the most poorly functioning members of my family, I had more perspective than Karen and was less inclined to leap to dire conclusions about the connection between sleeping patterns in infancy and eventual mental health.

For me, the more fractious issue was my desire to be the Greatest Father in the World. My own father loved my brothers and me fervently but, like many men, had difficulty expressing this love in an emotionally satisfying way. He was also a man who appeared to me to be in tremendous pain, pain that he struggled to hide from everyone in many ways, but that I could not help but see, feel, and be affected by, nonetheless. Yet because he either could or would not articulate it, I could only futilely plumb, without comprehension, its mute depths, and found myself left with an intense but unfocused desire to heal him without knowing where, when, and how he had been injured.

This unfulfilled, and at times subconscious, desire to minister to my father was certainly one of the things that motivated me to become a therapist in the first place . . . perhaps by healing others, my father, the man I cared for more than any other, would somehow be magically healed too. After all, I remember myself as a young boy marching around with a toy toolbelt and announcing to everybody who was interested that I was going to be a Fixer Man when I grew up, and, in a funny way, that is exactly what I became. But the motivation to *father*, which had always been a transcendant one, a calling that emanated from my deepest being, surely arose from that same fertile wellspring. For at some level I hoped that in providing my son with the deep sense of belonging and connectedness that my father couldn't provide for me during my childhood, not only Josh, but my father and I, would also be the beneficiaries. In fathering a child, I could re-father myself, and symbolically father my own father, and thus ease the ache that we had silently struggled with all of these years.

The problem was, of course, that I was grandiosely anticipating that this could be accomplished by sheer will and intense involvement alone, that a laserlike convergence of all of my energies on any distress or problems that Josh displayed would mean they'd be instantly extinguished, as would mine and my father's. For better or worse (most probably the former), this grandiosity was deflated very early on in parenthood by Josh's obstinate insistence on irregular, disruptive sleeping.

In an attempt to compensate for this utterly unanticipated sense of helplessness and incompetence, which of course reminded me of how helpless and incompetent I had been when it came to understanding and helping my father, I redoubled my efforts at being a Good Father. Soon, almost every minute that was not spent at work was spent being with Josh, or talking with Karen about Josh. Because I stoically refused any breaks from what I had defined as my emotional responsibilities, I naturally became depleted and demoralized, and found myself with less and less patience for Karen. And because she was so tormented by the swooping ghosts from her past, she didn't have much patience for me.

So we not only needed to realize that each of us had a role in perpetuating the exhaustingly unproductive dance of blame and criticism that we were dragging ourselves through, but also that these roles had their roots in our earliest childhood experiences.

It was when these, and other, themes and memories became more conscious for us that we finally were able to realize how trapped we were in our respective pasts, and to see that so many of the more difficult moments of parenthood were daunting because of what they stirred in us. Yet this enhanced consciousness, hard won as it was, did not by itself move us to a better marital place. It was when we decided to see a therapist together as a couple that we started to disentangle from the past, stop the faultfinding cycle, and once again begin collaborating in fruitful and affectionate ways.

Once you have brought children into this world, and faced the challenge of incorporating them into the context of even the most loving of marriages, you have embarked upon one of the most extraordinarily difficult as well as liberating experiences life has to offer. You are engaged in a remarkable adventure, one that will fill your life with untold pain, uncertainty, and delight, and that will force you to confront yourself and your partner in ways that you have never had to do before. But it is in this confrontation, this cauldron of intimacy, that you will achieve your fullest, most meaningful humanity.

While our society tends to view the beginning of family life as the end of a satisfying marital life, I believe that the beginning of family life is a re-beginning of marital life, and that opening yourself up to the shared experience of raising children can be the most passionate and redeeming experience a couple can have.

This book, through enhancing your awareness of the true impact of parenthood on your relationship, will help you choreograph a marital dance that moves more gracefully and lovingly to the rhythms of family life.

CHAPTER ONE

A Bi-cycle Built by Two

Carl and Suzanne plodded slowly into my office and took their seats with a collective, dispirited sigh. "If I had known that being a parent was going to be this hard on our marriage, I really would have thought twice about whether it was worth it to have children," Carl began. A forty-two-year-old professor of English literature, Carl and his thirty-five-year-old wife, who was a history professor at the same university, had come to meet with me because they felt their marriage "was on the brink," particularly since the birth of their first child a little more than a year ago.

Suzanne, currently on a combination sabbatical/maternity leave, spoke with the same resignation: "I mean, I knew it'd be rough, and I was expecting a challenge, but I feel like we had the neatest relationship with each other before, and now that we're parents, we're just killing each other."

When I asked them to describe for me what felt so disturbing, each had a different response. Carl admitted, "I may not be the Father of the Year, but I do more than most guys . . . yet she's never happy, either with herself or with me. It's like she's been depressed since she became a mother and keeps criticizing everything that I do, so I back off. I just don't feel like being with her or listening to her anymore, 'cause I'm really getting sick of hearing about it."

Suzanne elaborated: "I don't know what's happening, either. I thought being a mother would make me feel more grown up, sort of whole, but instead I feel incredibly needy and empty. And I feel like he's not really there for me, that even though I keep trying to get him to listen and understand how hard this is for me, I'm not getting through, so we wind up having these awful fights, which I feel horrible about, and then the whole thing starts up again."

In their initial efforts to convey to me how out-of-control their marital life feels, Carl and Suzanne have actually pinpointed with remarkable accuracy the essence of the cycle that they are stuck in.

Both are assuming that their partner is the cause of their marital distress. Carl is certain that if Suzanne were more content and less depressed, he'd feel more appreciated and be more likely to be involved with and supportive of her. Suzanne is certain that if Carl were more attentive and nurturant, she'd feel more confident and less needy and provoke fewer arguments. Their troubling two-person dance is seen by each of them as a solo performed by one person: the spouse.

Neither is yet aware that the negative influences flow in both directions; husband and wife are reciprocally influencing each other, *inadvertently catalyzing and reinforcing the very actions that are getting them so upset.*

So while Carl is thinking, I wouldn't withdraw if you weren't so critical and needy, and Suzanne is thinking, I wouldn't be so critical and needy if you wouldn't withdraw, Carl is neglecting, for now, the possibility that his own withdrawal in fact contributes to Suzanne's criticalness and neediness, and Suzanne is unable to see that her criticalness and neediness contribute to his withdrawal. They have gradually become each other's psychological prisoners.

How can parenthood, that most culturally sanctioned and sanc-tified of states, take a loving, comfortable, and solid couple like Carl and Suzanne and hurl them into such seemingly inescapable cycles of behavior? Why is parenthood, an event experienced by more than 80 percent of all adults in the world, so universally problematic and perplexing?

While it is natural to think otherwise, babies can never, by themselves, ruin their parents' marriage. Not that you'd know it from the kind of advice new parents are given about how to enhance their marriages once they have started a family, as we discussed in the Introduction, or the ways in which they are encouraged to focus on alleviating the child's problems as a way of solving their own.

They are consistently enticed with store shelves and catalogs filled with devices that are designed to reduce their child's distress. Teething rings, bottle warmers, cradle rockers, lullaby tapes, and thousands of similar products are sold on the premise that easing the child's pain will in turn ease the parents' own. The voracity with which they gobble up such items, however, tells us more about the intensity of the pain parents are feeling than the origins of that pain or the best way to quell it. The quietest, most peaceful baby in the world can still be reacted to in a way that causes severe marital distress, and the loudest, most cantankerous child can be responded to in a way that minimizes such distress and promotes growth. The more parents learn to look within themselves, rather than to their children, for an understanding of what is happening in their marriages, the better their chance of dampening the tension that comes with the new territory of parenthood and finding adaptive ways to grow and learn from the experience.

Let us now take a look at the typical balance between a husband and wife so that we'll understand how and why it is so dramatically altered by the transition into parenthood.

Dances in the Dark

It is part of our nature to try to understand complex matters in simple ways. Often these understandings work up to a point, and then collapse into disarray. Isaac Newton's theories on mass and gravity functioned beautifully until Albert Einstein applied them to what happens at the speed of light. Then, new and infinitely more sophisticated theories had to be constructed to take these bizarre circumstances into account, theories that made little intuitive sense, and in fact seemed to contradict common sense as we understood it. It wasn't that Newtonian physics was "wrong" and Einsteinian physics was "right": It was just that there were severe limits to how well Newton's work could be applied to the more extreme interactions in the universe, while Einstein's work was more versatile.

The same holds true when it comes to theories of interpersonal relationships. Take the basic behavioral principle of reinforcement, for example. The thrust is a simple and elegant one: Behavior that is rewarded will occur more frequently; behavior that is not rewarded will occur less frequently, and eventually be extinguished. This does, in fact, account for the outcome of many interactions, and there is a reassuring "justice" that inheres in cause-and-effect thinking.

What happens in interactions at the extremes, however, in relationships that are intimate and intense, is not fully explained by this theory. To go back to Carl and Suzanne for a moment, one would think that she would just stop badgering him for more support, since badgering doesn't seem to be "rewarded" with supportive behaviors, and in fact seems to turn Carl off. Likewise, one would think that he would just stop retreating, since retreating doesn't seem to be "rewarded" with her giving him more room, and in fact seems to facilitate an even more determined attempt at encroachment on his domain.

Yet they not only continue engaging in the very actions that are not reinforced, but actually intensify them, despite getting nothing but criticism in return for them.

Therapists who work with couples and families have developed an approach to intimate relationships called "systems" thinking that helps to explain apparent paradoxes like these.

Systems thinking is not our natural mode of cognition, and can sometimes be, like Einstein's theories, conceptually difficult and counterintuitive. But it is a powerful way of understanding how people in close relationships interact with each other, and, consequently, worthy of a more in-depth look.

The foundation of systems thinking is that the principles of cause and effect have little relevance when it comes to understanding how family members engage with each other. There is no point to trying to understand "why" we act the way we do, as if our actions have an independent logic of their own. Instead, it is assumed that there is a reciprocity inherent in all of our encounters, and that how we behave is related not only to what we have learned and how we feel, but, just as important, to how our relationship partner behaves.

According to this approach, our actions have both an intra- and interpersonal logic: They emanate from within us as a consequence of our personalities, physiologies, and upbringing, and they are also actively elicited and maintained by our partners in the context (or system) of our relationship. An interaction cannot be reduced solely to the "problem" that one person has with a particular issue or task, but needs to take into account the ecology in which that "problem" arises.

This leads to two very important statements about a couple's relationship. One, *when two partners are alert to their mutual contri-*

butions to an interaction, they can effectively amplify or change that interaction. When we can avoid merely blaming our partners for what it is that they're doing or not doing, and see their behavior not only as originating from within them but also as something that is engendered by our *own* behavior, we can conceive of strategies of change more effectively. When we become aware that we, perhaps inadvertently, help to create the very behaviors that cause us the most distress, we are much closer to diminishing that distress.

Two, *a change on the part of one partner will automatically create change on the part of the other.* It is as if we are each a component in an ever-shifting mobile: Once we make a move in one direction, it shifts the balance and forces another piece to move, which will in turn affect us. We cannot actually change another person directly, try as we might, but we can change how others impact upon us, and consequently how we behave. Once we make that shift, the overall framework of the relationship changes, which *in turn heightens the odds* that our partner will change.

Carl, for example, does not "make" Suzanne accusatory or clingy by his tendency to withdraw from her, and Suzanne does not "make" Carl want to avoid her by putting too much pressure on him. She does not criticize him *because* he withdraws any more than he withdraws *because* she criticizes. But the modus operandi of each affects and influences the other. The actions of one person are both cause and effect of the actions of the other person. They are in a reverberating cycle of behavior in which each unintentionally encourages the other to continue doing the very opposite of the behavior that is desired.

This early in treatment, I cannot guarantee that Carl will become more involved with Suzanne if she merely stops being depressed and critical. I *can* pretty much guarantee that if she *doesn't* change, he'll continue to withdraw. Likewise, I cannot guarantee that Suzanne will become more content if Carl merely stops retreating. I *can* pretty much guarantee that if he *doesn't* change, she'll continue to be depressed and critical. But more than the simple act of making these changes, Carl and Suzanne need an understanding of what is going on within themselves that causes them to behave in such counterproductive ways.

Some amount of reciprocity can contribute to, and in fact is necessary for, a growing relationship. None of us is a complete human being, and all of us benefit from contact with someone who fills in the gaps in our personalities. We may do better when we are in contact with our psychological "complement." Take-charge individuals may feel lost without somebody to direct, for example, and more subordinate individuals may feel lost without somebody around to direct them.

Our marriage may be perturbed into a state of *unhelpful* reciprocity, however, by anything that stresses it. Stress underscores the vulnerabilities in our relationship and makes us feel less secure and more anxious. Anxiety is an uncomfortable state that we intuitively seek to diminish. It is felt inside of us but can also be transmitted *between* us, much as electricity can be transmitted between two poles, and once begun, it has a current that exists independently of what switched it on. Let's take a closer look at the role anxiety plays in our marriage.

Anxiety: The Great Magnifier

When we are experiencing anxiety about our relationship, we automatically tend to look to our partners for some kind of relief from that anxiety. We might experience a greater need for them to behave in the way we would like them to behave. We might focus more on who is right and who is wrong and become more convinced that it is we who are right and they who are wrong. We might become more preoccupied with whether or not we're getting great enough amounts of hopelessly subjective commodities like "love" or "trust" or "affection." We might raise our implicit or explicit expectations of our partners and decide for *them* what they can and should do for *us*. We might insist that they address the reasons for our anxiety and devote themselves diligently to alleviating it.

We may focus on a presenting issue that we differ on, such as time, attention, money, work, or sex, and assume that *that* is what is making us unhappy. But these "issues" are really only metaphors for a disturbance in our marital homeostasis. The trouble we have in getting along with each other is *not* due to our differences in values, beliefs, outlook, and priorities when we deal with these issues. It instead corresponds to the ways in which we handle the anxiety that results from the shifts in relational balance that these issues provoke.

When we deal with anxiety in some of the relationship-defeating ways listed above, we are being more "reactive" than self-reflective, engaging in a kind of psychological knee jerk that leads to a similar reflex on the part of our partner. Our insistence that our spouses always adapt or accommodate to our needs is a manifestation of reactivity, for example. Its opposite would be a thoughtful deliberation on the origin of the anxiety that so troubles us, and a conjointly planned approach to reequilibrating during a turbulent time.

When reactivity is high, though, we tend to focus on changing someone other than ourselves, which leaves us unable to see more than one of the many facets to a dilemma. Focusing outward does temporarily reduce our anxiety, but permanently inhibits our capacity for genuine mutuality. Anxiously trying to correct our partners' "flaws" can quickly escalate and catalyze greater ones, as they begin to feel criticized and defensive, and then try to countercorrect us.

What happens then is that we each become the emotional hostage of the other. We blame them for not changing, and for "making" us the way that we are, while they do the same. And the more we do this, the more we exaggerate the very things that so irritate and enrage each other, and the less able we are to discover our role in the relationship pattern that is keeping us so immobilized. This does, in fact, stabilize the relationship, but the stability comes with a high cost, that of paralyzing conflict that gradually infects all of our interactions with each other.

There are many different kinds of reciprocal interactions that couples engage in as a result of the anxiety that flows between them. Two are particularly worthy of mention when we are examining the transition into parenthood because they are so common. One we'll refer to as the "pursuer and distancer," and the other as the "hyperparent and hypoparent." Although I'm discussing them separately, they are often simultaneous and overlapping systems (as Carl and Suzanne's situation demonstrates).

Pursuers and Distancers

A colleague once complained to me for several days in a row about the sleepless nights that she and her husband had been having since they had purchased the electric blanket that was designed to ensure a better night's sleep. They had been optimistic when they purchased it, since she was always cold and her husband was always hot, and this was a "high tech" blanket, with each half having an independently operated control that could be regulated by its inhabitant.

So when she felt that the bedroom was too cold, she kept turning her dial up, and when her husband felt that the bedroom was too hot, he kept turning his dial down, but somehow, neither of them wound up very comfortable. Finally, they realized that the manufacturer had accidentally reversed the controls, and that she had been controlling his side while he had been controlling hers.

My colleague's anecdote fits nicely with family therapist Carl Whitaker's observation that the "marital temperature never changes: we just alternate turning the thermostat down." All of us engage repeatedly in vigilant attempts to maintain the balance between independence and connectedness in our marriages, and to define an acceptable amount of relational space.

We oscillate between suggesting that our partner back off so that we can breathe and inviting our partner to come closer so that we feel safe and secure. This exquisitely shifting equilibrium is a dynamic one, constantly readjusted in response to the shifts in "temperature" that come with the thousands of interactions and events that we encounter in our lives with our partners.

Our oscillation between the two poles may, at times of low stress, be smooth and flexible, and closeness and distance can confidently and methodically be navigated by us. Sometimes, however, under more intense pressure, this oscillation becomes a wobbly one, and we start to swerve into eccentric and dizzying orbits.

Each of us brings to our marriage certain rules about the "appropriate" way to negotiate and achieve sufficient contact and space. We are also wired to detect the small deviations from these rules that our partner will inevitably display. When the needle on our own internal gauge hits the "danger" area, a series of countermaneuvers that seek to reinstate the equilibrium we are most comfortable with goes into action, which in turn sends our partner's needle into his or her danger area, catalyzing the opposing countermaneuvers. Our periods of distance are then filled with a tense irritability rather than a relaxed separateness, and our periods of togetherness feel like a strangling suffocation rather than an enjoyable engagement, as each of us struggles to find a midpoint that is comfortable for ourselves.

In the case of Carl and Suzanne, for example, he feels that the marital mooring lines are too taut and wants to pull away to get some space. She feels that there is too much slack in these lines and wants to tighten up those bonds of togetherness. Carl reacts by pulling away even more, while Suzanne reciprocates by fighting for more closeness.

They are each then constantly insecure, never far enough apart for Carl to feel satisfyingly separate, or close enough to allow Suzanne to feel satisfyingly engaged. The attempts each desperately makes to restore balance in the relationship elicit the very behaviors that throw their relationship further and further out of whack.

Thomas Fogarty, a family therapist who has carefully studied the origins of marital conflict, designated this sequence the "Pursuer-Distancer" drama. The pursuer is the individual who feels that the marital gap is becoming too great and seeks to narrow it by chasing after his/her partner. The pursuer's partner is the distancer, who flees from the oncoming embrace of the pursuer in an effort to avert too much closeness.

Pursuers blame distancers for distancing, and believe that they wouldn't pursue if the distancers wouldn't distance any longer. Distancers blame pursuers for pursuing, and believe that they wouldn't distance if the pursuers wouldn't pursue any longer. In the meantime, both keep doing more of what they are already doing while bitterly protesting it.

There are several important details that we must attend to in order to understand this maddeningly common dance completely. One is that nobody is at fault for "starting" it: Each plays a role in initiating and maintaining it, and either has the capacity to end it, too.

Second, one can be a pursuer in one aspect of a relationship and a distancer in another aspect of the *same* relationship. While more men have trouble with closeness and tend to become distancers, and while more women have trouble with separateness and tend to become pursuers, rarely is this breakdown consistent across gender. The desire for independence and the desire for mutuality are not gender-determined, but on the contrary play out depending on the nature of the marital issue, other patterns of marital interaction, family history, and personality characteristics.

The woman who *pursues* her husband in search of more verbal intimacy and self-disclosure, for example, is the same woman who may *distance* her husband when he is seeking more sexual intimacy and physical contact. The husband who pursues his wife in an effort to get her interested in watching a football game with him is the same man who will distance his wife when she seeks to include him in her bridge club.

Another thing to keep in mind is that while both the pursuer and distancer complain that the other must stop doing what s/he is doing, often it is the case that each *needs* the other to do just what s/he's doing so that s/he can feel complete. While it appears that the pursuer is *more* interested in intimacy and the distancer is *less* interested in intimacy, in reality both are just about equal in their uneasiness with intimacy, and engage in this two-step as a way to regulate how close they really become.

While it appears that the distancer is the one "without any feelings," in reality the distancer feels just as much as the pursuer feels. Distancers don't have fewer or less intense feelings than pursuers—it's simply that they *manage* these feelings in different ways. What looks like indifference is often just the flip side of preoccupation.

Distancers flee pursuers because they're fearful that their feelings will become exposed if they're caught. They protest the pursuit but would be lost without it, since they would then have to encounter their own inner world.

Pursuers are also uncomfortable with their feelings, although they'll deny this. They chase distancers because they're aware, at some level, that this protects them from having to encounter *their* inner world. The supposed lack of connection between the two of them is actually a way to handle what might be a very intense connection that both of them in their different ways find overwhelming.

The way that we know this is that whenever either of them

stops, the dynamics of this drama often can shift abruptly. If the pursuer actively stops pursuing, the distancer may stop running, get anxious, and begin to pursue the original pursuer, who then may become the distancer. If the distancer actively stops distancing, the pursuer may stop running, then become anxious and become the new distancer.

When the stress on a couple raises their anxiety, they will become vulnerable to an ever-more frenzied pursuer-distancer interaction. The system's reciprocity begins to quickly spin out of control.

Carl and Suzanne had choreographed a pursuer-distancer dance that had met both of their needs nicely before the arrival of their child but that spun out of control when the stress of child rearing destroyed their equilibrium.

For example, up until the time they became parents, there was plenty of room for the two of them both to connect and to maintain some separateness. Carl was a man of quiet strength and introspection who had a social life confined to a couple of close friends and his wife. Suzanne radiated intensity and thrived on close, verbal contact with a wide range of colleagues and friends, as well as with her husband.

In the course of therapy, Carl admitted that he benefited from the rich social life that Suzanne orchestrated, and that he didn't have the energy or self-confidence to initiate and maintain as many relationships as she did. He also said that while he sometimes felt intruded upon by Suzanne, without her around to facilitate their shared talks or activities, he would be likely to retreat a bit too much and start to feel lonely and alienated.

Suzanne acknowledged that she could go overboard when it came to doing things with friends, and that Carl's ability to refuse an invitation helped her not to get carried away. She also said that while she sometimes felt that he was a bit too walled-off and wished that he would take responsibility for initiating their talks and activities, she also valued his calming presence, and had learned a lot about "staying still" from him.

Once they became parents, however, and the amount of time and energy available to them was curtailed, the fulcrum of their marital seesaw began to shift, and they both tried urgently to restabilize it.

Suzanne, cut off from many of her social outlets because she was no longer working outside of the home, felt isolated and depleted by motherhood and started to pursue Carl more vigorously for contact. Expecting him to fill in the gap that her friends and colleagues used to fill, she frequently decided that it was time for them to talk about "important things, like our relationship and the kids."

This would make Carl anxious, and he would try to pull away, professing to not "know how" to talk. Suzanne pursued harder, suggesting that they enroll in a parenting class together. He agreed, then bailed out at the last minute, saying that his department chair had requested that he start teaching an evening class.

Suzanne got more frustrated, decided it was time to just "leave him alone," but without substituting any new sources of support and contact found herself feeling more and more besieged by anger and resentment.

At first, Carl felt some relief at being left alone. However, he was also troubled by how much he resented, rather than loved, his infant daughter's entrance into their lives, and frightened by how much more his wife was needing him, so the relief was only temporary. This buildup of internal turbulence left him feeling isolated and irritable, unable to focus effectively on his work and unwilling to turn to anyone for support.

Naturally, the tension between the two of them would sometimes mount so high that they would wind up in a disastrous fight over a trivial issue, such as a phone message that hadn't been promptly relayed, or a scheduling mix-up at the pediatrician's office. Their marriage had become like a room filled with combustible gas: Just toss a tiny match in and BOOM!—a giant explosion ensued.

After the fight, both would feel remorseful and apologize, but would nevertheless refuse to alter their basic thinking. Carl would plead with Suzanne to help him create "peace" by not being so tense, Suzanne would plead with Carl to "just talk to me." Yet because both of them were refusing to acknowledge their own roles in the cycle, it would inevitably start anew.

At this point, trying to get them in sync would have aroused the invisible forces of opposition that arise when you try to push two powerful magnets together: The closer they are, the more potent the resistance.

In a moment, we will get to some solutions to the dilemma that Carl and Suzanne found themselves in. Before we do that, however, let's examine another problem that arose in their marital system once they became parents, one that many other couples also wrestle with.

Hyperparents and Hypoparents

Rarely does each member of a couple function at exactly the same level. In fact, *some* differential in functioning between a husband and wife is natural. One spouse may derive benefit from being the care-taker, and feeling benevolent and responsible, for example, while the other may derive benefit from being taken care of, and feeling attended to and temporarily free of responsibilities. Particularly if each person in the couple gets to experience *both* sides of the dichotomy, depending on time and circumstances, this arrangement can be a healthy and enjoyable one.

Differences in level and intensity of functioning can also be *useful*, enhancing a couple's efficiency and intimacy. One spouse's easygoing manner, for instance, can complement rather than conflict with the other's earnest intensity.

When the system is stressed and in transition, however, such as during the child-rearing years, a marriage's typical differential may become less moderate, and each member's functioning can become stuck in more extreme positions. One parent, for example, may, for a variety of reasons, take on too much of the burden of family life, and become the "hyperparent," while the other, the "hypoparent," appears to be getting off easy.

The distinction between how much hyperparents and hypoparents do may not initially be a source of distress for new parents, but if they become *reactive* to this distinction, it can gradually get out of hand. For example, hyperparents may start off feeling comfortable with the initial distribution of labor. However, once family life is in full swing, they may begin to feel overwhelmed and troubled by the physical and emotional responsibilities of parenthood. They may try to avoid confronting this discomfort, which they may feel a little guilty or abnormal about, by doing even more. This, however, will accentuate the difference in functioning between them and their partners, and they'll begin to wonder why they're doing so much while their partner is doing so little.

They'll anxiously respond to the continuing burden of carrying a disproportionate share of the family load, not by examining the origins of their *over*responsible behaviors but by trying to change their partner's *under*responsibility.

Hypoparents may also have been comfortable with the initial breakdown in responsibilities, but as the novelty of having a newborn around wears off and it becomes clear that the baby is "here to stay," they may start feeling uneasy. One response they may make is to begin withdrawing from some of the parenting activities that need to be taken on, as if to deny the permanence of their new status.

Already in a retreating, "anti-parent" mode, they'll react to their partners' effort to make them "grow up" not by examining the origins of their underresponsibility, but by self-righteously wondering why they're always being nagged and why they're so unappreciated. They rebel against this perceived tyranny by doing even less, or by "doing what they're told," but in a lethargic and incomplete way. This precipitates further motivational efforts from the hyperparents, which produce the exact same nonresults.

A few rounds of this exasperating battle essentially convince hyperparents that their partners are indeed not reliable, and solidifies their assumption that they have to do everything themselves. The same battle convinces hypoparents that they have good reason not to do much, since they're being treated so unfairly, and "everything's getting done anyway, so why bother?"

The two partners become so locked into this cycle that they lose all sense of any way out of it. Though they are unaware of what they themselves are doing to keep the hypo/hyperparent cycle in motion, it couldn't keep going without the active participation of each. Just like the pursuer-distancer roles, these roles are reciprocal, each influencing the other simultaneously. *Hyperparents account for and make possible their partners' underparenting just as much as hypoparents account for and make possible their partners' overparenting.*

Hyperparents devote themselves to being responsible for addressing the needs of others but don't always acknowledge that, to justify this, they have to persuade themselves that others need their help. To do this, they encourage the very dependence that so drains them. Hypoparents want to be free of being "told what to do" but don't always acknowledge that it is their direct or indirect opposition to responsibility that invites their partners to try to change and control them.

Neither is morally or ethically "right," or better than the other. Like pursuers and distancers, they confidently assert that life would improve dramatically if their partners would just become more like them, but they are in reality mutually addicted to each other, and would suffer greatly, at least at first, if the pattern was to change at all. In fact, it is their intuitive understanding of the suffering that would accompany change that keeps them trapped in these positions.

I remember the first year that a friend and I coached high school soccer, we would finish pre-season workouts by asking the players to do a two-mile run around the practice fields. A motivated but obviously out-of-shape freshman named Jeffrey started heaving violently about halfway through the run, and the co-captain, a talented but somewhat lazy center forward named Pete, broke out of line and went running across the field to him.

I was at first touched by this display of caring between a senior and a freshman, as I watched Pete hold up poor Jeffrey and encourage him to relax and take some deep breaths. This routine happened several days in a row. One afternoon, however, when Pete was not at practice, Jeffrey "miraculously" was able to complete the run by himself without incident.

The following day, when the senior had returned, Jeffrey once again had difficulties and needed Pete's "assistance." Not surprisingly, when Jeffrey wasn't at a practice a week later and Pete had no one to "take care of," he excused himself from the run, saying he didn't feel well.

This was one of my first clear examples of how a couple can influence each other and affect each other's functioning. Jeffrey's deficiencies led him to "need" to be taken care of by Pete, but Pete also "needed" to be needed, to cover up his own deficiencies. Without Pete around needing him, Jeffrey did fine, but without Jeffrey around to be needed, Pete ran into trouble.

Let's see how Suzanne and Carl have become entrenched in another version of this same ballet. Suzanne complains constantly about Carl's lack of skill at bathing the baby, but refuses to create opportunities for him to learn. She often suggests that he do the baths, but has little success in getting him out of his study and near the tub. After a few tries, she sighs and decides to take care of the bath herself.

Once in a while, after a particularly lonely or discouraging day, she blows up and "demands" that he do it, and he does, but at these times she hovers around the bathroom, listening for signs of her daughter's distress, providing a running commentary on what Carl is doing right and what he's doing wrong. This does little to enhance the possibility that Carl will learn to enjoy bathtime and develop competencies with his daughter on his own. Not surprisingly, the next night he's holed up in his study once again.

The lassitude and incompetence that she helps to induce make Suzanne resentful of him, but also reassure her that she's needed, which is a crucial building block in the foundation of her self-esteem.

Carl whines that he's tired of her always nagging him about this. However, taking on more intimate contact with his daughter makes him feel scared and uncertain. He's never had to care for a baby and is not certain that this is in his "job description" anyway. He certainly has no memories of his own father being involved with bathing him or his baby sister.

By not displaying much initiative and interest, he induces the nagging and overresponsible behaviors in his wife that allow him to feel safe and justified about not doing much fathering. He needs *not* to be needed, and is resourceful at sabotaging Suzanne's efforts to cajole him into more engagement.

Carl and Suzanne have, in fact, reequilibrated their functioning differential and achieved some stability, but it has come at a high price—that of a constant state of threatening tension.

Yet as is the case with pursuers and distancers, these roles can flip depending on the issue at hand. Carl, for example, complained in their third session with me that Suzanne was irresponsible when it came to the use of their credit cards. However, he was secretive about how much money they actually had, and found inventive ways to refuse her offer to take over balancing the checkbook. When yet another disapproved-of expense was reported, he would sigh and toss up his hands, reestablishing for himself how "impossible" *she* was and how essential *he* was. He did not acknowledge that his own withholding of financial information and his rejection of her offer to assist in budgeting were contributing to this problem. He also did not take the time to notice that Suzanne spent more when she was feeling less taken care of by him, and that being more attentive to her might help her to curtail some of her purchasing.

Suzanne would tire of his ongoing accusations regarding her spending but refuse to see that by backing off from her insistence that Carl be more accountable to her about the status of their finances, and by continuing to buy somewhat impulsively, she was eliciting these very judgments. She also had not yet noticed that she was choosing to express her anger at being neglected by Carl indirectly, through this spending, rather than directly, such as by setting some firm limits about what she would and wouldn't be responsible for around the house. So the same hyper/hyporesponsibility circuit, with reverse polarities, emerged around the issue of money.

Hyperparents typically have supporters rallying around them. After all, they look much more responsible, more involved with the family, than do their partners, who in their stubborn refusal to shoulder their share of the burden appear inexcusably selfish.

"Hypers" often feel a great sense of self-righteousness: They've "tried everything" to get their underparenting spouses to contribute more, and nothing works. Furthermore, they dismiss the complexities of the relationship process and their role in sustaining it by focusing only on their partner's deficiencies. When it comes to balancing the accounts, the marital ledger is always in their favor.

Hypoparents, however, have their own side of the story, and their own supporters. After all, many people readily identify with the beleaguered victim of a perfectionistic and chronically dissatisfied spouse, the "nice guy/gal" whose partner treats him/her like dirt. But hypoparents, too, ignore the relationship dynamics as well as the ways in which they influence it. They grumpily believe that if they were just left alone or treated better, everything would work itself out.

The danger of a distorted reciprocity of this sort is that the spouses organize themselves around their marriage in a contrary, competitive way. For one to feel positive, the other has to be seen as negative. Both derive their self-worth from a sense of superiority to their "other halves."

So where does this leave a couple like Suzanne and Carl? Although we will be focusing more fully on solutions to problems like these in subsequent chapters, a brief summary of how they went about changing things is worth presenting here.

In both the pursuer-distancer and hyper-hypoparenting dances, couples are stuck because they are having difficulty acknowledging their own contributions to the cyclical state of affairs. Many times, refraining from an insistence that their partner change and becoming more aware of these personal contributions is the first and most important step toward improvements.

To assist Carl and Suzanne with this process, I asked them to work together on a couple of assignments. One involved their each making two pie charts, the size and number of the slices of one pie depicting how their time was divided up before they became parents, the slices of the other depicting time allotments after they became parents. The second involved their plotting along the circumference of a circle the alternating sequence of behaviors that each engaged in on the path to one of their fights.

There were several reasons for these assignments. The pie charts enabled them to see more graphically the ways in which their lives had changed once they became parents, and why they were finding it necessary to fight so hard for more of what they were needing. For example, when they saw on paper how much less time Carl was able to spend alone on his work, and how many fewer hours Suzanne was able to spend with friends, they were better able to understand the origins of some of their disputes.

The sequence-of-behavior chart enabled them to see more graphically that each had a role in the buildup of tension that led to their wars, and that it indeed was a cycle that had no beginning and, at this point at least, no end.

Perhaps most important, however, both assignments forced Carl and Suzanne to begin seeing themselves as partners, rather than adversaries, in parenthood. By looking together at the profound life changes that each of them had experienced since becoming parents, and by charting a mutually agreed-upon depiction of their combative behaviors, they had no choice but to become more attuned to their respective roles in their conflicts, and more sensitive to the alterations in their own and their partner's lives.

As a follow-up assignment, I asked each of them to look over the sequence-of-behavior chart and find two different places where they could intervene to disrupt the cycle and create a new, more pleasing interaction.

Suzanne decided that when she was feeling frustrated with motherhood, she could make a call to one of her old friends, rather than insist on Carl talking to her, and also that she could back off from being judgmental about the efforts he was making to be more responsible.

Carl decided that he could make sure that he reserved some time each evening to be solely available to Suzanne so that she could talk about and process her day, and also that he would give her a break by taking over all child-rearing responsibilities on Saturday and Sunday mornings, as long as she was available to help him should he need it.

At this point, Carl and Suzanne were well on the road to adapting more successfully to family life. It is important to keep in mind, however, that there was nothing magical about either Carl or Suzanne's solutions: It's likely, in fact, that the practical steps that they took toward change were old ideas that one or both had thought of before. What is significant is that it was only when they could recognize the systemic nature of their distress, and join together to pinpoint the ways in which each of them were responsible for creating it, that these ideas could flow more freely and take root. If I, or anyone else, were to suggest these interventions to them prior to their new understanding of things, they wouldn't have worked.

We have been learning to think "systemically" in this chapter, to acknowledge the reciprocity that is inherent in our marital relationship, the ways in which we invisibly and inadvertently influence each other's behavior. We have also examined the ways in which an external stressor, such as child rearing, raises our anxiety and disturbs what may have been a comfortable state of reciprocity into an imbalanced state that leaves us feeling angry and uncomfortable.

I wanted to start with an emphasis on reciprocity since too often the focus in analyzing marital conflicts is on personal problems, seeing the hypoparent as someone who can't accept responsibility, for example, or the distancer as someone who is frightened by the new levels of intimacy required by life with a baby.

Sometimes, as is the case with Carl and Suzanne, the very recognition of reciprocity leads directly to solutions. Sometimes, however, as was the case with Karen and me when it came to dealing with Josh's sleeping, the recognition itself doesn't help, and a look at the origins of our parental behaviors and feelings is required. This is what we will examine in the next chapter.

CHAPTER TWO

The Reverberating Journey

*"So we beat on, boats against the current, borne back
ceaselessly into the past."*
—F. Scott Fitzgerald,
The Great Gatsby

F rank, a forty-two-year-old veterinarian, was known to everyone as a rock-solid fellow. Immensely capable at almost everything he took on, he was admired for his remarkable ability
to remain calm and self-assured no matter how much stress he was
under. His wife, Vera, who was also a vet, appeared to be a bundle
of raw nerves next to his granitic demeanor.

Sometimes she found his solidity to be reassuring, a great comfort during her more strung-out moments, but other times she felt
exasperated by her inability to pierce his composure, to get at something more spontaneous, more earthy.

This changed when they became parents for the second time.
The birth of their Down's syndrome baby completely upended Frank's
sense of certainty and faith, and left him, for the first time, feeling
strangely incapacitated. The harder he struggled to regain emotional
control over this disheartening situation, the less control he had.

Frank's behavior changed radically during the year following the
birth of that child. No longer unflappable, he became erratic; tearful
one night, enraged the next, warmly optimistic the night after that.
Vera was completely dismayed by this development. "I need his
strength more than ever right now, and he's falling apart on me . . .
I've never been able to not count on him," she complained to me
during our first session.

Yet I felt that the falling apart that she was alluding to was in

45

fact a process that Frank *had* to undergo to allow the two of them a greater flow of adaptability and bonding during this painful time. He was finally being given a chance to explore his own wounded, cut-off childhood experience, one that had become a kind of paradigm for how he lived his adult life. Perhaps this might have happened at some point along the road even if he hadn't had another child, or if that child had been healthier, but either way, the opportunity was on the table right now.

My first glimpse of the pain Frank had stored up from his child-hood years came the day he began telling me about having to be hospitalized when he was seven years old. There was a defect in the structure of his chest cavity that required surgery, followed by a lengthy stay at a recuperation facility that was miles from his home-town, his first experience with being away from home.

In our sessions he recalled his desperate desire to fight off the terrible loneliness and desolation that he experienced then. The youngest of two sons (like his own son), he had always tried to catch up to his big brother, who seemed to capture all of their father's attention with his unusual athletic abilities. In fact, there were several different weekends when only his mother visited him because his father had decided to stay back and watch his brother's baseball games. At some level, he understood this decision—why should his brother be completely deprived of attention?—yet he remembered feeling miserable and spurned.

In one session he spoke of his recollection of overhearing his mother telling his father about the necessity for surgery, and his father's upset response, which at first had to do with how much the hospitalization would cost. Fearful of further angering and disappoint-ing his father by expressing his own terror about the operation, he walled it off, and strove to "be brave," recuperate rapidly, and keep his fear hidden.

The disappointment that Frank now felt in his son's disability and ultimate limitations brought all of these old emotions to life, however. All of the imperfect parts of himself that he had sought to conceal by his manifold competencies were becoming reactivated by the birth of his own, imperfect child. It was as if he were seven years old once again, "damaged goods" strapped into a psychological bed far away from home, and unable to ask for help.

As I helped Frank to feel more comfortable reaccessing his childlike needs for empathy and love during a lonely time, and to feel entitled to ask for help in meeting them, Vera began to appreciate and support him in ways that she had never been allowed to do before. She commented during one session in fact, "I don't think I've ever held him before. The other night when he started to cry it was so sad, but it was so wonderful—he's always the one holding me, and finally it was the other way around."

When both realized that certain needs can never be outgrown but stay with us our whole lives, they were better able to enjoy caring for each other without feeling self-critical or diminished. His psychological "regression" resulted in his dropping the shield that had protected his lifelong sense of loss and mistrust.

Since they so courageously stayed involved with each other while Frank allowed these previously unacceptable feelings of loneliness and deprivation to surface, and reexperienced his wound in all of its depth, the integrity of their relationship was promoted, and it became richer, and more soulful. But it was only when parenthood yanked Frank back into his own childhood that these changes could come about.

We are led by many to believe that the major stressors associated with parenthood have to do with the tangible challenges that we are presented with, such as physical fatigue, increased decision-making responsibilities, less free time, fluctuations in sexual desire, etc. This is deceptive, however, for although these difficulties are indeed real and impactful, they are in and of themselves *not* the major reason that parenthood is such a fertile breeding ground for marital conflict. Similar difficulties may appear in couples' lives at other times and under different conditions, for example, and not create nearly the same amount of commotion.

Something else besides the daily vicissitudes of child rearing disturbs our lives when we become parents, something that leaves us vulnerable to experiencing profound frustration and discontent. I believe that it is the simple but elemental fact that *having children sends us back into our own childhood* that creates such stress. The content of our surface marital *battles* may vary, but the fundamental reason that a war is raging in the first place has to do with the fact that we have each temporarily regressed into a childhood state and are desperately doing anything we can to remain afloat in these turbid waters. And it is often the very desperation of these attempts that creates, rather than solves, our problems.

One of our fantasies as we make the transition into parenthood is that having children will deepen our foothold in the world of adulthood and help us finally to put our childhoods, and our childishness, to rest. Safely in grown-up territory, we will no longer be at the mercy of those turbulent and irrational feelings and conflicts that poke up their heads and disturb the mask of placid and confident maturity that we struggle to display to the world.

We will be healed and transformed, cleansed of all that is unlikable, freed of all that is troubling, blossoming radiantly with an abundance of warmth, love, and generativity. Parenthood will gently nudge us into finally becoming the person we have always wanted to be, and our rebirth will be a painless and serene one.

No longer confined by the petty concerns of the workaday world, we will magically become lost in a paradisiacal state of rapture and tranquillity as our baby teaches us all that we need to relearn about intimacy and love. And of course *all* of our relationships, foremost among them our marriage, will simultaneously evolve in response to this metamorphosis, and transcend the irritants and resentments that had built up over the years so that we can soar in joyous union.

In fact, quite the opposite happens at first. Parenthood, for all of us, drives home some painfully sharp emotional nails, and we find ourselves becoming not someone different, but someone who is unfailingly the same, so much the same that we can't stand it sometimes. Our worst, rather than our best, qualities seem to be magnified, and we become more, rather than less, susceptible to what appear to be our most juvenile and despicable impulses. We feel that we're growing "down," not up, and the harder we fight against this reality, the faster we sink.

Like the horse drawing the milk wagon in the Russian folktale, who continues to stop at the houses of customers who have been dead for years, we, too, find ourselves stopping in front of the ancient emotional landmarks that dot our childhood maps. When our child is crying, we have difficulties responding in calm and rational ways because it reminds us of our own tears from long ago, or of our parents' distress when we were fretful. When our child is throwing a tantrum, we feel violent rather than sympathetic because our own childhood fury is being jump-started, or because we're identifying with our parents and their upset with our tantrums.

While there are ultimate advantages to this reconnection with the past, as we learned from Frank and Vera a moment ago, it is important to keep in mind that *nobody* reexperiences his/her childhood without powerful feelings of fear, trepidation, and anxiety. Try as we might to romanticize to the contrary, being little, helpless, and dependent is a perplexing, bruising experience.

Even in the best of circumstances, with a solid nuclear family, food on the table, good health, and roofs over our heads, we are constantly buffeted by forces whose origins we know little about, and even less about how to handle.

Even the most loving and tolerant caregivers were imperfect. Whether they thought they were letting us know this or not, they were often feeling preoccupied, despairing, lost, depressed, or overwhelmed themselves (often for the same reasons that we are now). They grew irritable with our constant demands, impatient with our bewildering storms of emotions, and angry with our need to test out and bump up against their infuriating limits and rules.

And this is what happened under "ideal" conditions. How much more our childhoods must have roiled if we came from homes with unhappy marriages or divorces, chemical dependencies, poverty, verbal or physical abuse, mental illness, diseases, handicaps and disabilities, sudden or out-of-sequence deaths of important people, and the other unfortunately common calamities of family life.

When we raise our own children, we once again encounter the anguish and pain that characterized our childhood struggles, and must lure these struggles to the surface for another, closer look. This can be a foundation-shaking experience, making us relive past feelings of powerlessness and need that we thought, and wished, we'd left behind.

The cavities in ourselves, the places in which we lack substance and strength, will once again be exposed. Conflicts around themes like dependence and autonomy, power and impotence, sexuality and aggression, constraint and spontaneity, will recur. Unruly emotions and unkempt thoughts surge back into prominence. Troubling questions about mortality, gender identity, and injustice will be raised with ever greater urgency. All of the unresolved aspects of our relationships with the members of our first families will once again surface.

The journey back to our own childhoods that parenthood engenders obviously has tremendous impact on how we raise our children, and less obviously, but just as powerfully, on our relationship with our spouse. This is because whether we realize it or not, whom we chose to be our marital partners, and how we interact with them, is very much rooted in these childhood experiences. Let's turn our attention to this, and see how it plays out more fully when we have children ourselves.

The Presents of the Past

"'Til one can see the family in oneself, one can see neither oneself, nor any family, clearly."
—R. D. Laing

Is there any couple that doesn't realize with a shudder that, at one point or another in their marriage, they are acting exactly as their parents did in their marriage? I once caught a glimpse of myself in the mirror while feeling critical of Karen for being caught up in a telephone argument with her mother, and noticed an annoyed, skeptical squint as I listened to her.

During a visit to my parents later that month, I heard my mom getting involved with her own mother on the phone in a way that I knew infuriated my father. As I turned to take a look at him, I was startled to see that same hard, squinty gaze that had framed my countenance being directed at her from him. In that moment, I felt both intensely connected with him and intensely respectful of *all* of the connections that bound my father and me as we each strove to resolve the intimate matters of marriage.

Our desire to fulfill our personal "declarations of independence" compels us to ignore the impact that our heritage exerts on us. We imagine that because, in these modern times, our marriage has not been "arranged" in any explicit way, we can stroll confidently down the aisle and with each step shed all that we have endured and absorbed through the years of childhood and adolescence. We like to believe that because we enter the marital covenant with "free choice," we have the ability and the right to etch whatever messages of happiness and delight we wish to on our partner's equally blank slates.

And the person whom we marry will not be just anyone, but the idealized healer who will, with the glance of an eye or the stroke of a hand, eradicate the pain that we have so conscientiously sought to avoid and free us up to live a life unencumbered by the ache of old wounds and the fear of new ones. We are certain that our partner will join with us in constructing a shelter to protect us from the psychologically damaging elements that have swirled so darkly around us, someone who will plug the holes in our identity and help us to feel complete. S/he will lead us to re-create all that felt wonderfully melodious about our early lives while damping all of the minor chords that have resounded insistently for so many years.

Alas, as all of us at some point realize, this is hardly what happens. It is difficult to acknowledge that our relationships in the new family we form through marriage are profoundly affected by relationships in our first family, the one we're born into; but that, sometimes regrettably, is always the case.

Our culture prides itself on self-determination, but the exasperating fact is that while we are busily determining our selves, we are doing so in a powerful force field that has affected everything about us, from the kind of people we are, to the kind of things we do, to the kind of relationships we have.

We all play the part that our first family rehearsed us for, without our fully knowing it, and this determines in important ways the kind of spouse and parent we ultimately become. We bring to the families that will be *our* creation a temperament and style, a set of assumptions and beliefs about family life, a constellation of hopes and fears, that was honed and conditioned by our childhood circumstances.

For when a marriage is transacted, it is not just a bride and a groom who wed, but also their two bulging narratives of influence and experience. Much of what comprises these narratives is the ever-shifting web of past and present bonds.

There are relatives we know well, and those we don't know well at all. There are people who affect us in the present, those who affected us only long ago, and those who indirectly affect us by affecting those who *directly* affect us. There are the projections onto us of individuals we may never have known well or met, figures whose spectral presence may have dogged us for a lifetime without our even being aware of it.

There are supporters of our union, enemies of our intimacy, and competitors for our attention. *Any* of them may change places at any time, depending on what is happening in their lives and what they see in ours. *All* of them add to the emotional process that fuels or inhibits our growth as a couple.

The nature of the intersection between our history and our partner's history, and the way in which we synthesize these histories into a new marital paradigm, is what will determine the success of our union.

Just because our childhood influences our choice of spouse and the ways in which we interact with them, however, why would this create such problems for us? Why would the reconnection with our childhood that parenthood fosters also foster the conflicting interactions of pursuing and distancing or hyperparenting and hypoparenting that seem so sticky and unproductive?

One answer lies in what family therapist Ivan Boszormenyi-Nagy describes as the "invisible loyalties" that link us with our first families. He conjectures that we are all bound to our original caregivers, despite their flaws and imperfections, and that the character of this bond is what will determine the strengths and weaknesses of the intimate relationships we initiate as adults.

Often, our loyalties to our first family insinuate themselves into our lives in a positive way. We all are aware of our similarities to one or both parents, or our adherence to our family's values, when those qualities work out well for us. The conscientious ways in which we incorporate their traditions guide us, and can serve us well as we strive to define our own identities.

Sometimes, however, these loyalties wind up constricting rather than enhancing our lives. The ways in which these less productive loyalties come into play are complex, deceptive, and often quite hard to identify.

For example, Barbara, a twenty-nine-year-old physical therapist, is proud of the fact that she works in a private practice with an orthopedic surgeon three days a week in addition to raising her three-year-old son. She is certain that the fact that she is employed outside of the home distinguishes her from her own mother, who had always been a full-time caregiver and had often complained about how worn out she felt.

Yet Barbara, too, is worn out, her energy dissipated by her desire to be as physically available to her son as her mother was to her. Her chronic refusal to acknowledge how unrealistic this is leads her to feel just as depleted as her mother always did. So although she is *behaving differently* than her mother by working outside of the home, she has set up her life so that she is *feeling similarly*. And these feelings, as discomfiting as they are, may be easier for her to contend with than the fear and uncertainty she might encounter were she to be disloyal to her mother by putting her own needs on a par with her family's.

Ian, a thirty-one-year-old father of two, came to me for therapy because he was feeling depressed and exhausted, and troubled by his short fuse with his kids. In one of our first sessions, he conveyed his sense that his own father was unavailable to him because his "grown-up" pursuits took priority over his "parenting" pursuits. His dad would make time to play on various athletic teams, for example, but rarely have time to play ball with Ian and his siblings. Even when he *was* around, he was more standoffish than playful, as though he begrudged them whatever time he did spend with them.

Ian is so devoted to righting this wrong that he works overtime to be available to his children by constantly submerging his own interests. He doesn't ever feel comfortable saying no to his children when it comes to playing with them, and never chooses to do anything for himself when it conflicts with doing something for his kids. In fact, in another therapy session it became clear that they did not even know he had any interests outside of work and fatherhood, despite the fact that he was a talented woodworker and an avid movie buff.

The paradoxical result of Ian's relentless determination to be different from his father is that he totally neglects himself and thus ends up being just as resentful of the time he forces himself to spend with his children as his father was. Ultimately, he was loyal to his father's style of parenting in that he, too, withheld something important from his children. While the withholding looked very different on the surface (his father was physically absent from his children most of the time while Ian, by not sharing any of his personal interests with his children, was emotionally absent), the outcome is remarkably similar; a father who doesn't share himself with his children and is hard for them to be around because of his irritability.

Of course, it is not just his father Ian is being loyal to in this scenario, but his childhood self. By refusing to set reasonable limits on his involvement with his children, he is trying to avoid causing his children the pain his father caused him. Both sets of loyalties are being expressed in ways that might seem the very opposite of loyalty; his father would not be pleased to know that Ian lives a life dedicated to being different from his, and his children are not pleased with the fretfully obsessive attention they receive; but these are manifestations of a deep-seated, if not fully acknowledged, loyalty.

Sometimes our loyalty to the past takes the form of all but compelling our loved ones to participate in painful reenactments of early life situations. If, for example, as children we were abandoned by someone important, through divorce, perhaps, or even death, we're then likely to be sensitized to other abandonments in our lives. We find ourselves reacting with unwarranted intensity to our partner's withdrawals, even when they are only momentary or minor ones. This, ironically, precipitates the very withdrawal we fear, as when one partner's anxious clinging becomes a turnoff to the other. By re-creating the original scenario in a new theater, we maintain our connection with our lost loved one and to the hurt child inside of us.

That is one of the reasons that individuals who have been abused as children often find themselves in adult relationships that are also abusive: The reassuring familiarity of the abuse, and their loyalty to their victimizers as well as to their victimized childhood, is sustained, and they've come home again.

It is all of these loyalties, in all of their varieties of expression, that for better and worse are revivified by the shadowy journey back in time that accompanies parenthood. And it is here that we find the most elemental answer to why the process of becoming parents is so hard on a couple's marriage.

For it is the way that we as a couple manage and negotiate these often conflicting, tormented loyalties to our first families that is at the root of each of our contributions to the reciprocal dances that we engage in.

Let's take a look at a couple of examples that will show how this happens.

Hal, a thirty-eight-year-old pharmacist and father of two boys, contacted me because of the disagreements he and his wife were experiencing around issues of disciplining their children. His thirty-four-year-old wife, Jeannine, a chemist who had recently gone back to part-time work after taking several years off to be a full-time caregiver, informed me that the problem was that Hal was constantly rescuing the boys from punishment.

"Anytime I implement anything, you're in there talking me out of it, or trying to get me to negotiate. They don't learn anything but that you're the nice guy and I'm the witch, and I'm sick of it," she declared.

"If you weren't such a witch with them, I wouldn't have to be in there rescuing," Hal countered darkly. "I mean, you don't let up, you're constantly on them for every little thing, and I feel like you're really making them feel bad all the time."

When I asked Hal how he thought limits should be set with the boys, he said, "It's just a matter of talking softly but firmly to them, that's all. They'll come around, they're good kids."

"You don't have to be around them as much as me," Jeannine almost screamed. "If you were, you'd have to deal with all the crap they pull, and it wouldn't be all of this talk-softly-and-sweetly baloney. You'd be on them at least as much as me, you just don't see it."

In getting some background, I learned that Hal's mother had been an unpredictable disciplinarian when he was a child. He recalled that one time she had laughed gleefully with him when he had used his crayons to color her checkbook, but another time she had smashed him across the face because he was accidentally making pencil marks on the kitchen table while drawing her a picture. His father worked "round the clock" and apparently had little authority in their home. Hal remembered his mother talking angrily to him about his father and his paternal grandparents when his father wasn't there, which was most of the time, and he recalled his father's frequent and surefire exits to the bathroom in response to his mother's harangues whenever he did make an appearance.

Jeannine never knew her father, who had walked out on her mother shortly after Jeannine was born. The youngest of three, with two older brothers, she had angrily watched her siblings wear her mother down with their constant stream of "druggie friends" and scrapes with the law.

These aspects of Hal and Jeannine's histories hadn't come into play much before they had children. Times when they had had to agree on some kind of limit-setting of one sort or another were few and far between, confined to relatively benign (for them) issues such as how frequently they'd have dinner at Jeannine's mother's, or whether to let their dog sleep on their bed or not.

But the demands that all children make on their parents to draw the line were made on them, too, and it was at this point that some of their destructive reciprocity was coming into play. When it came to the realm of discipline and limit-setting, they had become polarized, she playing the role of hyperparent, in this case more actively involved with discipline, and he the role of hypoparent, and thus less actively involved.

Jeannine's mode of discipline naturally reminded Hal of his mother's violent temper. When he rushed instantly to the boys' defense, he was defending not only them but his father and himself as a child, in a way that his father never did for either of them. His loyalties were not with his wife but with the beleaguered Boys and Men who are always besieged by Women.

Hal's "absence" as a disciplinarian reminds Jeannine of her own absent father. Her vigilant attempts to get her boys to behave appropriately, and to get her husband to provide her with 100 percent backing, are rooted in her bond to her mother, and her wish that her father could have been there with her mother to help her to raise and control her unruly brothers. Her loyalties are not with her husband, but with all of the Women who have been abandoned and mistreated by Men.

Hal feels that Jeannine is violent and assaultive. Jeannine feels that Hal undermines and sabotages her. And each acts in ways that are intended to get the other to change. The problem is that their vision of the present situation is being viewed through the lens of the past. They have become people who are more symbolic than real for each other at this juncture in their conflict, which prohibits them from viewing with clarity the ways in which each of them unintentionally fuels the fire.

For progress to be made, both Hal and Jeannine need to recognize their respective contributions to the problem, and to become more aware of the ways in which his/her past is influencing the present as a first step toward diminishing this influence.

In a later chapter we will be discussing in more detail the ways in which problems like these can be addressed, but let me briefly present some of the pathways Hal and Jeannine found to lead them out of their ongoing conflict.

When childhood experiences are interfering with adult problem solving, we have to revisit our childhood, with the wisdom and perspective of adulthood, and take a closer look at what was actually happening back then. Our insight and understanding as children were quite limited, and this second or third look often sheds light on hitherto hidden realities. Sometimes this insight alone is curative, and not a whole lot more needs to be done for change to come about.

For example, I asked Jeannine to talk with her brothers a little more about their memories of their upbringing, particularly their father, whom she had never gotten to know and who had died several years ago. She was surprised to find out that they remembered him fondly, and that their sense was that even though he no longer wanted to be married to their mom, he wanted to remain involved with the children. Their mother felt so abandoned, however, that she couldn't tolerate this, and worked hard to shut him out of the family's life. One brother, who had been in therapy, told Jeannine that his therapist had told him that one of the reasons he was probably such a problem during adolescence was that he was hoping to create enough of a ruckus that their mother would have to call their father back and make room for him, if only as co-parent.

Of course, her brothers' version of the family history was no more "correct" than the one she had been walking around with up until now, which was her mother's version. In every family, there are as many stories as there are storytellers. But this new slant on the situation helped Jeannine to feel less negative about "Men," such as her father and brothers, and a little less beholden to her mother.

"She obviously didn't have to be parenting alone, after all, and she certainly didn't have to ignore my brothers' requests to see our father as forcefully as she did," she explained in our next session. "In a way, I feel kind of used by her, as if I was supposed to be her husband, and supporting her like a husband would do."

I asked Hal to talk with his mother a little bit more about his upbringing (his father also had died several years ago), and to ask her to focus some on the challenges that he presented to her.

She was surprised and pleased to be asked, and exuberantly chatted away about how "hyper" he was as a child, which reminded her of his own oldest son. She also said that she was the one who had wanted to get him involved with Little League baseball and other activities, thinking that this might mop up some of his excessive energy, and it was his father who had vetoed the idea, saying he didn't want Hal to get hurt. So Hal, like his wife, started developing a richer and different set of impressions of childhood, in which his mother, although less predictable than his father, also seemed more sensitive to his needs and more invested in meeting them.

"I always thought of my mother as the bad guy and my father as very tolerant, but in a funny way she seems to have keyed into me better than he did—he was so busy avoiding her, he probably was avoiding me, too," Hal commented in the same session.

These insights didn't by themselves solve all of the conflicts that Hal and Jeannine were experiencing around discipline. Additional work had to be done, work that was built upon their acknowledgment of their past and their new and more complex understanding of it. However, their journey into the past *took the edge off* of these conflicts enough that the two of them were able to begin thinking differently about them.

Once Jeannine was freed from her single-minded loyalty to herself as an abandoned daughter and to her victimized mother, and once Hal was freed from his single-minded loyalty to himself as an "abused" son and to his victimized father, both found it easier to compromise on their differing child-rearing philosophies.

*   *   *

In another case, Judy and Jonah were both thirty-one-year-old psychologists who came to see me while she was starting to wean their two-year-old son. Judy was mourning the loss of this connection with him, and Jonah was sympathetic to her pain but unaware of its intensity as well as of any feelings that he himself had about his son's weaning.

He would blithely reassure her that there'd be other ways to enjoy their boy without nursing him, and that they'd probably have another child anyway, so it wouldn't be the last time that she would ever nurse. These well-intentioned but ineffective efforts would provoke an anguished outcry from Judy, who would bewail the fact that Jonah couldn't possibly understand the nursing experience or he wouldn't say "such insensitive things" to her.

This made the conscientious but hurt Jonah back off, for fear of saying the wrong thing, which led to Judy feeling even more unsupported and pursuing him for "support" even more intently. She became more and more invested in Jonah understanding exactly why weaning was so difficult for her, and spoke about it more and more frequently with this goal in mind.

Naturally, this effort backfired. Jonah became less willing to deal with the whole subject, and began avoiding other sensitive topics, too, for fear that they would inevitably blend into this one, which was indeed quite often the case. Thus, they were beginning to cut off from each other at the very point where they needed each other the most. She had become the pursuer, and he the distancer.

When I questioned Judy about why it was so important that Jonah appreciate the difficulties she was having, she replied that this was the only way she imagined he could help her with weaning their son.

Judy: "If I knew he understood, I'm sure he'd be there for me."

BES: "And what would it be like if he were there for you?"

Judy: "I don't know . . . you know, be there, support me. . . ."

BES: "Which would mean what, specifically?"

Judy (tearful): "I need somebody to help me through this. . . . "

BES: "Does it need to be Jonah?"

Judy: "Who else could it be? He's my husband, it's his son we're talking about."

Jonah (emotionally): "I'd really like to help her through this, but I don't know how. . . . "

At this point, Judy and Jonah are locked into thinking there is only one solution to their problem. Anything short of his complete understanding of her experience is deemed by both of them to be a failure in communication, and with each failure, they struggle even harder with each other, resulting in more failure still.

In response to this sense of failure, both partners have become hurt and disappointed, placing blame on each other to ward off these feelings rather than looking inward for the origins. This not only makes it impossible to attain their original goal, that of mutual understanding and support, but unlikely that they can meaningfully sort out and come together around the fundamental theme that is on the table, which is their *shared* sense of loss as an important stage of child rearing comes to an end.

As I helped each of them to explore their conflict using a wider-angle lens that included data from their past, rather than just the present, they gradually found themselves with a greater capacity to bond.

BES (to Judy): "Can you think of anyone besides Jonah who might support you through the weaning process?"

Judy: "I'd have to think. I mean, a couple of my friends have been helpful, particularly the ones who've been through this themselves . . . but somehow, it's not enough, that's why I keep going back to Jonah."

Jonah (feeling relieved that he may be off the hook for a moment): "How about your mom?"

Judy (darts him a look and laughs): "My mom? She's probably delighted that I'm weaning. I mean, she didn't understand what all the fuss about nursing was in the first place—she thought it was kind of indulgent, and not very efficient. I think she can't wait for this to be over with."

BES: "Did she nurse you?"

Judy: "Nah... well, maybe, actually I think she did, but not for very long—of course I don't remember... but she never talks about it fondly, just says, 'It wasn't done in our day,' like it was something she tried and then ditched... too much trouble... she's too efficient for that... you can't measure how much milk he's getting, and she always wants to know how much he took."

BES: "What would you like her to know about what it was like to nurse, and what it's like to begin giving it up?"

Judy (angrily): "You mean, if she could possibly deign to understand? I'd want her to know that it was the greatest thing I've ever done, that it was worth the struggle, and the sleepless nights, and that I'll do it again for our next child and you can't understand how wonderful it is to be asleep with your boy, all warm and snuggly (sadder)... and that I don't know what it's going to be like to not have that anymore (starts to cry)."

Jonah (softly): "You know, it's kind of weird for me, too, now that I think about it. It's been so much a part of having a child, you nursing him, that I'm not really sure how it's gonna go, either, without it. It's hard to picture him not having that contact with you every day...."

Judy (doubting and baiting him): "Oh, you'll be pleased, too, you're kind of tired of it.... you kind of roll your eyes when he asks to nurse and it's not one of the regular times, and none of our friends with two-year-olds still nurse, and you're embarrassed... admit it!"

Jonah: "Well, I do get a little sick of it, I'll admit, and frankly, I'm looking forward to your not having to drag your breast out in public, because it is still embarrassing for me, but all I'm saying is that I'll kind of miss it, too."

At this point, Judy and Jonah have finally begun to make contact around the theme of weaning in a way that they hadn't been able to before. It came not from her exerting more and more effort trying to *get* him to understand her, or from him exerting more and more effort trying to *be* understanding, but from her encountering more fully her relationship with her mother, and the ways in which she had not been there for Judy.

BES: "Tell me more about what you think influenced your mother to not nurse you."

Judy: "Well, *her* mother was kind of a tyrant, and didn't think anything that she did was good enough, so if *my* mother didn't master something right away, if it wasn't going to be just right from the get-go, she just stopped trying, to avoid being criticized, or being a failure. My mom was kind of all alone when she had me, they had just moved because my dad was in the service, and had no friends and family in the area . . . and it *was* kind of frowned on by her doctor, too, now that I think about it, he just told her to try bottles if I wasn't taking the breast."

BES: "Do you think that your mom had reactions to your being a success as a nursing mother when she had been deprived of that experience herself?"

Judy: "I never thought of it that way, although we are kind of competitive in a way—maybe she feels like I've defeated her (angry again), and in a way, you know, I have, I think I've given my son something that she never gave to me, and it's so precious, and that's what I want her to know. . . . "

As Judy talks, it becomes clear that the theme of getting her husband to identify with the complexity of the weaning process is a smoke screen. What she needs to do is not persuade her husband to understand her, but to see and reconcile with her mother more completely. Her most basic desire right now is to have her mother understand what motherhood has been like for her, as well as to understand more about what kind of parent her mother was for her.

This work is crucial to her expanding maternal identity, and if she can embark on it, with my help as well as that of her mother and any other extended family members (aunts, grandmothers, etc.) who might be helpful, she will be well on the way to finding new dimensions to her relationship with both her son and her husband.

Meanwhile, Jonah has his own reverberating journey to contend with. While his conflicts are farther from the surface, they are still agitated by his son's weaning.

BES (to Jonah): "While we're on the subject, did your mother nurse *you?*"

Jonah: "No, her doctor was dead set against it, too—she said it just wasn't done, she didn't nurse any of us."

BES: "What was it like to see your son nursed by your wife?"

Jonah (distant sounding): "Nice, really nice . . . it looked so pleasant for them."

BES: "Stir any other feelings?"

Jonah (edgy): "No, I guess not . . . I really liked the fact that he was so taken care of by Judy, and liked thinking that he was getting all those antibodies you read about through the milk, and not having to deal with bottles and formula—I've heard that's a mess. . . . "

BES: "When Judy said earlier that sometimes you seemed exasperated by his nursing, what was she referring to?"

Jonah (jauntily): "Oh, I don't know . . . I guess I'm still a little embarrassed about the nursing in public."

Judy (almost jumping out of her chair): "That's not what you tell me!

You tell me that you think he shouldn't need it anymore, that it's enough already, he's a big boy, he can talk and everything."

Jonah (embarrassed): "Well, I don't know . . . maybe so, I mean, sometimes he does seem like he's a little too dependent. . . . "

BES: "Was your independence important to your father?"

Jonah: "God, yes, the last thing he would want would be for me to be dependent. He was terrified of our needing anything from anyone, and so proud of his own self-sufficiency, really tried to pass that on to us. I mean, he grew up during the Depression, and he knew what it was like to have to depend on someone else . . . it was humiliating for him and his parents."

BES: "Did your need for security ever get short shrift due to the emphasis on your being independent?"

Jonah: "What do you mean? I mean, we were secure. . . . "

BES: "In what ways?"

Jonah (sounding defensive): "We knew my parents would always be there for us, and that there'd always be food on the table and presents at Christmas. That's secure . . . it's more than a whole lot of kids have."

BES: "Could you ask them to hold you if you were hurt?"

Jonah: "You mean my parents? Well, my mom, I guess . . . not my dad, I'm not sure he would have been too happy about that. He wouldn't have been happy at all . . . "

BES: "But if you needed a little extra tenderness, a little extra soothing, could you turn to him for that?"

Jonah (smiling sadly): "No way . . . I mean, there was just no way I would have taken the chance. He cared, I think, but not in that way."

Judy: "That's how I feel about you and me—you never turn to me when you're hurt... you always take care of it yourself, and then wonder why no one cares about you. You're just such a machine, that nobody can ever help you."

Jonah (tearful): "I feel like I'd be letting you down if I needed something from you, you're so busy and preoccupied with the baby and everything. . . . "

Judy: "But that's what infuriates me, I think I get so busy and preoccupied because you've never turned to me, and I've just never felt that important to you. You seem to do so well without me... I'd love it if you'd turn to me for once."

As we edge closer to Jonah's childhood experience, his fear of being abandoned or humiliated for needing help becomes more prominent. Watching his son's ability to ask for and get "fuel" through nursing begins to stir in him some of his own unmet needs for refueling, and his steadfast and prolonged efforts at denying these needs for fear of exposing them to those he cares about and fears rejection from.

Once some of his vulnerability has been acknowledged, Judy is able to voice her concerns about her husband's lonely sojourn and invite him to open more of himself up to her. Thus, an interesting switch has taken place. Instead of her complaints that he doesn't understand *her* at this delicate time in her motherhood, and pursuing him for more contact, she is now offering to better understand *him* at this suddenly delicate time in his fatherhood.

The cycle of pursuit and distancing has finally begun to slow down, and the original conflict, which was his supposed lack of understanding and support of her as she began to wean their son, has been transcended. Without their intentionally working to enhance this understanding, they've found entirely new and hopeful avenues of engagement by acknowledging the influence of the past.

We have learned in this chapter that the origins of reciprocal marital conflicts like pursuing and distancing or hyperparenting and hypoparenting often lie in our childhood experiences. The main reason that parenthood is so stressful for us is because having children breathes new life into these childhood conflicts and sorrows that we thought were long since buried.

When this happens, our often invisible loyalties to our first families reemerge, loyalties that, however indirectly or paradoxically expressed, dictate the behaviors that either help us to adapt to child rearing or lead us directly into our reciprocal marital conflicts.

Now that we know what the problem is, however, we need to examine more closely how to grow beyond the loyalties that constrict our adaptability to parenthood, so that new marital behaviors and interactions can begin to take root. For the couples described in this chapter, simply adopting a broader perspective and becoming more aware of their pasts was a healing experience and unstuck them.

Often, though, we need not just to think differently about our family of origin, but to act differently with them, too. The next chapter will explore this process in more detail.

CHAPTER THREE

Change and How It Happens: Differentiation and Selfhood

"I was a revolutionary when I was young, and my only prayer to God was 'Lord, give me the energy to change the world.' As I approached middle age and realized that half my life was gone without my having changed a single soul, I began to pray, 'Lord, give me the grace to change all those who come in contact with me—just my family and friends—I shall be happy.' Now that I am old and my days are numbered, my one prayer is, 'Lord, give me the grace to change myself.' If I had prayed for this right from the start, I would not have wasted my life."

A cartoon depicted a friend confiding to his bartender, "We were getting along fine—then she began trying to bring out the best in me."

We all have the understandable urge to find our partner's faults and weaknesses, assume that these are at the root of our problems with each other, and conscientiously set about to fix them. Although this feels right and appears to make enormous sense, most of us need to become aware that such endeavors not only don't solve problems but also generate new ones.

As we learned in the first chapter, if we want to resolve the problems in our marriages, we must first determine our own role in the creation and maintenance of those problems. If we don't do this, if we view our unhappiness as the direct result of our partner's behavior, we're left with only one option, which is to somehow try to get our partner to change through coercion, pressure, withdrawal, or persuasion, none of which ever work.

Differentiate, Don't Blame

Thinking "systemically," we see that what we judge, blame, and condemn our spouse for doing is partially engendered by our own actions. Once we recognize that, we realize we can alter the dynamic between us by changing our role in it. But I don't mean to suggest that making personal changes is always easy. Often, it will require us to examine the core dramas from our family of origin, and the way in which we reenact them in the present so as to preserve the loyalties to our past. This can be a foundation-rattling process because it takes us to the heart of our identity; to the Self and the degree to which Selfhood has or has not been fully realized through the process of differentiation.

When I refer to Selfhood, I mean that nonnegotiable part of our identity that guides our lives from within, and that we bring to all of the interactions in our intimate relationships. *Individuals whose Selves are differentiated are ones who are both* aware of *their loyalties to their first families and, because of this awareness, capable of* growing beyond them. They can successfully function both in, and, if necessary, out of contact with, their nuclear family and larger kin network.

People who have not achieved sufficient differentiation will live their lives in one of two ways. They will either attempt to avoid and escape their family of origin, meaning that they are ignoring their loyalties. Or they will remain too fused with their family of origin in a conscious attempt to honor these loyalties. In both scenarios, they are imprisoned by these loyalties, even though it may not seem so at first.

What is essential to keep in mind when understanding this concept, known as Bowen Theory after family therapist Murray Bowen, is that *avoidance* and *fusion* are flip sides of the exact same phenomenon. Those who insist that they have "no loyalty" to their extended family are saying the same thing as those who insist that they have "nothing *but* loyalty" to them. Those who always rebel against or hide from their family are doing the same thing as those who never leave or oppose their family. The only distinction is that they are *managing* their lack of differentiation in dissimilar ways.

The danger for members of a couple who have not been working at psychologically differentiating from their families of origin is that they will have few options when it comes to their own evolution as a couple.

If they are undifferentiated in the manner of still being too "glued" to their families of origin, they will ceaselessly demand more "intimacy" or "support" or "closeness," from their partner without ever feeling satisfied.

If they are undifferentiated in the manner of being "cut off" from their families of origin, they are likely to retreat into a fragile and isolated emotional cocoon in an attempt to protect themselves from the stresses of family life; both their first family and their new family.

Of course, what often happens is that the two members of a couple are undifferentiated in opposite ways, but to approximately the same degree. Bowen believed that whether one or both partners are too glued or too cut off, they generally marry someone who has achieved the same level of differentiation as they have, for they will be intuitively drawn to their like, even (or especially) if the likeness is disguised by a difference in style of differentiation.

Ron and Linda, a couple who came to see me because of a variety of conflicts around family issues, are typical of couples who are dissimilar in style of differentiation but similar in degree. Ron felt that he and their two children had to take a backseat to Linda's parents, since "she spends as much time with them as she does with us." Linda felt that Ron was always "nitpicking and criticizing—I never do anything to his satisfaction, and I'm sick of it."

Linda, an up-and-coming twenty-eight-year-old management trainee at a large corporation, was the only offspring still living in the same town as her parents: All four of her siblings had married and moved out of state. Her parents, who were still in good health, relied on her for advice and entertainment, and she gladly provided both. Linda complained at times about not having enough time for herself, but blamed this on the demands of her nuclear family, rather than on the demands of her parents.

When I asked her if she had ever refused her parents' request that she stop by or talk on the phone for a while, she said, nervously,

that she never had and never would: "I care for them too much...
they're wonderful people." When I asked her what would happen if
she did choose to decline, without suggesting that she actually do
so, she responded irritably, "I don't know. There's no reason not to
see them, is there? They're not going to be around forever...."

Ron, meanwhile, a thirty-four-year-old businessman, proudly
viewed himself as free of the "malignancies" of his family of origin.
"My mom's a drunk and my dad's an enabler, and I decided I just
needed to be free of that crap and start anew" was his explanation
of why he hadn't talked to either of them for almost a year.

Both Ron and Linda felt justified in their handling of their parents.
Linda felt that her parents needed and deserved at least one child
who would care for them in their old age. She was unwilling to
acknowledge that in immersing herself so totally in the caretaker role
with her parents, she was alienating Ron and distancing herself from
her own children.

Ron felt that his parents were a bad influence, and that he
therefore had to distance himself from them to prevent their "dys-
function" from leaking into his own life. What he was unable to see
was that by doing so he was virtually guaranteeing that he would
create in his new family relationships the very problems he was
running from. He was so afraid of and stuck in the position that he
was in with his parents, that of being their "victim," that he had
become overly sensitive to being "victimized" by his wife and children, even when this was far from their intent. His intolerance of
their imperfections set up an interaction in which he, then, became
the new victimizer.

Neither Ron nor Linda was really differentiating from his or her
parents: Both were suffering from an overly intense attachment to
them, but via opposite strategies.

Though Ron and Linda came into therapy hoping to change their
relationship, they each remained convinced that the only way to do
that was to change the other person. Neither was willing to consider
looking beyond the confines of their relationship with each other to
look at the influence of their relationships with their families of origin.
In fact, they declared that such a discussion was outside the bounds
of anything they were willing to deal with in therapy. When couples
don't differentiate from their original families, they place unrealistic

expectations on the "refuge" of their marriages, and expect them to do what no relationship can ever do, which is to help each member of the couple become more of a person. Couples who strive to "finish" themselves solely by investing in a bond with their partner have not fully finished their childhoods. Another way of saying this is that what is lacking in the connection between spouses is often a mirror image of what is missing in their connections with their parents. Missing intimacy or honesty or autonomy in a marriage reflects the intimacy, honesty, or autonomy that was missing from those earlier relationships.

Because I was never able to find a way to help Ron and Linda broaden their viewpoint to include the influence of their past, the therapy never really took off, and they terminated without having experienced much change after several sessions. Ron, in particular, left saying he was offended by my inviting him to examine his estrangement from his parents. With the ascendance of the concept of the so-called "dysfunctional family" in this society, it has become almost a given that individuals who grew up in families like Ron's, families marked by chemical dependencies and abuse, should detach from their families of origin. When we have been mistreated, neglected, abandoned, or violated by our parents, this is a natural and understandable tendency, and the concept of "divorcing" one's extended family in general, and one's parents in particular, has a certain immediate appeal to it.

The problem is that parents and extended family cannot be divorced from our lives any more than children can be. We have no choice in the matter, and if we attempt to artificially "create" a divorce, through cutting off from them, we seal off the possibility that we can ever be different.

Cutoffs ensure a repetition of unresolved relationship problems in several ways. One, because so much of our energy is utilized to maintain the cutoff and fend off emotional "toxicity," we have little energy left over for the relationships that we are currently more invested in. We then become like a nation that devotes so much of its budget to defense that it has little left over for the care of its own internal resources.

Second, while we imagine that what has us feeling hurt or stuck or frustrated with our parents is unique to our relationship with them, in reality this point will be reached in any important relationship we participate in. So when we leave our relationship with our parents at an unresolved crossroads, we then lack the confidence and maneuverability needed to unstick our new relationships when they reach, as they inevitably will, the same impasse.

Third, when we abandon a connection with our parents and extended family, we eliminate a potential source of belonging, support, and ideas that might be of assistance during turbulent times. This is a particularly risky thing to do during early parenthood because the demands on us tend to be so extraordinary.

Fourth, when we attempt to reduce our own discomfort by becoming more superficial and disconnected vis-à-vis our family of origin, we inadvertently ask our nuclear family to act out our loyalties for us, raising *their* discomfort. What we try to *uproot* from the garden of our upbringing, we often find *taking root* in our marriage and new family.

Poet Robert Bly wrote, "In marriage, each holds the leash of the Nethermost beast," which I take to mean that we often ask our spouses to be the container of those traits and longings that we associate with our childhoods, and that we may be most cut off from and uncomfortable with.

When we turn away from our first family, we are turning away from our own self-knowledge, and insisting that our partners carry the burden of our more troubling characteristics for us. We then find ourselves in the midst of what family therapist Robert Beavers calls the Unholy Bargain, which he describes as: "You have unresolved mixed feelings and so do I . . . resolving these in ourselves means growing up, declaring ourselves, and this is painful and possibly dangerous . . . so you take one half of my feelings, and I'll take one half of yours, then neither of us has to resolve our internal conflict, but we'll fight like hell for the next forty years."

Our culture often equates maturity with independence, and places a premium on rupturing our alliance with the past. But while it sounds more grown up to say that we're "done" with our parents, this can never be the case. We may be "done" with being a *child* for our parents, and this, in fact, is one of our goals, but we're never done with our parents. They may be "former parents" in the sense that we have grown to need them less intensely, but they are still an inextricable part of our lives no matter how convinced we may be that we have successfully removed them.

Not all cutoffs are as dramatic as Ron's, but other, subtler versions of cutoff are no less injurious and constricting to marital life.

Philip Guerin, who has studied the ways in which the extended family influences relationships between husbands, wives, and their children, has coined the phrase "ritualized cutoff" to describe one common variant. In families in which there is ritualized cutoff, there is in fact regular contact between family members, but it is usually only during family rituals (birthdays, holidays, funerals, etc.). At these times, there is a glancing, tangential quality to all of the interactions that take place, with little of significance being touched upon. Relatives *appear* to be involved with each other, but what they are actually doing is devoting most of their time and energy to an *avoidance* of involvement of any depth. The cutoff remains, but subterraneously.

Scott, for example, a thirty-six-year-old salesman and father of two small children, saw his parents and siblings at family dinners on birthdays and holidays, yet the range of what could be talked about was severely restricted. While these evenings appeared to be filled with banter and cheer, in reality the tension level was quite high, as everyone worked conscientiously at *not* talking about his mother's continued dependence on pain killers for hypochondriacal aches and pains, his brother's impending divorce, and the cloudy future of the family business.

Another form of cutoff I have often seen is what I term the "oppositional" cutoff. In this case, there is also some form of regular contact between an individual and his/her parents that is not strictly superficial, but the contact is characterized by eternal conflict, by an adamant refusal to "give in" on any issue. Self-definition is limited to simply and predictably opposing or thwarting everyone else. Identity can only exist *in reaction to* the family's standards, instead of growing autonomously out of and beyond those standards.

The eternal state of protest does create a *sense* of Self, but it is a highly dependent and, consequently, ephemeral one, because it is completely symbiotic with what it protests against. When we are so reliant on the existence of someone to defy in order to establish our boundaries and know that we exist, our hollow sense of Self will quickly give way under even the slightest pressure.

Abigail, a twenty-six-year-old manager of a clothing store and mother of a six-month-old, saw her parents and older sister at least once a week, but these encounters were generally characterized by her picking a fight with them about what she felt was their parochial approach to child rearing. She was as intent on being the rebel as her family was on providing her with something to rebel against, and everybody left these visits feeling critical of everybody else, and vowing not to reengage, but only for a few days, when the next round would begin. Her mother thinks, She doesn't care about me, she's always angry, but in reality Abigail cares deeply about her mother, and is so antagonistic because that is how she deals with the discomfort she feels about how much she cares and about how undifferentiated from her mother she still is.

The apparent flip side of cutting off that Linda engaged in above is a third kind. I call this the "accommodating" cutoff, because it *looks like* engagement but in fact produces the same results as a cutoff. Accommodating cutoffs occur when we choose to live two separate lives, one for ourselves and one for others, be they the members of our first family or our new family.

When someone like Linda says that she "couldn't spend enough time" with her parents, that does not mean she's not cut off. On the contrary, what it probably means is that while she seems intensely engaged with them, she's in fact extremely cut off from her *real feelings* about them. Idealizing them is a way of sanitizing her feelings so that she never has to examine the relationship more closely.

We often feel guilty for growing up and leaving our family of origin, and sometimes this guilt becomes a heavy burden that we tire of bearing. When this is the case we try to be the Best Child we can possibly be to make up for the "betrayal" of having grown up.

Sometimes being the Best Child means wearing a mask and acting like the person we know our parents would want us to be, regardless of whether this is who we truly are. Like Linda, we edit what we have to say, censor what we really think, and in general give in and act the way we know others would be most comfortable with.

Sometimes, however, being the Best Child means creating a continuous stream of problems for our parents and remaining dependent on them to perpetuate the myth that nothing has really changed. This may convince them that they're "still parents after all," and help them to resist acknowledging what is different between the two of them and what is different between them and us.

Bonita, for example, is a forty-year-old civil engineer and mother of twin boys. Over the years, she has made a name for herself in a traditionally all-male field, but regresses whenever she is with her mother to the extent that she insists on seeking her advice on everything from child rearing to her wardrobe. If her mother is unavailable for or uninterested in such consultations, Bonita intensifies her demands or withdraws in a huff until a new problem surfaces.

Linda and Bonita are both, in their respective ways, *pretending* to be different from who they really are—Linda by being extra "loving," Bonita by being extra "childlike." Whenever pretending is our best or most common mode of navigating the tensions that come with family interaction, we are actualizing a form of cutoff that leaves us prone to paralysis and dissatisfaction in our current family relationships.

Mature differentiation does not depend on geographical distance at all. Whether we're thousands of miles away from our families or across the street, we can remain entirely enmeshed and dependent on them, emotionally isolated from them, or connected with them in a way that allows for respectful, rather than intrusive, engagement.

The extent of our differentiation from our parents does not even depend on whether our parents are alive or dead. In fact, the death of our parents may have limited the opportunities we have for differentiating from them, meaning that we remain overly attached or avoidant, longing for them or unilaterally refighting the same old battles despite their having been buried years before. This may seem like a hopeless trap, but there are also tangible strategies, as we'll discover in a later chapter, to catalyze further differentiation from someone who is no longer physically alive, but remains very much alive inside of us.

Becoming Self-Centered

So what does successful differentiation of Self look like? How do you know when you're "there," or at least headed in the right direction?

As we've discussed, differentiation is based on an understanding of the nature of our extended family system, of how that system continues to influence us, and of what our own participation in that system, does, and should, consist of.

When we have differentiated from our parents, we can acknowledge and appreciate what they gave us and let go of what they couldn't and can't. We are free to belong to our first family as well as to grow out of the family circle. And when we *do* grow and leave, we do so not suddenly or urgently, because we "have to," but thoughtfully and gradually, because we "choose to." Even upon having left, we remain psychologically connected in a way that leaves room for our confident and ultimate separateness from them, and theirs from us. This separateness is not a *state* of having simply gone, but a *process* of letting go that leads ultimately to a more vibrant and supple form of togetherness.

When we can function in our parental and other extended family relationships with low levels of anxiety, fear, or rage, and still be true to ourselves, we can be sure that we are indeed differentiating and building the necessary foundation for Selfhood.

Bringing that Selfhood into our marriage is characterized by some of the following attributes:

- Being aware of your need for both contact and independence and being able to move comfortably between the two poles based on your, your partner's, and your family's needs.

- Staying emotionally connected with your partner even when the two of you diverge in your thoughts, ideas, or actions.

- Being free of the compulsion to either *control* your partner's life or be controlled.

- Having an awareness of your strengths as well as your vulnerabilities, and the ability to present a balanced portrait of both to your partner without needing to exaggerate either.

- Taking a stand on important issues and clarifying what you are and are not willing and able to do for your partner, and what you are and are not willing and able to tolerate from your partner, and conveying this stand with congruent words and actions.

• Asserting yourself and making requests when the situation calls for it as easily as you are able to give in and accommodate at other times. Your choice is based on the realities of shared life and what is best over the long haul rather than on what will temporarily reduce discomfort or anxiety in the short run.

• Advocating for yourself and establishing your own position on an issue rather than trying to please, change, or rebel against your partner.

• Doing for yourself in a way that doesn't leave you feeling overly selfish or greedy, or undermining anyone else, and doing for others in a way that doesn't leave you feeling overly burdened or martyred.

• Respecting your partner as an equal and expecting the same kind of respect for yourself.

• Valuing yourself as both a self-actualizing, self-propelled individual, and as a partner in a relationship that promotes growth and self-worth in each person.

When the participants in a marriage have differentiated from their first families and embody a lot of Selfhood, there is an interpersonal synergy that injects their bond with resilience and strength, that allows them to heal and be healed, to nourish and be nourished. Selfhood works like an antibiotic against a wide range of marital contaminants.

When the participants in a marriage have an *absence* of Selfhood, their interchange is characterized not by respect and sensitivity, support and openness, but by *reactivity* to each other. A reactive marital system is a cycle of intensifying and unending complaints and conflicts that grow out of a husband and wife's response to the level of anxiety between them. The reactivity keeps them both from *connecting* effectively and from *separating* effectively. It is a glue that prevents free movement within the context of their intimacy with each other.

Anxious reactivity can never be fully eliminated, but the more of a Self we are, the more we defuse rather than amplify it. The best way to do this is to observe carefully our tendency to be reactive with each other, and to develop perspective, which is a balance between our objective and subjective states. Having perspective means that we can think about our feelings, rather than just experiencing and being buffeted by them. It is not intellectualizing, justifying, legitimizing, or obsessing about our emotions but reflecting thoughtfully and courageously about them while finding constructive ways to articulate and act upon them.

When we are freed from automatically reacting to our own or our partner's feelings, but can instead process, understand, and communicate them in meaningful ways, we develop the flexibility to make choices, solve problems, and change. We are then guided and fueled by our emotions but not ruled by them: They become our friends and colleagues rather than our enemies or dictators.

Let's now take a look at a couple who had slipped into a hyper/hypoparenting dance during the initial years of their transition into parenthood, and how increasing their sense of Selfhood through further differentiation enabled them to grow beyond their loyalties to their first families and develop a more equitable, satisfying, and efficient distribution of labor.

Roger and Annette, both lawyers, had two daughters, four and two years old. They came to my office at Annette's insistence, because she was feeling "burned out" by motherhood and unsupported by Roger. While it was not his idea to come, Roger had agreed to do so without much resistance, and appeared genuinely concerned, but equally confused, about his wife's frustration.

Annette jumped right in, declaring that "I've tried everything to get him to do more, but nothing works." When I asked her to tell me about what actions she had already taken, she quickly ticked them off on her fingertips: "I've reminded him, nagged him, even gone on strike and let the laundry and the dishes pile up, but I couldn't stand it after a while, even though *he* apparently could. He said one time if I just made a list and didn't say anything or nag him, he'd do what was on the list, but that didn't help either. . . . I've blown up at him sometimes, too, when it all comes crashing down on me, and then he'll do a little more for a little while, but that's about it—nothing really seems to matter."

Roger didn't disagree with much of what Annette said, but still seemed bewildered by what all the tension was about. "I earn about seventy-five percent of our money, because Annette only works part time now, and she doesn't get paid as much as I do 'cause she does contract work, so I'm not sure why I get all these hassles. I make a good living, I'm around for the kids, and I help out whenever she asks."

"But I've got to ask you half a dozen times, and even then, you do stuff in a half-assed way!" Annette fairly shouted.

"But I *do* it," Roger replied emphatically. "At least I get to it eventually, and do it . . . you're never satisfied with what I do anyway, so why bother trying? And I can't be expected to run the show at work *and* at home, so what's wrong with needing some reminders from you about what needs to be done now and then?"

"But it's not now and then, it's like you won't do a single thing unless I think of it—there's nothing that you take charge of," Annette ventured.

"Sure there is—I make sure the cars are serviced, I took care of painting the basement; I walk the dogs each evening. There's plenty that I do—you just don't appreciate it," Roger insisted.

Turning to me, Annette sighed and said, "This is where we get stuck. I want more from him, he's sure he's doing enough, and I can't seem to get him to change."

If you are thinking systemically, it is probably clear to you by now what was keeping Annette and Roger stuck in this exasperating interaction. Both were feeling overwhelmed by the stress of parenthood, and while they were managing their stress in different ways, each felt that the real answer to their problems lay with the other one.

Annette, who is in more obvious discomfort than Roger, is convinced that for *her* to feel better, *he* needs to change. She assumes that the origin of her distress is his lack of motivation for and involvement in family life.

While increased motivation and involvement on his part *might* temporarily help her to feel a little better, that doesn't mean that his lack of motivation and involvement is the *origin* of her distress. That would be like saying that because aspirin helped to ease the pain of a broken leg, the source of the pain was lack of aspirin in one's system. The aspirin eases the *symptom* of the distress, not the distress itself.

However, because she is convinced that his selfishness is the root of the problem, she has no choice but to insist that he change. Even when *she* tries to change by "backing off" and letting the dishes and laundry pile up, she has not really changed much at all. Her actions are a little different, but her belief that Roger is to blame for her distress is unaltered. She has become powerless because she depends on *him* to make *her* life better.

Roger is locked into a similarly limited logic. He is convinced that Annette is to blame for *his* distress, and often mutters to himself while under attack that if she would just ease up a bit, life would be much smoother.

If she did, in fact, ease up a bit, he *might* temporarily feel a little better, but it would not last, because his thinking has not changed, either. Even when he now and then decides to "do more," it still comes from a place of wanting to get her off his back, rather than a more thoughtful commitment to shared family functioning or an understanding of how he elicits her being on his back in the first place. She, of course, senses this, which is why his help never really satisfies her and remains nothing more than a glitch in their standard cycle of interaction.

Annette contributes to Roger's hypoparenting by never setting any reasonable limits or boundaries to her herculean efforts for very long, and by "supervising" the efforts he *does* make in a supercilious way. This makes it easy for him to remain passive, since everything gets done anyway, and most of what he *does* try isn't valued, anyway.

Roger contributes to Annette's hectoring and overparenting by rarely initiating or contributing in the ways that would be meaningful for her, and by often doing half-assed jobs. This makes it easy for her to remain critical and disappointed.

Neither sees that their reciprocal functioning is an outcome of *both* of their styles of interaction, and that each could have enormous impact on the nature of that reciprocity simply by changing himself/herself, rather than trying to change each other.

They remain stuck because each is focusing on the other's "problem" without being fully aware of the fact that they are relying on their partner's problem to help them avoid issues and dilemmas that are deeper and more troubling ones.

Their cycle of overfunctioning and underfunctioning was not just an outcome of gender, character, or personality but also of issues dating back to their childhood. Both had family backgrounds and loyalties that predisposed them to manage the stress of parenthood in their particular ways.

In exploring Annette's family of origin, I learned that she was the oldest of three children and had a chronically ailing father and a mother who wanted to be a sister rather than a parent.

"She was more interested in her social life than the 'trivia' of making meals and paying bills, so everything kind of fell on me. I was cooking dinners for my sisters by the time I was in third grade, so my mom would be free to talk on the phone and schmooze with her friends." Enlisting her retiring husband rather than her obedient daughter in a more cooperative parenting arrangement seems not ever to have been seriously considered by Annette's mother.

Her father, a kind but meek and lethargic man, presented a never-ending series of physical complaints to Annette, since his wife had long since stopped being interested in him. Annette was expected to minister lovingly to him, since her mother had chosen to be unavailable to do so.

Despite the fact that Annette eventually left home to marry, become a mother, and carve out a successful legal career, not a great deal had changed in terms of her relationship with her parents. When they came to visit, her mother would not offer to help out with housework or baby-sitting, but instead expected to be entertained and escorted like a tourist from one museum to another. Her father would sit passively in the living room, counting out his pills, and asking Annette upon her return what was for dinner and if she would mind reading some articles he had brought about a controversial new treatment regimen his doctor was considering for his as-yet-undiagnosable complaints.

As we discussed this, it became clear that Annette had learned early on that to be accepted and cared for, she had to parent her own parents, an exhausting undertaking that completely deprived her of her own childhood, and that convinced her that her self-worth was directly proportional to how much self-sacrifice she could muster.

As an adult, then, the more she sacrificed, the more she fulfilled and remained loyal to the legacy prescribed for her by her first family, no matter how depleted she got. To bring more Self to her interaction with her husband, she would have to further differentiate from her family of origin by breaking this habit of ignoring her own needs and attending to those of her parents.

Roger grew up with a younger sister and an older brother, but his brother was hit by a car when Roger was thirteen, an accident that left him paralyzed and severely brain-damaged. This brother had eventually died only a few years ago, right around the time that Roger became a father for the first time. As Roger told this story, it became clear to me that the family had not completed, or even commenced upon, the grieving process that would help them to come to terms with this tragedy. Instead, his father had retreated into his work from the time of the accident on, leaving his mother and his sister turning to Roger for comfort and support.

He remembered a number of times when his dad was working late, and he'd hear his mother crying in her bedroom and go in to comfort her. During her adolescence, his sister would detail for him all of her scary encounters with sexual promiscuity and drugs, yet ask him to keep it a secret and refuse his suggestion that she get some professional help.

Not much had changed for *him*, either, despite the fact that he, like his wife, had eventually left home, married, and become professionally accomplished. His sister, to this day, still turned to him for support, asking him to loan her money when she was divorcing her first husband, and to continually advise her on the subsequent custody and child-support issues that always seemed to crop up, even though this was not his area of expertise. His mother would sigh to him on the phone about the fact that his father wouldn't retire as all of her other friends' husbands had, and that she envied them for being able to travel or relax when she still had to wake up and make his lunches for him as she had been doing for years.

It was clear, then, that Roger, like his wife, had been asked to take on so much responsibility that he, too, had grown up without having much of a childhood. He bore the lion's share of his mother and sister's rage and mourning, and tacitly agreed to be the lightning rod that protected his fragile, workaholic father from these same feelings. He was pre-wired to avoid his wife's needs because he had always been and continued to be so attentive to his mother and sister's needs. And Annette's "going on strike" was no different for him than what his father had done, which was to "psychologically" go on strike and avoid dealing with the family's loss.

To bring more Self into his interactions with his new family, and to not be so fearful of being overwhelmed by the needs of others, particularly females, he would have to further differentiate by asking his first family to take more responsibility for their own lives.

Until they had children, Roger and Annette had been able to balance their lives nicely, and the extent to which they had differentiated was fine. They both had enough time and energy to continue catering to their families of origin and still be there for each other, since neither's needs were particularly intense. Once they started their own family, however, their resources were severely compromised, and they were no longer able to care for their first families, each other, and their children.

Also, parenthood spun them into their own version of a Reverberating Journey. Annette was predisposed to react anxiously to any withdrawal from her husband because as a child she had lived with parents who had withdrawn from each other and from her. Taking on the role of parent stirred up all of her unmet needs, and they were coming out in a torrent, with Roger as the sole target.

Roger was predisposed to react anxiously to any neediness on his wife's part because the presence of two new girls, his daughters, may have subconsciously reminded him of his clingy mother and sister. In addition, parenthood commenced for him around the time that his older brother died, so he may have been associating being a father with losing a brother. Holding back from his new family enabled him to temporarily stave off some of his unprocessed grief, and prevented him from getting too close in case he should someday be confronted with another tragic and premature loss of a loved one.

So for all of these reasons, their marital conflicts emerged at this stage in family life, and further differentiation became necessary so that their marriage, and their new family, could grow.

Because Annette was in more admitted discomfort than Roger, and thus the one with her "motor running" and more motivated to change, I began our work by telling her about the proverb that states, "If one wishes to catch a squirrel, one does not chase it, but lies down and falls asleep with a nut in one's hand." She instantly picked up on the metaphor, admitting that chasing after her husband seemed to push him farther and farther away. "But how can I fall asleep when there's so much to do, and what nut would get him coming toward me?" she wondered.

I suggested that she make a list of what she was and was not willing to do, and present it to Roger. Right away, she admonished me, "I've done this before, and it doesn't work. I've set limits and backed off a dozen times, and it never gets me anywhere."

"But you may have done so without altering your appraisal of the situation. I am asking you to *begin* by setting some limits, not to end there. Setting limits will not by itself result in change, but will lay the groundwork for enduring change to come about," I replied.

When she came back for the next two meetings with excuses for why she had not come up with such a list and presented it to him, I guessed that something else was blocking her progress. Not doing her assignment was not resistance, but the only way she knew how to tell me that a larger issue needed to be addressed.

As it turns out, her parents were due to come for a visit the following weekend, so I changed the assignment by asking her to think about ways that she could set limits with *them,* rather than with Roger. She seemed delighted: "I'll tell my mom that I'll take her on one touristy trip, but only one, and I'll tell my father that I'm not doing any cooking—if they want something special, we can do carry-out; otherwise, they'll eat what everyone else eats."

I asked her to prepare herself for what might be their hurt or confused reactions, because whenever anyone breaks a family pattern that has a long history to it, this will be sure to incur enormous resistance and produce redoubled efforts by everybody else to get the initiator to "change back."

She came for our next session with some interesting insights: "You were right—my mom wasn't in the house more than five minutes before she showed me a page from a travel book that listed all of the places she wanted to get to on Saturday and Sunday, and when

I told her that I'd had a hard week, and I didn't want to schlep the kids all over the city with her, she suddenly withdrew and sulked for most of the rest of the weekend.

"And my father really wasn't any better—he was feeling decent this weekend, for a change, but seemed perturbed that I wasn't taking requests for meals and that I hadn't made their room up nice like I usually do.

"And yet in a funny way, even though they were clearly disappointed with me, I felt very free, and I wondered why I hadn't started doing this long ago. The kids and I got along better than we usually do during these visits, and because I hadn't spent the days gallivanting around to keep my mom happy, Roger and I had some time for each other, too, and that's *never* happened when my parents visit."

In the following meeting, she informed me that she had finally gone ahead and completed the original assignment that I had given, letting Roger know what she would and wouldn't do for him, and what she expected him to do, and that after some intense discussions, they had worked out an agreement that she felt satisfied with. Setting limits with her parents had given her the confidence to do so with her husband.

Not surprisingly, however, despite the fact that such an agreement was in place, Roger was not instantly faithful about adhering to it. He, too, had some important work to do before changes that he had agreed to could actually become a reality.

Hypothesizing that he wouldn't be able to accommodate to some of his wife's and daughters' needs until he disengaged from the needs of the other females in his life, mainly his sister and mother, I asked him to embark on the same process with his first family that Annette had with hers.

"What exactly do you have in mind?" Roger asked.

"Well, it seems that you're still seen as some kind of pump that they use to fill up their tanks when they're running low. Your mother treats you more like a husband than a son, your sister treats you more like a father than a brother, and I can't imagine that you have much left over for your own life and the life of your *own* partner and children if you're constantly being so attentive to everybody else."

"I see what you mean, but how could I do it differently? They all seem to need me."

"Well, they may need you, but you also seem to need being needed *by* them just as much. You have so effectively provided partnership for your mother over the years that your parents haven't had to deal with their relationship with each other. And you're so willing to clean up your sister's messes that she's never learned to clean them up herself. No wonder you feel like avoiding your wife when she comes at you with some needs of her own—you're already overbooked."

With this framework in mind, Roger decided after some discussion that as a first step, the next time his mother complained about his father's work, he would simply suggest to her that she complain to his father directly, rather than sympathetically give her room to ventilate. And the next time his sister asked for legal help, he would agree to help her find a lawyer close to where she lived whose work he could endorse, but would not remain "of counsel" in an area in which he had no special expertise.

Roger reported that both seemed stunned by his response. When he wondered aloud during their next telephone conversation if his mother could talk to his father about the retirement issue instead of to him, she snapped, "I haven't talked to your father in years... why start now?" Roger had resourcefully responded, "Because you're married to him, not to me." She slammed the phone down, went into a funk and didn't call again for two weeks, but then re-established contact and acknowledged that "this must be a big burden to you, hearing how unhappy I am all of the time."

When he offered his sister the names of a couple of lawyers who were expert in matters of family law, she seemed hurt and asked Roger if this meant he wouldn't help her. He replied that he didn't think he had been of much help to her, getting involved with an area of the law he knew little about, but that he would be happy to talk with whatever lawyer she chose to fill him/her in on the background.

He then suggested that maybe he could be of more help to her by being her brother, rather than her lawyer, and dealing with some of what had been so difficult about their past. At this she broke down and started to cry, saying that she had always felt guilty that she didn't want to visit their older brother at the rehabilitation facility where he had lived his last years. Roger, too, acknowledged his own feelings of regret and loss, and for the first time in years they began to process the impact that this trauma had had on all of them.

Over the next few months, Roger gradually took over more and more of the responsibilities that Annette had asked him to share with her, and she noted that, in particular, his relationship with the girls was characterized by more play and good-natured teasing than usual.

Only when he had shrugged off the shackles of catering to his first family's needs and began attending to his own did he find within him the capacity to more fully address those of his wife and daughters.

It was clear, then, that Annette had found it easier to be frustrated with her husband than to acknowledge the ways in which she remained beholden to her parents, and that Roger found it easier to stay aloof from his family than to deal with his own loyalties to his first family and his grief for his dead brother. Remaining polarized in their reciprocal dance served the function of keeping them from revisiting the unhappiness of their past until they were more ready to do so.

There was still more work to be done, but over the next year Roger and Annette continued to gradually reequilibrate their marriage and find constructive ways of asking for and getting help and support. Less prone to over- or underfunctioning, they were better able to adapt successfully to the constantly shifting circumstances that are an integral part of marital and family life. The creation of their new, more enjoyable family dance was made possible not by directly tackling the issues that had seemed to divide them but by enabling each of them to sort out the influences of the past on their present lives and take steps toward achieving more differentiation from their families of origin.

In this chapter, we have been considering the possibility that the "high road" to changes in our marriage is a focus on changing ourselves rather than our partners. We are best able to change ourselves when we are willing to undertake the process of *differentiating* from our first families. Differentiating means becoming more truly our Selves, acknowledging and honoring our loyalties to significant figures in our past while *growing beyond* those loyalties that stunt our growth or distort our relationships with people in the present.

In a later chapter, we'll go over a number of specific strategies that will enhance our differentiation from our family of origin and catalyze the development of our Selfhood. But first, let's take a look at how we can use our new knowledge of Selfhood and the dynamics of change to address an issue of supreme importance during the early stages of parenthood.

CHAPTER FOUR

Dia-logic: The Art of Self-Focused Communication

"In every house of marriage, there's room for an interpreter."

—*Stanley Kunitz*

D uring graduate school, I worked on a research project that examined the relationship between marital communication and marital satisfaction for couples who had been married more than five years, using a combination of clinical interviews, structured exercises, and psychological tests. There were two couples in particular who forced me to reexamine some of my preexisting assumptions about that relationship.

One of the exercises involved videotaping the participants as they attempted to resolve a marital disagreement. Adam and Nancy were a couple who informed me in their initial interview that they had in fact taken a six-week communications-skills seminar given at their church a couple of years before.

When they did the disagreement exercise, their expertise was evident immediately. They followed all of the golden rules of healthy communication, such as using "I" statements and speaking calmly and listening attentively to each other. Not surprisingly, they rather quickly got to what appeared to be a positive resolution to their conflict, which had to do with whether or not they would use a baby-sitter or their parents for an upcoming vacation without the children (they chose the latter).

Another couple, David and Dawn, took no more than half an

hour to break almost every rule of good communication that I had learned to hold sacred. As they struggled with the issue of whether to invest money in keeping one of their old cars running or ditch it and plunk down some money for a new one, they interrupted each other, raised their voices, and glared at each other with murderous eyes. At one point, each dragged in old and somewhat unrelated issues, Dawn complaining about her husband's tendency to leave abandoned parts on the floor of the garage when he was working on the cars, David complaining about his wife's overemphasis on their "status" in the neighborhood. At another point, they wound up basically just sputtering with rage at each other and not making much logical sense. They eventually came to an agreement, which was to stick with their old car, but this agreement, forged under such stormy conditions, sounded as if it would last about as long as the car would.

The surprise came when I examined the results of the written assessment that each participant had to fill out individually. The reflective and articulate Adam and Nancy both scored very low on the scale that measured their satisfaction with their marriage; the volatile and unruly David and Dawn each scored high.

The follow-up interviews confirmed these results. Adam and Nancy were so intent on being polite with each other and maintaining their dignity that the relationship had been bled of its intensity. There was no room for any high voltage, and the two of them had very quietly, and with good manners, grown apart from each other over the years. When the videotape was played back for them, they watched solemnly, but with little observable reaction.

David and Dawn laughingly acknowledged some embarrassment about how the exercise had gone when they watched the videotape, and apologized for having "lost control." On the other hand, they said that they knew that sometimes they had to "clear the air" before they could get to the resolution of a problem, and had built enough trust in each other over the years to be able to overlook things said in the heat of the moment and to hang in there with each other until things cooled down. Afterward, they reported, they were often able to deftly revisit the original problem and address it successfully.

Our marital differences only begin to lacerate our bond when we are unable to talk effectively about them, so there is an understandable emphasis on communications skills in our culture. Unfortunately, we seem to have got away from the basic reality that communication is an art as well as a science, an emotional process as well as a cerebral one. What is being communicated goes from heart to heart as well as from mouth to ear.

I have encountered so many patients who, like Adam and Nancy, have taken communications-skills workshops, or studied books and manuals on the subject, and yet who still come to me complaining that they're not communicating well with their spouse, or they're simply miserable, "good" communication notwithstanding. The reason is that, quite often, couples have acquired raw skills without addressing any of their more elemental affective issues. In such cases, no amount of strategic eloquence will replace what is missing.

This is not meant to undermine the importance of communications-skills training. However, my experience has been that such training has a positive impact on a couple not so much because of the learning that takes place, but because the joint decision to take on the important project of improved communication helps remind a couple that they are on the "same side of the fence" in their marriage. The value of this realization generally exceeds that of any "rules" of good communication they may learn.

Using "I" statements, for example, is effective only if you have enough Selfhood to be able to define an "I" that has strength and integrity. When there is a distancer-pursuer or hyper/hypoparenting dynamic, each may be using "I" statements, but if the "I" is simply in reactive mode, an unwitting partner in a destructive duet, nothing is likely to change.

The pursuer insists on contact by saying, "I need you to let me in on what you're feeling," while the distancer insists on separateness by saying, "I have said all I'm going to say, and think you should leave me alone." The pursuer concludes that the distancer's fear of intimacy is the "real problem," while the distancer concludes that the pursuer's obsessive neediness is the "real problem."

The hyperparent says, "I need you to do more," and the hypoparent says, "I've done plenty, you need to back off." The hyperparent concludes it is the hypoparent's underresponsibility that is the problem; the hypoparent concludes that it is the hyperparent's judgmental nagging that is the problem.

In both scenarios, the partners absolve themselves of any responsibility so that they remain stuck in their respective ruts, all while scrupulously following prescribed communications guidelines.

Family therapist Edwin Friedman believes that how well messages between two people are heard is not really based on the actual words they choose at all. He instead focuses on the *direction* they are moving in, their *distance* from each other, and their *anxiety* level.

His sense is that people can only hear you:

1. When they're moving *toward* you, rather than away from you.

2. When there is enough separation for data to be transmitted, but not so much that you're out of each other's broadcast range.

3. When the anxiety in the system is low. During verbal transactions, the anxiety will operate the way static does on a radio: Turning up the volume will not enhance the clarity of transmission, but only increase the static. The best alternative is to be more differentiated, so that you can tune in better.

With this framework in mind, a successful dialogue that results in two people understanding each other and cooperating better is the outcome not just of good elocution or careful semantics, but of two people who know where one ends and the other begins, who are experts on themselves rather than on their partners, and who can effectively manage their anxiety without insisting that their partner be different.

Let's now examine one of the aspects of married life in which Self-focused communication is most essential.

Owning Our Needs

I recently heard a joke about a guy who got a flat tire on an isolated country road and opened his trunk to discover that he had a spare tire but no jack. Beginning to despair, he looked around and saw a gas station on the horizon.

As he walked with relief toward the station, it suddenly occurred to him that the manager would probably realize what desperate straits he was in and charge him a bundle for the use of the jack. As he continued to walk, his fantasies intensified, and he started thinking that the manager would probably toy with him a bit and hint that he didn't have a jack to offer him in the first place. Nearing the station, he was so worked up that he imagined that the manager probably had an entire *roomful* of jacks, and would sadistically refuse to let him have any of them, for any price.

When he finally got to the station, sweaty and enraged, he immediately stormed into the office and screamed at the shocked teenager behind the cash register, *"You can take all your jacks and shove them!"*

One of the truest measures of our Selfhood is the ways in which we acknowledge and address our needs. For a relationship to survive, and grow from, the experience of having children, both parents have to be able to recognize their own needs, as well as their partners'. "To want and want but not to have," in Virginia Woolf's words, is the surest way to make a wreck out of a marriage, as well as your children.

All of us subconsciously hope that when "two become one" *we*, rather than our partners, will be the "one." But in a healthy marriage that is not unusually stressed, we find ourselves easily, equally, and unbegrudgingly giving to each other so that both of us end up feeling restored and renewed. Our mutual "usury" enables us to feel okay about the sacrifices that come with molding ourselves to some of our partner's expectations.

Pouring children's needs into the marital stew changes things, however, because, particularly during early childhood, their needs have to come first. Our fantasy of a partner who exists just for us withers even further, and we are forced to constantly give up, compromise, share, and accommodate at a point when we are needing a lot ourselves. In trying to give our children what *they* need, we often lose out on what *we* need.

The growing discrepancy between what we want and what we get depletes our capacity for understanding, such that the family may at first resemble not two caregivers and a child, but three orphans who are all fighting for nonexistent parenting. We vacillate between asking, demanding, and giving up, and feel enraged that we have been so quickly forgotten and abandoned by our partner.

Why is it so difficult to build a healthy and mutual dependency into our bond? Why do we feel so ashamed of the depths of our needs, and so illiterate when it comes to reading them? We have surely noticed that our babies have no difficulty with *their* needs: They'll squall in a moment if they're dissatisfied, no matter what the reason. How, at some point, did we become so inhibited, so cut off from experiencing and expressing our deepest needs?

Like the stranded motorist in the aforementioned joke, we often fight off dependency because when our needs are exposed, we are vulnerable to being humiliated, repudiated, or taken advantage of. Both males *and* females do this repressing, although usually in different ways. We've seen the results of these differences when we examined hypoparents and hyperparents, and pursuers and distancers. Now let's take a look at how these styles evolved.

Men quickly ascertain that they are not supposed to *have* any needs, that they are "big boys now" and should be self-sufficient. If they *do*, in fact, have some needs, this situation can be dealt with by:

1. Taking care of them privately, without their being acknowledged

2. Projecting them onto someone else, who then carries them for us, or

3. Getting someone else, usually a female, to figure out what they are and unhesitatingly meet them

A perfect example arose frequently during the writing of this book. I often felt guilty about being less available to my family during the more arduous periods of writing. On evenings and weekends, I was torn between wanting to work on the manuscript and get through whatever impasse I was stuck at and wanting to spend time with my family.

Rather than address this directly, however, and deal head-on with whatever disappointment would entail should I make an actual request in one direction or another, I would make a nondecision and hang out with them in a distracted and mildly moody way, while thinking nonstop about the book.

Eventually, Karen would sense some tension in the air, get exasperated, and wonder if I might be wanting time to work on the book, a suggestion with which I would gladly concur. I was unable to speak up about my own needs because unconsciously I felt that wanting time away from my kids would mean that I was a Bad Father, so instead I got my wife to express my needs for me by proxy.

The transition into parenthood accentuates a man's denial of his neediness. One study showed that fathers who participated more in child care had happier wives and healthier children but felt less pleased with their own lives. A possible explanation for this is that these men had begun to subordinate their own needs in an attempt to live up to their new role and responsibilities.

Left to his own worries about impending parenthood when his wife becomes consumed by the changes entailed with pregnancy, uneasy when it comes to connecting with other men about these worries, and unable fully to enter the dreamy, slow-moving world of his infant, a new father can gradually become weighted down by the burden of all of this anxiety and confusion. Unwilling to saddle his exhausted wife with any additional demands on her capacity for care-taking, he ironically ends up being even more of a drain on her, as I did with my own family because of my inability to ask for what I needed.

Participative-childbirth classes instill this subordination of needs into their male students. The "coach" is designated as a kind of all-night service station, and the ways in which he is to meet his wife and newborn's needs are vigorously drilled into him. This is not such a terrible thing, except for the fact that his own concerns are not sufficiently dealt with: Classes almost never, for example, have a male co-instructor to focus on the expectant fathers.

Also, he is typically not invited to tap into a supportive network of classmates, friends, or kin, so that he can be "served," too, at this vulnerable and scary time. There is no biological ritual, like pregnancy, and no psychological ritual, such as a baby shower, that affirms his ascension into parenthood. So he learns early on that his needs are relatively unimportant and are supposed to be diverted.

This attitude is often carried along from pregnancy into parenthood. The following is only one from my private collection of dozens of quotes from reputable child-care books that broadcast the same biased message: "If you are the father, your support is needed to help your wife through this period so that she, herself, does not become emotionally depleted." And that is the only reference to fathers in the entire book! The expert writes as if men have no connection with their wives outside of parenthood, no investment in their children, and no vulnerabilities of their own.

Some fathers do what previous generations of men have frequently done, which is to back out of the active nurturance of their mate and children. "She's so needy," a man will complain. "She wants too much from me." Yet he is *just as much* in need, in this case in need of both solitude and support, as *she* is in need of contact. He uses *her* demands as a decoy so that his own inner wants avoid detection.

Other fathers ignore their needs in a different way, by trying to become Superfathers in the same way that mothers a generation ago began (and continue) trying to be Supermothers. Running themselves ragged by attempting to heroically provide everything for their growing families, they quickly encounter the deficits in how they were parented and bump into their own limits.

Yet they continue to gut it out and stagger through their lives, unwilling to take the risk of surrendering and asking for help. They resentfully wait for somebody else to discern how they're feeling while paradoxically feeling proud that nobody notices how drained they've become.

And if somebody does, finally, notice their needs, they are grateful but also irritated, because they have been "found out." It is as if they are so embarrassed at having been offered assistance that their belief in their masculinity is undermined. They are then quite naturally unable to receive and relish this care, making it less likely that they'll get any more of it in the future.

Women find it just as hard to acknowledge their needs as men do. The problem for women is not that they aren't supposed to *have* needs, but that they are supposed to meet *their* needs through addressing those of everybody else. They become skilled at putting their own interests, wants, and ambitions on hold until everybody else's are satisfied. They feel guilty about reaching for something that is for them rather than for others.

This outlook becomes even more pronounced during the transition into parenthood, in which they are more closely identified with their mothers and encouraged to more completely deny their "inner child" needs to attend to those of their "real" child.

Already socialized to be self-sacrificing, they become, as psychologist Samuel Osherson has observed, the "emotional switchboard" of the family. Valiantly trying to fulfill the multiple requests that are continuously and urgently being relayed to them, they put their own needs on hold.

When the results of socialization are compounded by the biological imperatives of pregnancy and nursing, which dictate that the mother truly is more responsible than anyone else for meeting the baby's needs, it seems all the more inevitable that the woman should take on the larger burdens of family life. This reality can quickly become regimented into the self-reinforcing system we have been examining, in which the more she does, the less her husband needs to do, which means there's more for her to do and less for him to do, and so on.

In the extreme situation, a new, first-time mother starts to feel she has two kids, her child and her husband. Already overwhelmed by the unnerving tasks of new motherhood, and urgently in need of nurturance herself, she finds herself in a panic as her husband starts to become more childlike. She begins to imagine, somewhat justifiably, that her life would be better as a single parent, because although she'd be left without a spouse, at least then she'd have only one dependent to contend with.

If she were truly comfortable with her ambivalence about motherhood and its difficulties, and with the fact that she still has not outgrown some of her own neediness, she would be able to be straight with her husband about how drained she feels, and what would help her to feel restored. However, because she feels that she'll be devalued and rejected if she's not consistently the nurturer, she hides her inner struggles. These, then, emerge not as direct requests, which are more likely to be heard and addressed, but as complaints and attacks, which are more likely to be dismissed.

Being unable to comfortably acknowledge that "I *can't* do everything around the house," she operates on the assumption that "I *should* be able to do everything around the house," which, unexamined, eventually leaks out as "You never help me do anything around the house!"

The husband, under attack, will feel cornered and defensive, determined to dodge her so that he isn't done in by her "constant nagging" and her "need to control." "She expects me to read her mind," he'll mutter, self-servingly, or, "She's not satisfied no matter what I do, so why bother."

Meanwhile, she'll keep feeling ever more tired, more uncared for, more invisible. Alienated by his stubborn refusal to minister to her, she'll push harder and harder for support in a way that winds up antagonizing and distancing the man she's looking to for that support.

Regardless of our gender and our chosen style of denial, we do no one, least of all our children, any favors by circumventing our needs, and having them spill over indirectly, or containing them until they explode at lethal levels. This ensures a constant state of indebtedness, dissatisfaction, and depletion, which will make it impossible for us to function well as a family, no matter how much we love each other. If we are always there for everybody else, we cannot really be there for them at all: It *is* possible to be too good for our own, and our family's, good.

So, there is really no way around it. To make it through parenthood as a viable couple, we have to be able to share our vulnerability with our partner, in full acknowledgment of both our own and our partner's needs. Here, then, are some ways for new parents to put their Selves into action and communicate their neediness in a respectful, growth-promoting way:

1. MAKE SPECIFIC REQUESTS

This sounds simple, but it's not. As we have already learned, we are ultimately responsible for the changes that do or do not come about in our relationships. If we consistently but ineffectually complain about the inequitable distribution of labor in our marriage while simultaneously submitting to this unfairness, we will never be taken seriously by our mates. If we angrily vent or hysterically shriek at our partners *only* at the height of our and their anxiety, this will guarantee that they will not clearly hear and respond to what we have to say.

If we attack them for the current state of affairs without examining our *own* contribution or defining with clarity our *own* positions, we maintain the status quo and keep the marriage stuck. If we drop hints without specifically declaring what we are hinting at, we ensure that we will feel insignificant and starved.

The best way to get our needs met, and to depolarize our hyperparenting-hypoparenting or pursuing-distancing dance, is to determinedly ask ourselves three questions: "Exactly what is it that *I* want changed? Exactly what am *I* doing to make it come about? Exactly what am *I* doing that is inadvertently preventing it from coming about?"

If what you want is your partner to be "more involved," specify what that involvement consists of. Is it doing the wash? Feeding the baby? Listening more attentively to your concerns and worries?

Once you know what you want, think about what you have done up until now to get it. Have you asked directly? If so, *how* did you ask—in an open way or in a way that faulted your partner for not having read your mind and known what your needs were? Did you suggest that this change is important for *you*, or did you try to force your partner to agree that such change is in his or her best interests?

What opportunities have you created for your request to be made a reality? How congruent have your words and your actions been, and has your desire to appear accommodating or unselfish muddied the clarity of your request?

At some level, for any significant change in a relationship to be initiated, one partner has to decide that s/he is uncomfortable or fed up enough to draw a bottom line and stick to it. This is usually the overfunctioner, and while it may feel unfair, and like even *more* overfunctioning, to have to be responsible for taking a stand, if the overfunctioner doesn't identify and speak to those needs that *must* be met, chances are no one will.

Of course, there are two ways to define a bottom-line position.

One arises from a sense of hopelessness and desperation. Armed with threats that probably won't be made good on, fueled by petulance and rage that are either terrifying, anesthetizing, or off-putting to our partners, driven by a fierce conviction that it is *their* obligation to know how to make *our* lives better and to do so promptly, we draw these bottom lines; but like chalk marks in a violent rainstorm, they dissolve and are indecipherable in no time.

The other kind of bottom-line position is an outgrowth of an increasing awareness of our own needs, rather than our need to change or control our spouse. It is expressed in precise and succinct ways, without guilt-inducing complaints or defensiveness-inducing attacks, and expresses, in no uncertain terms, what we are and are not willing to accept and do.

Spoken with dignity from a standpoint that is pro *us* rather than anti *them*, out of a commitment to our Selves rather than an attack against our counterparts, it is heard loud and clear, and backed up with concrete behaviors that signify our belief in it.

Of course, many of us have difficulty sticking with these bottom lines because, as we just learned, we were not always raised to value our needs or to know how to address them. Moreover, once we do begin to address them, describing our bottom-line positions as honestly and directly as we can, we may find that our new candor is not greeted with enthusiasm by our partners.

After all, once we begin to address our needs straightforwardly, it means that we are being different. And change is always difficult, even change for the better. We must be open to whatever response we get from our partners, remembering that we are responsible only for how we *act*, not for how our partner *reacts*. If our bottom line is met with anger or sadness, withdrawal or aggression, we may be tempted to back down and decide that change is not worth it.

"S/he's making me feel guilty," we may howl defensively, as if our spouses were to rejoice supportively and join in with every move toward separateness or self-care that we make. Yet nobody can "make" us feel guilty: It is our own, dormant guilt that is leaping into consciousness as we strive to be different.

If we can resist rushing in to smooth the waters, and tolerate some of our partners' temporary discomfort without withdrawing from or abandoning them, we and they may quickly discern that the depth of their pain is not quite as profound as first imagined.

2. REMEMBER THAT IT IS MORE IMPORTANT TO HAVE OUR NEEDS HEARD THAN IT IS TO HAVE THEM MET

We sometimes hedge when it comes to communicating our needs because we're absolutely certain that even if we went to the trouble of owning up to them, they'd still be ignored or repudiated, and we don't feel like subjecting ourselves to that kind of dismissal. "Why go to the trouble?" we ask in a disheartened way. "It won't matter... nothing's going to be done."

It's true that not all of our needs can be met, and *certainly* not all of them can be met by our partner when we're both under the duress of early parenthood. But a couple can still come together around this disappointing realization and embark on a shared exploration, if not satisfaction, of those needs. Though the specific needs may not be met, the more general and overarching one—the need for support and connectedness—will be.

It is not our partner's job to have solutions to our distress and fulfillment for our needs at the ready: That is neither possible nor realistic. But simply being there for each other as we share our needs may be the basis for the most important and tender connection that we can forge with each other.

I used to rely on my long runs as an escape from having to think about parenting responsibilities, particularly after some interminable discussion with Karen about one or another aspect of child rearing. Upon my sweaty and breathless return, she would usually ask, "Did you think about what we were talking about?"

Generally, of course, the answer was no, because I was going for a run with the conscious intent of *not* thinking about it. Saying this left her feeling neglected and unheard, certifying my unwillingness to focus on what she couldn't *stop* focusing on. Faking it by stammering "Sure," but not having anything halfway intelligible to offer, naturally got the same result. Yet the thought of using my potentially head-clearing run to ruminate even further on issues that I was already sick of dealing with was a distasteful prospect.

My personal compromise was to spend the first five minutes of the run thinking over what we had been talking about, and to bring up with Karen whatever I had arrived at, even if it was nothing more than a continued and shared sense of frustration with whatever the problem was. This initially felt dumb, and somewhat artificial, as I really didn't want to be thinking about the kids, and I was sure my inability to have arrived at a cogent solution would betray this.

However, as it turned out, what was important to Karen was the mere fact that I was willing to do the thinking at all. When we both realized that what she needed was not necessarily a solution but a sense of shared commitment from me, this small five-minute shift in behavior became a healing part of our interactive repertoire.

3. TAKE THE RISK OF TRUSTING YOUR PARTNER

If we're in an overfunctioning/underfunctioning dyad, the hardest thing in the world for the overfunctioner is to believe in the under-functioner's competencies and strengths. If the underfunctioner lets us down, we wonder why we once again made ourselves vulnerable by asking for something. If s/he does come through for us, we wonder why it took so long to happen.

We have to learn to assume the best, that our partner is solid and grown up enough to be there for us. This can be an anxious prospect, indeed, but it opens up the possibility of deepening our bonds with each other.

I cannot count the number of times that I have worked with couples and heard one member confess to the other, "If only you had just *asked* me for [fill in the blank], I would have tried to give it to you." Ruling out your partner's potential before giving it a fair shake will leave both of you feeling unnecessarily deprived.

4. Learn Both to Receive and Give Graciously

Not only do we need to ask directly for our needs to be met, but if our partner is making genuine efforts to address them, we have to respectfully receive what is being offered. Being able to receive is an art in itself, and not an easy one to master. But unless we make progress in this area, we are consigned to getting only limited amounts of what we really want.

A woman I worked with despaired of ever getting her husband to "really talk" with her. She complained that whenever she wanted to have a serious conversation, he would soon decide that it was time to walk the dog. We spent a couple of months working on her being less of a pursuer, and on his learning more about why his withdrawal engendered her pursuit.

She then described an incident in which she invited him to sit and talk for a while after dinner, and he replied that he didn't feel like talking at that time; he needed that period to decompress from his day at work. She was smart enough to realize that this was a change: Instead of leaving, he was talking. He was in fact saying that he didn't *want* to talk, but he was interacting rather than withdrawing just the same.

When she thanked him for letting her know and suggested that perhaps they could catch up with each other some other time, he agreed. She was shocked to discover that later that evening when she came down to say good night to him, he shut off the TV and asked her what she had wanted to talk about at dinner.

By respecting his need for a quiet time after dinner, she had helped him to see that communicating his feelings did not automatically result in fierce condemnation from her. This was all that he needed to encourage him to begin experimenting with sharing more of his life with her. She had repositioned herself as someone he could draw closer to, rather than someone he had to fear and run away from.

Sometimes we, like our children, just have to be gently wooed into a form of relatedness, particularly when our childhoods have been notable for the dangers that accompany true relating. Openly receiving whatever is offered, even if it is tiny and incremental, is the most successful way of wooing.

Conversely, when we are being asked *for* something, we need to be as clear in defining what we're willing to do as our partner is in making the request.

"I'd be willing to take over the breakfast preparation on Mondays and Wednesdays when I don't have early morning staff meetings" is a whole lot easier to trust than a disgusted "Okay, okay, I'll do all the breakfasts from now on," or a snarled "I'll help, but not every day, that's for sure."

As much as possible, don't commit to something that you feel you're not going to be able to make good on, just to temporarily silence your partner. "Is what s/he's asking for reasonable, and can I in good faith, without resentment or recourse to vengeance, promise to do it?" would be one query to start with.

And when we *do* give, we have to give without any expectations of repayment. Family life can't be based on feelings of indebtedness. It's a joint enterprise we have embarked upon; we and our partners are on the same side. We may like the feeling of being "owed," but once our spouses feel this way, they are less likely to comfortably ask for anything for themselves, and we're less likely to summon the philanthropic gestures that help to carry us through tough times.

5. SUPPORT YOUR PARTNERS' RIGHTS TO HAVE THEIR NEEDS RECOGNIZED AND EXPRESSED

While we all harbor, at some level, the wish for a spouse whose only need and purpose in life is to satisfy *our* needs and purpose, such a scenario is the stuff of fantasy. We have difficulty understanding our partners' needs, and encouraging them to put their needs out on the table, because we're fearful this will result in a reduced likelihood that our *own* needs will considered.

And in some ways, of course, our fear is well founded. Marriage would be easier if only one of us had any dependence, if our mates were available on a twenty-four-hour basis to soothe, comfort, and nurture us, and if they wanted only what we wanted.

Given that this is never the case, the next-best scenario is one in which we allow for and reinforce each other's vulnerability, and attend to our partner's needs without feeling compelled to meet all of them. When both of us learn to acknowledge and express our neediness with each other, the larger need that all of us have for reassurance and love is already met.

One of the most frustrating marital encounters occurs when one partner would really *like* the reticent other to be more forthright in expressing needs, and tries to do this on his/her behalf. "I think what you really want is for me to———," we volunteer at such times. We need to remember that we can *never* advocate effectively for anyone else. What we *can* do, however, is create the conditions under which another person's self-advocacy can develop.

This might mean encouraging other people to focus on themselves, rather than our doing it, and/or going out of our way to respond positively when they *do* summon the courage to focus on what they want and directly request it.

6. BEWARE OF WHAT YOU WISH FOR: YOU MAY GET IT

Many times we think we need help from our partners, and yet when we get this help, we still feel frustrated and deprived. That is because what we want may not be help, but some sense of shared responsibility and energy.

When somebody is *helping* us, it implies a kind of temporary and limited support in an endeavor that is mostly our own. This feels very different from a sense of partnership in a project we are equally invested in.

Asking for "help" around child rearing, for example, maintains the skewed belief that only one of us is really in the business of parenting, and the other is a hired hand who cares significantly less about the outcome. That's when we get into situations in which one partner, typically the husband, tells the other, "Sure, dear, I'll baby-sit tomorrow night while you go to your meeting." There should be no such thing as baby-sitting for one's own child.

If what we want is help, it is fine to ask for this. But if what we want is a more equitable distribution of parental commitment and responsibility, then we need to be clear about this, too, or it's unlikely we'll get it. And we need to understand that if our partners do begin to assume this sense of commitment and responsibility, we are then obligated to share our *control* over the parenting, in the same way that we expect our contributions to the earning or management of finances would also afford us some control in this area.

Staying in Our Own Skin

Let's now take a look at a parent who was able to bring more of her Self into the process of addressing and communicating her needs.

Helen, the forty-two-year-old mother of three young boys, came to see me wishing to change her partner's behavior, but soon became aware that these changes would have to begin with adjustments in her own behavior.

A common breakdown between the two of them occurred when her husband, Jake, would come home from work feeling worn out, and Helen, worn out from her own day with three lively children under the age of six, would look to him for instant relief and assistance. Not surprisingly, things never went the way either of them wanted.

Jake would find some project that "had to be done" as soon as he came home, and Helen would either martyr herself and continue her solo parenting while raging to herself about his selfishness or begin complaining out loud, but not directly to him, about his lack of participation, which he responded to by burrowing further into his private activities.

Both, of course, felt justified in their actions. Jake reminded Helen that he worked hard all day and didn't want to be given responsibilities as soon as he stepped in the door without a moment to catch his breath. Helen reminded Jake that she was working all day, too, and that she didn't get any "breathers" herself. And there the two of them remained for several years, glaring at each other across the chasm of their unmet needs.

Some family-of-origin work with Helen pinpointed the source of her reluctance to be straightforward about what she needed. Briefly summarized, she had been raised, as many girls are, to take care of men. She had always been expected to "be there" for her three brothers and her father, whether this meant becoming a cheerleader and attending her brothers' football games in high school rather than actually playing a sport herself, which was her real wish, or joining her mother in helping out in her father's dental practice during the summers, which her camp-attending brothers did not have to do. Asking for or doing what she wanted would certainly be a radical departure from her upbringing.

Before supporting her in making any changes in her marriage, I helped her do some work changing these original family patterns. These involved, among other things, no longer agreeing to join with her mother in doing all the cooking for special family events, but instead asking her sisters-in-law, and even her brothers, to chip in, and looking into reenrolling in a graduate program in special education that she had taken a leave of absence from once she had children, even though her mother was horrified that she would neglect her children, which the mother viewed as an assault on the values she had tried to inculcate in her daughter. These actions strengthened Helen's confidence in her capacity to make changes, and helped to prepare her for doing so in her marriage.

In the meantime, an opportunity arose for her to put her new skills to work with her husband. Jake had been away on a business trip for two days and came home shortly before dinnertime. As they were sitting down to eat, he received a phone call from a good friend whom he hadn't spoken to in weeks. He didn't want to miss the opportunity to check in with his buddy, whom he had been playing phone tag with for quite a while, and leaving Helen and the three boys alone at the dinner table, he went off to the den to take the call.

Helen typically would have begun ranting at Jake for this decision while he was still on the phone or shortly after he got off. This would not only ensure that what she said wouldn't be heard, but would virtually guarantee that the rest of their evening together would be characterized by tension and irritability, with him being walled off and dismissive of her and the children for not being more "welcoming" and for giving him such a "hard time," and her simmering with resentment of him. This cycle they knew all too well.

On this occasion, however, Helen swallowed her impulses along with her dinner, and continued to monitor the children as calmly as possible until after Jake returned to the table and finished eating. Then, explaining that she had some calls to make herself, she told him to take care of giving the children their baths, instead of following her usual practice, which was to hope (usually in vain) that he would offer to do so and end up angrily doing it herself when the offer never appeared.

Jake fulfilled her request after some mild protests, which Helen ignored. She was tempted to dash upstairs to intervene when she heard a fight erupt between two of her sons during story time, but sat still long enough to let the temptation pass.

When the kids were finally in bed, and she and Jake had a chance to reconnect, Helen again handled the encounter differently from before. Instead of waiting for Jake to apologize for taking the phone call, or resentfully asking him how his trip went while fuming inside, she said that she was interested in knowing more about what the last few days had been like but had something that she needed to get off her chest before she could give him her full attention. This automatically *gave* her his full attention, which was half the battle right there.

At this point, with the turmoil of the last several hours behind both of them, she said that while she knew he valued his friendships, she would have greatly preferred to have had him offer to call his pal back at a more reasonable time. She added that by the end of the day she felt overwhelmed by the kids, and the sound of his steps in the driveway always seemed to offer some hope of respite. When no interest or assistance was forthcoming from him, she invariably ended up feeling disappointed and resentful.

She said nothing more than this. She did not ask him how he could have been so thoughtless. She did not wonder "why it was so important" that he talk with his friend right then and there. She did not ask him to "put himself in her shoes" or intimidate or humiliate him into expressing "in his own words" an understanding of how this made her feel. She did not ask him to "promise" never to do this again. She did not insist on an apology. Any of these gambits would have guaranteed a defensive, nonlistening spouse, and incurred less, rather than more, caring behaviors on his part, the very opposite of what she was wanting and needing.

By staying in her own skin and defining her stance in a moment of relative calm, she raised the odds that she would be listened to, and got more across in a minute than she used to try to hammer home in hours of bitter recriminations.

By neither blaming Jake nor insisting that he change, but instead by changing her own response to their standard duet, she opened the door to change on his part.

Jake responded not with the contempt for her that she had been accustomed to anticipating, but instead with a Self-focus of his own. He admitted to having been inconsiderate, and did promise to be more attentive to her needs when he came home.

He also mentioned that he was tiring of his travel schedule, and of not having the time to do things like talk to friends on the phone at his leisure. Beginning to reevaluate his commitment to his work, he wondered if they could talk over some options together that weekend.

Interestingly enough, when Helen was reporting this incident to me, she sounded quite angry, something that surprised her. "I got almost exactly the response I've been wanting—why am I still so pissed off?" she wondered.

My experience has shown me, however, that when we have remained submissive for a long time and finally begin to assert ourselves, it is not unusual to feel anger. Usually, this is a combination of anger toward our partner, for having engendered and enjoyed the unequal state of affairs for so long, and anger at ourselves, for having agreed to it all these years.

It may also be fear of change. I felt that in Helen's case part of her response was uncertainty about who she would be if not the all-important, all-sustaining matriarch of her family. She had a lot of ambivalence about whether she really wanted to reenroll in school and take on the challenge of working on her career. Total absorption in motherhood had thus far saved her from having to make those decisions. Acknowledging all her feelings of anger and ambivalence without condemning either Jake or herself will eventually enable Helen to sort them out, however, and to become more comfortable with both assessing and asserting her real needs.

Helen will surely slip again, and become irritable or reactive in the ways that she used to do in the past. And Jake will certainly not transform himself overnight; it will take a long time for him to make significant changes, to commit himself to doing more to fulfill Helen's needs and temporarily overlook some of his own.

But she has made a major shift in her capacity to relate to her first family and her husband. Understanding the origins of an unpleasant cycle of behavior helped her create the circumstances in which a new, more nourishing cycle could begin.

With time, and some diligent practice, Jake and Helen will find dozens of new resolutions to what felt like inescapable problems.

We have learned in this chapter that effective communication comes about not just by the words that we choose, but by knowing more about the Self who is behind these words.

Particularly during the depletion and exhaustion that accompanies early parenthood, it is essential that we find ways to focus on what we want rather than on what our partners "make us" feel, so that we can discover successful and dignified ways of communicating and addressing our needs.

While thoughtful and deliberate communication of this sort is obviously appealing, because we are human it is not always possible. This means that we need to be resilient enough to handle our more tumultuous marital and parental moments with Selfhood, too. In other words, we need to fight our wars in a way that doesn't end in the demolition of our partner—hence, our marriage. How to go about doing this will be the next chapter's agenda.

CHAPTER FIVE

Hugs of War: The Fights That Need to Be Fought

*"The music at a wedding reception always reminds me
of the music of soldiers going into battle."*
—Heinrich Heine

I n one particularly memorable *I Love Lucy* episode, Ricky has
done something that has riled Lucy, and Fred and Ethel have
been listening to her fume at her absent husband all afternoon.
As Ricky finally and naively strolls in the door, he is greeted first by
the dour Fred, who protectively remarks, "You'll never get out of
this one, Rick . . . just turn around and go right back to Cuba."

Though we may all wish at times to "go back to Cuba" instead
of battling it out with our spouses, fights are an inevitable by-product
of two people living together. All couples, even the most committed,
will at some point experience bewildering difficulties that buffet them
for a time and lead to fights, unless they unhealthily conceal their
real feelings. We like to imagine that our love and affection for each
other will keep us in a paradisiacal state of giddy harmony that will
carry us smoothly over such rocky terrain, but we will always have
to do some tough slogging at various points in our journey together.

A one-panel cartoon entitled "Superman—The Husband" shows
the caped hero at the dinner table with his wife, poking crabbily at
his plate with a fork while asking, "What's in this?" Her acerbic and
disgusted reply: "You tell me, Mr. X-Ray Vision." Even Superpeople
get into it with their spouses.

In fact, family research demonstrates clearly that the marriages

111

that work best are *not* the ones in which there is the least amount of fighting. On the contrary, the marriages characterized by no fights and by unusual amounts of compliance and amicability are often characterized by tenuous attachments, fraudulent harmony, minimal potential for growth, and/or an insistence that others, such as children or in-laws, unwittingly do the fighting *for* them.

Likewise, research has shown that the children of parents who have regular and resolved fights have higher levels of interpersonal poise and self-esteem than do those whose parents have chronic, *un*resolved fights or those whose parents appear not to fight at all.

The families that work best, then, are the ones in which both marital partners understand the importance of fights, and learn to fight well enough that they can endure, complete, learn from, and laugh at their fights. When we come to terms with the need for us to "fight for our marriage," we can then put our heads together to understand and grow from our battles.

Sometimes, however, we do "go right back to Cuba" and avoid the fights that we need to have with our spouses. This is especially true during the early stages of parenthood when, despite the research cited above, we feel enormous pressure to keep things calm and happy because we are fearful that our discord will damage our offspring.

But it is our desire to avoid conflicts, and the ways in which we go about this avoidance, that amplify simple disagreements into the most damaging fights of all. All of the dutiful things that we do to steer clear of the darker side of our relationship are what ironically contribute to the creation of an even murkier, more inclement marital climate. The worst problems sometimes come not from the fights we *have*, but from the ones we *don't have*.

Often, when couples sit sluggishly in my office and comment that "it's too late" for them to meaningfully address their disagreements, my thought is not that it's too late, but that it's too early. They're sluggish because they refuse to slug it out, and the level of unspoken conflict is so high that it's impossible at this stage for them to know what they're feeling for and with each other. It's as if something fierce has to be transacted between the two of them before their marital lake can be drained of conflict in a way that will enable them to see with more clarity what lurks at its bottom.

Without fights, our interactions will be more careful than caring, more exacting than exciting. If we don't allow them to take place, we do ourselves the injustice of isolating our anger from every other emotion, rather than placing it in a context in which it can be understood in relation to our other emotions.

Sometimes it is in dealing with our children that we see the results of repressed anger most clearly. A four-year-old was brought by his parents to see me because he had recently started sucking his thumb again. I learned that he had become interested in guns since starting nursery school several months before, and that this made his parents so uncomfortable that not only did they choose not to let him have a small water pistol that he wanted, but they also didn't allow him to make believe that his index finger was a gun in play. My interpretation was that because he had been thwarted from having the opportunity to learn how to assert his anger in a safe, symbolic, nonverbal way, he simply asserted it in a more regressed way. When his symbolic "right to bear arms" was reinstated by his parents, the thumb-sucking gradually disappeared in a few weeks.

Likewise, the couple who decide that they are not allowed to fight may "suddenly" become bored with, critical of, or walled off from each other, because they have been thwarted from having the opportunity to learn how to assert their anger in a safe, verbal way. They "regress" into dissatisfaction or discord when they are not given the chance to practice their aggression and coherently integrate it into their psychological landscape. It is only when they learn that there are safe ways of expressing anger that this common kind of marital exile can be prevented.

There are of course some ways of fighting that are more productive than others, which we will discuss in a moment. However, it should be kept in mind that there are no stringent and universally applicable rules for equitable fighting that couples can always adhere to.

At times when I read books on communication that propose lists of these rules, it occurs to me that any couple who are actually *following* these rules are either not really married, or not really fighting (which may be the same thing). In any case, I have outlined some reasonable guidelines below that may allow for marital and parenting fights to erupt without their becoming frightening, overwhelming, or truncated. Use the ones that speak to your needs, and try not to think of them as rules.

1. LET THE ANGER OUT AND IN

Anger as soon as fed is dead—
'Tis starving makes it fat—

—Emily Dickinson

I have many patients who defend the terrifyingly honest things they say during their fights with, "I didn't mean it: I only said it out of anger." The implication here is that since the words came from an angry place, they were irrational and should not be taken seriously.

The truth is that what we say out of anger is just as genuine and meaningful as what we say out of love or loneliness or jealousy or any other emotion. This is not to imply that there won't be contradictions between what we say in one moment and what we say in another (as in "I love you" and "I hate you"). But even though the words we fire when our tempers flare may not express *all* of what we are feeling toward our spouse, they do express *some* of it, usually a part that we have been keeping to ourselves.

Folksinger Pete Seeger sings, "There can't be great love without great anger," and indeed interpersonal connections without some fury are connections without much passion. Nothing is more vital to our marital future than finding meaningful ways to express the exasperation and rage that are inevitable components of living with our beloved.

But still we may find ourselves dancing around this task, trying to stick, with gritted teeth, to communicating just the warm feelings, rather than the hot or the cold ones. When we do this, however, we, like the couple I described in the previous chapter, compromise our capacity to truly engage and cooperate with one another.

Perhaps the most common reason that we are reluctant to express our anger is that we walk around with a catastrophic sense that expressing our anger will make things worse than they already are for us. We may be fearful that we'll be abandoned if we get angry, or dismissed as impossible. We may be concerned that we'll lose control of ourselves and become destructive, or appear weak. We may be worried that our anger seems to run so dark and deep that there will simply be no end to it if we begin to let some of it out. We may be anxious that we'll have to actually back up what we say if we are visibly angry.

Often, there is little reality to any of our fears, even though they are powerful and appear to be well founded. Perhaps as children we were threatened with abandonment if we were angry. Perhaps we have seen an angry parent or some other person lose control and become violent and scary. Perhaps our anger's been buried within us for so long that we can no longer assess its beginning or end: It eats away at us like a hugely coiled tapeworm, its appetite insatiable. Yet in the vast majority of cases, adults find that once they feel more comfortable acknowledging and expressing their anger, these catastrophes rarely occur.

What we risk by venting our anger out loud is generally far less threatening than what we risk by suppressing it. Internalized anger causes emotional and physical symptoms like depression, alienation, ulcers, fatigue, backaches, and high blood pressure. Also, we have to remember that if we don't express it directly, it will come out anyway, but sideways, in a way we can't control. The phone message that we forget to deliver to our partner, the medicine we forget to give to the baby, the check we forget to deposit, can all be passive aggressions directed against our spouse when we're afraid of what we're feeling.

I remember during the very bumpy months after Josh was born that I was interviewed on television about some research I had done on fathering. I excitedly asked Karen to videotape it so that I'd be able to show off to my friends and relatives. When I came home later that evening to find that she had in fact taped it, and then "accidentally" taped *over* it, it did not take us long to conclude that she was not very much enjoying the scenario of my appearing to the general public like an expert father when neither of us was feeling particularly expert with our real-life son.

Since I chose not to address this directly with her, but instead to mope about it in solitude, it also did not take me long to just as indirectly retaliate by becoming noticeably less sympathetic to her mothering concerns the rest of the week. An hour of fighting about our disappointment in each other and how things were going would have saved us both a few *days* of vengeful neglect.

In addition to feeling comfortable expressing our anger, we have to learn to assist our partners in doing the same thing. The more you sense your spouse's anger and give him/her room to express it, the more likely that your fights will be fought cleanly and productively, as happened for Betsy and Ken, who consulted me because, in Betsy's words, "We're no longer in love, and this is a last-ditch effort before we separate from each other."

It quickly became clear to me that their conflict was rooted in a communication problem—*not* their inability to communicate loving feelings, as they were suspecting, but their inability to communicate *angry* feelings. Betsy, a thirty-two-year-old administrator at a government agency, had given birth to their first child eighteen months ago and was currently on an unpaid maternity leave.

Ken was the thirty-six-year-old owner of a landscape business that, after some early successes, had fallen on hard times. One of the first issues we tackled was the temptation he felt, each time another day went badly, to vent all his feelings on his unsuspecting wife and son when he walked in the door.

Not that that was what he did: He remembered his own father storming in the door after work in a menacing way and wanted his son to have different memories. Moreover, he was sure that he was a creep for being angry in the first place, and some self-hatred about not being a very good provider was also stirring the pot. Thus, he would instantly withdraw from Betsy as soon as she asked how his day had gone, so as to protect himself and his family from what he felt to be his inappropriate rage. She would notice the withdrawal, rather than the anger, and already feeling lonely for him after a long day at home with the baby, start prodding him to talk with her about their respective days.

What she was looking for him to communicate was love, warmth, and interest. This was only natural, as life with an eighteen-month-old was filled with enough tantrums and power struggles that she didn't particularly care to seek out any new ones.

What Ken was feeling, however, was not love, warmth, and interest, but frustration and anger, and because he was uncomfortable with this combination, he withdrew further, certain he would disappoint or anger her if he expressed what was really on his mind.

Of course, his withdrawal eventually *did* make her angry, which she, too, felt uneasy expressing, since she was concerned about alienating Ken any further, particularly after they had been apart all day, and because she didn't want to make the same mistakes she'd seen her mother make with her father (Betsy described her as having "driven my dad to drink with her nagging.") So she retreated further into her relationship with her son, while Ken got angrier still that she was not attending to him. This cycle would repeat itself for a number of days until a blistering battle would explode, and all of their pent-up rage would viciously spew forth. Living this way month after month, it was no wonder they felt that separating was a reasonable alternative.

The intervention was simple. Betsy was told to assume that Ken entered the house with mixed, rather than loving, feelings. Instead of sweetly asking him how his day was, expecting a positive response, she was to first give him an opportunity to change his clothes, and then give him some time alone with their son, which he agreed to. This allowed him to distinguish himself from his own father, and shift gears slowly from work life to family life.

When they were ready to talk as grown-ups, she was to inquire about his whole range of feelings, and encourage him to talk about any that seemed prominent. Ken was to answer that question first, and Betsy was to be as open as she could in hearing him out. This afforded Ken a nonjudgmental opportunity to have his feelings recognized and validated, and afforded Betsy the opportunity to gauge how much contact she wanted with him and was likely to have during the first hours he was home.

After he had settled in, Ken was then to ask Betsy the same question, and try to elicit the information in the same open-minded manner. Having the chance to acknowledge the full spectrum of their feelings early on enabled them to begin the communication process on an open, rather than a closed, note for the two of them.

With this business "out of the way," they could then proceed in a more balanced fashion through the rest of their time together, rather than walk on emotional eggshells as they each struggled to hide the feelings they felt so uncomfortable about having.

Keeping this framework in mind helped them to sort out the many other conflicts that they faced, and not only diminished the frequency and destructiveness of their fights, but enabled them to begin directing their energies to finding ways to convey the genuine affection that they each harbored for the other. But only when they gave themselves room to be angry could this renewal process begin.

A related problem can arise when we do begin a fight but then decide to "make nice" before the fight has really been completed. It's as if we're so distraught about being angry with our mate that we can't sustain it for more than a few moments, and feel compelled to become instantly empathetic and right away kiss and make up.

Most good fights are balanced on complex issues that probably cannot be resolved in two to three minutes of shouting, followed by a quick, remorseful hug. If apologies are premature, not only might they be insincere, but, worse, the differences that led to the fight remain essentially unaddressed. The groundwork is then automatically laid for another tangle to commence soon after.

The greater the tolerance we have to sustain the tension and endure such angry encounters, the more likely that they'll lead to enduring solutions, and the more likely a repeat of similar battles in the near future can be avoided.

2. Don't "Deride and Conquer"

"It is easy to fly into a passion—anyone can do that— but to be angry with the right person to the right extent and at the right time and with the right object and in the right way—that is not easy, and it is not everyone who can do it."

—*Aristotle*

There are lots of ways to know that you are beginning to venture into a fight that will ultimately create more of an adversarial than a cooperative environment. One is when you insist on making your mate understand that the conflict is your mate's fault, and that your mate ought to "know better." When phrases like "You should . . . ";

"You'd better start . . . "; and "You're being unfair" are being bandied about, something is going awry.

These words suggest that you are operating in a fantasy world in which there are universally defined and agreed-upon rules of justice and injustice, fairness and unfairness, right and wrong, fact and fiction. This stance will be certain to arouse your partner's self-protective instincts. When we are able to move beyond the thrust and parry of mere attacking and defending, new resolutions to our conflicts always seem to emerge.

If you are interested in finding *another* sure way to not be listened to, just label your counterpart in a pejorative way, and deafness will immediately take hold. Name-calling and character assassinations automatically make us slide into a defensive mode that leaves us completely unavailable for contact.

It is better to focus on actions, not personal attributes. Pointing out that when your partner does x in situation y, you feel z will give both of you a clearer shot at problem solving than will labeling your partner as irresponsible, insensitive, unloving, or some other defensiveness-arousing adjective.

Likewise, when you sense that you are doing nothing more than defending or justifying your*self,* you're most likely going to make your partner feel unlistened to, and increase the likelihood of further assaults. A colleague suggests to marital partners who take this tack that "you need defend yourself only in court," his point being that most intense emotional processes grind to a halt in the presence of defensive postures.

An alternative to this dance of attack and defense, which we have already learned, is to focus on your *own* role in the conflict. You could describe *your* contribution to the fight, for example, rather than your partner's. This is not just a shift in language, but more important, a shift in perspective. It can feel like a dangerous thing to do, but with practice, it'll feel safer, and may quickly become the most effective route to lessening defensiveness and improving everyone's auditory capacities.

"You know, I'm not crazy about the hostile way you've gone about telling me this, and we're gonna have to talk about that sooner or later, but the fact is, I know you've got a point, I really have *not* been pulling my weight when it comes to keeping things organized around here" is one way this could go.

You may think that this is like "giving in," that your partner will sadistically gobble up your words and use them against you, and in fact this does sometimes happen at first: "See, I'm right, that's what I've been saying all along, it's all your fault!" may be the initial response that you get.

However, this business of sticking with *your* contribution to the fight while understanding that its existence is a result of *shared* responsibility will, over time, help you and your partner to deal with each other more flexibly, as you each become less rigid about having to defend your platform.

Maurice, for example, dreaded nothing more than Joelle's all-too-frequent complaints that he was "lazy" because he didn't help out enough around the house. The accusation aroused his first and only instinct, which was to list for her all of the things that he had, in fact, done. This, not surprisingly, did nothing more than give Joelle reason to intensify her attacks. Most of the things he did she hadn't asked him to do in the first place, nor did she find them particularly helpful. And she wasn't all that pleased with how he did them anyway.

I suggested to Joelle that she focus on the specifics of what it was that Maurice was or wasn't doing, and how she felt about it, rather than attacking his character in a way that simply led him to defend himself. I suggested to Maurice that *his* way out of this cycle was to make sure he took a full minute or two to listen to Joelle's complaints, and then repeat them back to her rather than instantly jumping in to justify himself. Letting her know that he heard what she was saying, even if he didn't agree with it, would be a crucial step toward an exit from their painfully recurrent cycle.

Maurice was reluctant to consent to this, as he was worried that appearing open would give her greater license to complain and result in his being more brutally intimidated and unappreciated. In fact, the opposite happened. When Joelle focused on what Maurice had *done* rather than on who he *was*, he was better able to hear her. When she began to trust that Maurice would listen to her before beginning to defend himself, she became less bitter, and more open-minded. This in turn gave him the additional confidence not only to register what she was saying, but also to try to understand what was behind her words and deal with what led to her frustration.

A common instance was when she was irritated with him after he had given the kids their baths but hadn't cleaned out the tub. Saying, "When I see that you have left the bathtub dirty at the end of the day, I begin to feel overwhelmed because I know I'm the one who's going to have to clean it the next day" rather than "How could you be such a slob and leave the place looking this way?" allowed him to hear her, because he didn't instantly feel the need to counter her assault.

When he could acknowledge that this must be irritating for her, since she was the one who would most likely have to clean it eventually, and sympathize with her for the impact that this had on her, she felt understood. This in turn left her more open to hearing his point of view, which was that his priority was getting the kids dressed and in bed on time after bath, rather than cleaning the tub, and he couldn't do both at the same time. This was exactly what he used to say before, but it would always come at a time when Joelle wasn't ready to listen. He had learned that the best way to get understanding is to show it.

Once this old communication pattern changed, their energy wasn't all directed at finding new ways to attack and defend, but could be used to find a more even distribution of household labor. In this case, Maurice agreed to clean the tub himself rather than expect Joelle to do it, but she agreed that it did not have to be cleaned every night.

One additional note about derisive attacks . . . avoid perpetrating them not only on your partner but also on yourself. When you respond to your partner's anger or disappointment with instant agreement— "Yes, I am a wretch and a lout and a useless human being"—you intentionally or unintentionally make your partner feel guilty for having said anything. The result may be a short-term plus, some relief from being criticized, but the long-term outcome is that your partner may become reluctant to address any real issues with you, and that you will then be unable to arrive at any real solutions, for the problems will simply get buried.

You can acknowledge your partner's point of view without having to concede that you are an unfit, psychologically impaired adult. Whining about how terrible you've been or constantly lapsing into tears and self-reproach can be subtle ways of trying to disarm your partner and avoid dealing directly with his or her gripes. If you "win" with this technique, you both lose, because it will do nothing more than distract you from the issue at hand, and ultimately lead to more, rather than less, conflict, or an erosion of trust between you.

3. STAY FOCUSED

I know I'm in bad shape during a fight with Karen when I lapse into something that begins with, "Yeah, well what about the time that you . . . " It doesn't matter how I fill in the blank: It could have been something meaningful or trivial, something from the recent or distant past. But if I'm dragging in a theme that is not directly relevant, I know that we're headed into choppy, and usually unproductive, waters.

By now I'm aware that my tendency to dredge up floating marital debris has one of several origins: Perhaps I have started to realize that Karen is actually making a good point, one that I am not too comfortable acknowledging and not too proud of, and thus one that has to be countered.

Or, I fear that, given my usual reluctance to acknowledge anger, if I don't take the opportunity of the fight we're already having, I'll never have the strength to address issues I've been sitting on for weeks. So I use Karen's anger as a springboard, enabling me to leap into a litany of all of the things I have been wanting to say but haven't got around to. In this way, I manipulate *her* use of force to justify *mine*.

As you can imagine, "kitchen sinking" of this sort, for whatever reasons, rarely does anything but provoke irritation and detour a couple from the important matters at hand. All of these other issues that we bring up may, in fact, have some importance and relevance, but they will never be recognized if they're just randomly tossed into a disagreement that has another focus.

It can happen at any time, of course, but this pernicious habit often becomes most pronounced at 3:30 A.M. or so, after new parents have been reawakened several times by a crying baby. Typically, a husband will start off with an attack about this being his wife's fault because she provided (choose one) too much/too little (choose at least four) exercise/stimulation/love/food/discipline/holding/etc. before putting the baby to bed that night, and when the battle is joined by his wife, both of them half-dead from exhaustion, it soon escalates to the point where one of them arrives at the conclusion that the marital relationship always has been a disaster, always will be, and perhaps should be ended, now! It just so happens that tonight, at 3:30 A.M., is the extraordinary moment that he or she finally has this penetrating insight.

New parents are especially vulnerable to losing focus during fights because they generally feel so squidgy-brained from all of the responsibilities and issues that are assaulting their raw sensibilities. Yet because they have so few opportunities to engage, angrily or otherwise, it is essential that they find ways to maintain focus, or their interactions will repeatedly be uninspired or destructive ones.

Staying with the issue at hand is best, even if it's one that you feel "weak" on. If one of you does begin to lose focus, the best intervention is for the other partner to acknowledge that the new issue being brought in may well be important but is worthy of a separate discussion of its own. Reminding your partner that "Whoever brought it up gets the floor" is a useful comment to have at your disposal.

Vigilant and perfectly accurate counterattacks that begin with "That's beside the point," or "Yes, but that was different because. . ." will only serve to increase the probability that the new issue will become even more avidly pursued by your partner.

For example, after the third consecutive night that five-year-old Wanda has wet the bed and wakened her parents with a request for her sheets to be changed, Tina wants to talk with her husband, Darren, about why this has started happening two years after they thought their daughter had been successfully toilet-trained.

Darren doesn't really want to talk about it, and would prefer to just change the sheets one more night and see if this problem works out on its own. He certainly doesn't want to talk now, in the middle of the night, when both of them could use the sleep.

However, Tina, who was a bed wetter herself up until she was seven years old, is very nervous about this fledgling pattern, and insists that they begin making plans now for how this will be handled. Darren participates sleepily, nodding affirmatively to all of her ideas without choosing one to run with or coming up with any of his own.

Tina senses his lethargy and pushes harder for solutions to be developed, while Darren remembers how many meetings he has scheduled, meetings that, he notices with a beat of panic as he looks at the clock, begin just a few hours from now. Feeling the distant pounding that signals the daylong headache he gets when he hasn't slept enough the night before, he blows up at Tina, telling her he's sick of dealing with her, and that she's always been too dependent on him for "answers" since the day they met. Tina, also fully worked up by now, hollers that he's never been there for her, and that even from the beginning of their relationship she knew she couldn't count on him for "real support." Wanda straggles out of her room, wide-eyed, and watches this scenario without a word.

Darren charges out of the bedroom with his pillow to sleep on the couch downstairs, while Tina sulks in bed by herself after snapping at Wanda to go back to sleep. By the time they both get home from work the next day, they are crossly silent with each other, raising their daughter's anxiety and with it the possibility that she'll wet the bed again.

After a few therapy sessions, they had some clear ideas about how to prevent this conflict from blowing so far out of proportion. Darren explained to Tina that sleep was very important to both of them, and that they should generally avoid child-rearing discussions that are likely to take hours to complete. On the other hand, he did reassure her that he would be more fully available at some other time to discuss a troubling issue further, rather than just hope she'd never bring it up again.

Once she realized the role played by her own painful memories of her bed-wetting, Tina was able to explain to Darren why Wanda's display of a similar problem made her so anxious, and to help him understand that what she was really looking for during her late-night despair was not solutions to the problem but an opportunity for her nervous fears and old shame to be ventilated and heard.

Since at this early stage in treatment it was too much to expect Tina to completely quell her uneasiness, I suggested that Darren give her fifteen minutes, but no more than this, to blow off steam in the middle of the night should this or any other problem arise at that time, and that he make sure he stayed awake and held her hand while he listened. At the end of fifteen minutes, he was to reassure her by letting her know when in the next day or two they'd have a chance to talk things over further.

Interestingly, once they implemented these interventions, Wanda's bed-wetting stopped, not because they developed any new or inventive solutions, but perhaps because the lowering of their own emotional temperatures diminished the anxiety Wanda felt around this problem.

Knowing when we are too stressed or exhausted to interact productively is useful knowledge to have, and our best solution may be temporarily but honorably extricating ourselves from an interaction, or limiting its duration, while making a commitment to return to it at a more appropriate time. We thereby reduce the chances of becoming locked into hopeless and destructive squabbles that never reach real resolution.

4. HAVE YOUR OWN GENEVA CONVENTION

It never ceases to amaze me that countries that are at war accuse their enemy of not fighting fairly, as if war were a board game that was designed to be enjoyed rather than a violent attempt to eradicate a foe. On the other hand, marital wars *can* and should be fought fairly, since the goal is not eradication but unification. One thing that will help to bring this about is deciding which weapons are off-limits during a fight, and sticking to this as much as possible.

Such a tactic is never easy, because often what we want our partner to not do during a fight is the very thing that s/he is prone to do when emotions run high. Fights usually have a natural half-life, however, and if allowed to proceed at their natural pace, they will eventually wind down and conclude. If ended prematurely because a dangerous weapon is unveiled, however, they rarely get defused, which sets the stage for more tension and conflict later on.

I have noticed that therapy with the couples I work with is sometimes useful not because I provide them with specific interpretations of or solutions to their problems, but simply because the therapy creates a context in which a husband and wife can fight confidently, without being fearful of anything dangerous occurring. The containment provided by the observation and occasional commentary of an outsider holds them gently but firmly accountable to reasonable standards of interaction, and they find that within a half hour or so, they are able to create their own solutions, without needing me or anybody else to intervene.

What should be off-limits in a fight varies from couple to couple, and usually has something to do with the particular weapons that were brandished during childhood, because those are the ones that are most frightening to people. For some of us it's threats of separation or divorce. For some of us it's attacks on our family of origin. For some of us it's our partner's depression and refusal to fight. For some of us it's being walked out on in midsentence. For some of us it's the triangling in of other participants (friends, in-laws, children, etc.). No matter who we are, though, there is always some particular thing our partners can do to us in the context of a fight that will pretty much guarantee the derailing of the discussion and the heightening of feelings of fear and rage between us.

If we can reach some understanding and agreement about what these unacceptable arms are, we increase the chances that we can *both* feel optimistic and competent about the resolution of our conflicts.

Eddie and Darlene, for example, came to talk to me about their marriage because they were sick of having the same fights over and over again. What seemed to be happening was that their fights were always aborted by one of them, such that they never were able to pursue a conflict to its end point and put it to rest. Thus, the groundwork was always laid for the inevitable rerun, which would end just as inconclusively.

Darlene, whose father had abused her as a child, became understandably fearful whenever Eddie grabbed an object and threatened to throw it (even though he never had, in fact, hurled anything at her), so she'd leave the room. Eddie, whose mother had always abandoned him by leaving the house in response to her husband's resounding onslaughts, overreacted whenever Darlene disappeared, and chased after her in a terrifying way.

Once they were aware of this cycle of behavior and its ramifications for each other, Eddie volunteered to restrain himself from even threatening physical violence during his fights with Darlene, no matter how intense things got. And we worked out a plan for him to keep a hand exerciser nearby so that he could squeeze it if the impulse to throw anything ever began to get the better of him.

Darlene continued to have some difficulty staying in the room with Eddie during a fight, and still felt the urge to flee. I asked Eddie to promise that he would not chase after her should she feel she had to leave, which he agreed to do. I asked Darlene to allow herself to leave "in stages," such as by departing the room but staying in earshot of Eddie so that they could remain in conversation.

However, without the threat of being attacked, Darlene gradually lost the desire to leave. Knowing that she'd be sticking around, Eddie was calmer and less desperate, too. They found that their disagreements could then proceed toward a useful and appropriate terminus, and no longer needed to be reenacted again and again.

5. TRY TO LEARN RATHER THAN WIN

Every fight has within it dozens of potential learning opportunities, and is rich with lessons on everything from how we appear to others, to how we were raised, to how we handle our own or someone else's intense emotions, to how we cover up fear and guilt, to a host of other personal realities. If we see our fights simply as battles to win, however, we *always* lose . . . we lose the chance to understand something important about ourselves and our relationship.

The fights that Clarice and Greg demonstrated for me during their therapy sessions, for example, had a Vince Lombardi kind of feel to them: Winning wasn't the main thing for them, it was the only thing. Both were doctors, and the parents of three-year-old twins. When they fought, they went at each other like linemen in the Super Bowl, with grunts and curses and verbal flings to the ground.

Such intensity was fueled by their assumption that "losing" meant the erasure of their entire being. Both were raised by parents who intimidated and skewered them with biting logic and repartee whenever they began struggling to assert themselves. For their fighting as a couple to become more productive, they needed to find a way to join together and envision their fights as a shared learning experience, rather than as a life-and-death struggle for psychic survival.

With this in mind, I asked them to find the most fragile and valuable item that they owned and bring it to their next session. They self-consciously arrived the following week bearing a beautiful ceramic vase that had been Greg's great-grandmother's. I then asked only that as either of them sensed a fight erupting, they both had to place their hands on the vase before continuing with the fight.

This ritual helped remind them that what was at stake during their struggles together was not their personal survival, or an ephemeral rating of either's "rightness" or "wrongness," but the survival of their marital bond, represented symbolically by the vase. Their contact with this precious, valuable piece of shared ownership helped to keep them "in touch" with the importance of being softer with each other as they worked out their disagreements.

6. DISCOVER RATHER THAN GUESS, SPECIFY RATHER THAN GENERALIZE

"You're acting like I don't do anything all day!" a full-time caregiver shrieks after her husband has sighed heavily upon entering their clothes-scattered bedroom.

"I've had it with your belief that I'm the worst father in the world!" a husband bellows as his wife stares vacantly at her breakfast after hearing him say that he'll have to work late again that evening.

Don't leap to dire and extreme conclusions about what your partner is thinking about you. The problem with mind-reading is not just that we are usually off-base, but that it may so enrage or intimidate our partner that we never get the real story. Maybe that sigh or that stare had nothing to do with the present circumstances. But the wife who thinks her husband is attacking her will be so busy defending herself, and the husband who thinks his wife is disappointed in him will be so busy counterattacking, that neither will find out what is really troubling their spouses. So it is always better to ask and find out than to guess and imagine.

The same holds true with generalizing about your partner. It is unlikely that your partner has "never" cared for you, never helped you out, understood you, supported you, gone the extra mile for you, or whatever. The desired behavior may have occurred less often than you would have liked, but it probably did happen. If not, you probably wouldn't have got married, and wouldn't be so upset about it *not* happening right now.

Generalizing will only spur on the defensive posture that foils our futile attempts to get a handle on the situation.

7. Closing the Circle

I sometimes think that the most important aspect of communication between a husband and wife (or between any two people, for that matter) is not why, when, and how they fight, but whether or not they take the time to follow up their fights at some later point. A "postgame show" can be one of the most effective ways to assess your relationship's strengths and weaknesses, and to allow the intensity generated by the fight to forge closer and more lasting bonds between the two of you.

There are different ways to do this, none of which, of course, are applicable in every situation or to every couple. Psychologist John Gottman, for example, prescribes what he calls an "ABCD Analysis," which stands for "Antecedent, Behaviors, Consequences, and Doing Differently." When couples take the time to reflect upon what led up to the fight (Antecedent), what they did during the fight (Behaviors), what their behaviors provoked in their partner (Consequences), and then, with this data in mind, what they plan to Do Differently in the future, the marital system grows more supple and secure with each angry encounter.

Less formal and programmatic procedures can work well, too, such as negotiating a temporary agreement, asking each other for feedback on how you sounded or what you said, or summarizing your conclusions. More spontaneous responses, such as laughing about how ridiculous the whole experience may have been or celebrating the end of the fight with ice cream, can all contribute to a sense of affection and well-being that diminishes the fear that something "awful" happened.

Pretty much anything that "closes the circle" and gives you room to think about the fight without excessive remorse or malevolence will be all it takes to reframe your fight as just one more loving encounter.

8. "NOT IN FRONT OF THE CHILDREN"

New parents are always put in one double bind or another by the lay or professional "experts" on family life. "Never fight in front of the children" is one of the axioms of family communication that is always being touted, often by the same person who also insists that "you should never put off having a fight."

So what are we supposed to do in these situations? Have such self-professed experts ever actually *lived* with children? If they have, they would know that if you made certain not to fight in front of the children, you would constantly be putting off your fights, and if you never put off your fights, one time or another you'd be fighting in front of the children.

I certainly think it's important that serious fights be fought, as much as possible, during a time and place that provides some privacy for a couple. Personally, I hate it when a fight erupts in front of our children, and I see their confused, forlorn faces as they watch their mother and father raising their voices at each other.

But I also think it's important to remember that it is not such a terrible thing for children to see their parents fighting, particularly if they also see their parents resolving their differences and making up.

The adults I work with who have the most difficulty fighting either witnessed brutal, violent fights between their parents that overwhelmed them when they were children, or saw *no* fights between their parents, were deprived of the opportunity to learn how to fight fairly, and concluded that fighting must be such a terrible thing that it is to be avoided at all costs.

It is a scary, riveting, but ultimately healthy experience for children to see their mothers and fathers bravely express anger with each other, and then to see how the expression of this anger becomes another powerful source, rather than erosion, of loving attachment between the two of them. This gives them the confidence to recognize and honor their *own* tumultuous feelings, and find healthy ways to verbalize them without fearing the loss of love.

When you sense a fight brewing, you can ask the children to go somewhere else for a time, or agree together to postpone it until some seclusion is possible. If both are out of the question, however, you can simply let them know that "Mommy and Daddy are angry with each other, and we need to work this out. You may hear some yelling and things you don't like, but there's no reason to be worried— we'll work it out soon and be even better friends than we were before."

Then, when it's over, make sure you follow up with *them,* too, and articulate, in terms they'll understand, what the fight was about, and how valuable it is for people in love to be able to be intense, honest, and sincere with each other.

9. Break All of These Rules from Time to Time

The opening caveat to this section on rules and regulations for marital fighting was that there was little chance that anybody who was in love and actively engaged with their partner actually followed them all the time. So it is important that you not feel intimidated by these suggestions, or deficient in case you, like everybody else, have broken them from time to time.

When you're upset and frightened and face-to-face with your own and your partner's "demons," it may be impossible to completely stop the action and bring to mind the strategies we have been discussing, or to always react thoughtfully, blamelessly, and nonjudgmentally.

And some rules may at times be *worth* breaking, as long as nobody is threatened or hurt. Interrupting your partner while s/he's speaking is not usually a good idea, for example, but it's better than getting sullen and not speaking or listening: Sometimes we have to interject something or we feel that we'll disappear beneath our partner's vitriolic deluge.

Changing from the original topic of discussion or dumping out an overloaded laundry list of complaints or kicking a chair out of exasperation will *not* help the flow of information exchange, but *will* convey to both of you that the intensity is currently higher than your capacity to sort it out. This is a significant state of affairs, and one that needs to be understood for continued openness to be sustained.

Such rule-breaking may clear the air and provide the release of pent-up tension that is necessary for the search for a respectful compromise to begin to take hold. Just as an inner tube is easier to change when the *air* pressure has been reduced, an action or attitude is easier to change when the *emotional* pressure has been reduced.

CHAPTER SIX

What Mothers Should Know About Fathers

There is hardly anybody around who would balk at the concept of shared parenting these days, for the advantages cut in every conceivable direction. Women who are freed from the demoralizing entrapment of total domesticity feel less isolated and better able to have a career, should they so choose, without so much worry about the emotional cost to their children. Men who are freed from exclusive responsibility for wage-earning can better afford the formerly forbidden experience of real participation in family life. Women can bring to the workplace the relational skills in which they are so well schooled, while men can enliven their home life by bringing to their family the commitment, intensity, and drive that have been nurtured in them.

Sociological and clinical research has shown that couples in more egalitarian marriages are, in the long run, more satisfied with themselves as well as with their marriages, and not only stay married longer, but also live longer. Women who have more professional identity than the average woman, and men who have more parental identity than the average man, have higher self-esteem and report greater life satisfaction, too. Since the ways in which mothers and fathers adapt to parenthood are psychologically linked with each other, these positive feelings usually become contagious and bolster both of us.

Children who grow up with two actively participating caregivers also do better. They are more successful socially, cognitively, and psychologically, and are freed from the enmeshment that accompanies hyperparenting by one caregiver, usually the mother, and the alienation that accompanies hypoparenting by the other, usually the father.

Boys are encouraged to explore rather than repudiate the feminine aspects of their identity, and to feel comfortable with and express their needs for affiliation and contact, and thus have better "emotional muscle tone." Girls develop with less conflict and guilt, display an enhanced belief in their autonomy, and, like boys, become more psychologically buoyant and "fit."

So why do so many parents, even those with the best of intentions, have such a difficult time establishing the equality that they truly believe is in their, and their children's, best interest?

The reason, of course, is that, despite our intentions, a complex matrix of issues makes achieving this equality an uphill battle. No matter how promising such an egalitarian future might appear, there are profound societal and personal constraints in place that mitigate *against* change, and very little concrete, practical support *for* change. When a dissolution of stereotypes is encouraged without individuals being provided with adequate and acceptable alternatives, even the most liberated partners are filled with confusion and self-doubt.

Fathers, for example, having been absolved from parental responsibility for generations, are now being asked to be significantly more involved with their children, but they have no role models for doing so, nor have they been offered much of a chance to express their own, gender-specific parenting concerns.

Mothers feel guilty if they don't take advantage of increased opportunities to develop a career and become less family centered, but blame themselves, and are blamed by others, for any family problems that erupt if they *do* cultivate a professional identity.

So we are in the awkward position of entering parenthood in the nineties while having been schooled in the values and imprisoned by the public policies of the forties and fifties. The men who have built their self-images on their capacity to achieve and produce, and the women who have built their self-images on their capacity to connect and relate, feel baffled by the whirlwind of expectations that seize and suddenly displace them from their emotional home base.

How *do* we make the ideal world, described by Betty Friedan as the "Second Stage" of feminism, a world in which men and women alike are able to find fulfillment on both the homefront and the work-front, a reality? Certainly not by trying to make men into women, or women into men. There are and will always be differences between the sexes, some of which come about because of genetic inheritance, some because of our differing physiologies, some because of how we're raised and socialized, and some because of an interaction of all of the above.

My belief is that for shared parenting truly to take hold in our society, the differences that exist between men and women, no matter what their origin, have to be addressed, not ignored. This is not with the intention of *exaggerating* them, but more with the hope of *bridging* them by developing a mutual, cross-gender understanding of them.

What we learned in a previous chapter is that stress raises the anxiety of our marital system, which in turn raises our reactivity to each other, leaving us less flexible when it comes to resolving conflict. When anxiety is high, we feel out of balance and begin responding to each other in ways that lead us to become more polarized rather than more aligned. Differences in attitude, style, and opinion that formerly attracted us to each other begin to drive us apart. An "If-you're-not-with-me-you're-against-me" approach poisons the easy give-and-take that is essential for enduring intimacy.

One of the main reasons that couples may experience an increase in marital turbulence when they become parents is because, under the duress of parenthood, *all of our differences as men and women surge into even greater prominence than usual.* Psychologist Nancy Chodorow's feminist-centered critique of traditional psychoanalysis, *The Reproduction of Motherhood,* goes a long way toward explaining how some of those differences come into being.

She starts by noting that men and women of the current generation were *both* essentially raised by their mothers. Because we begin to shape our personalities by identifying with our same-sex parent, girls can begin defining a self by identifying with their caretaker. For boys to identify with their same-sex parent, they have to repudiate their connection to their mother and seek their father.

Since the last several generations of fathers in our culture have not been that intimately connected with their children, this means that boys' gender identification consists mostly of modeling their fathers' separateness and distance, leaving them ill equipped to handle intimate relationships. Girls, too, lose out. While a girl obviously doesn't identify with her father as a same-sex role model, her *connection* to this largely unavailable man is so tenuous that she misses the opportunity to get some important instruction in autonomy from him.

This helps us to understand why women are generally more comfortable with connectedness and less comfortable with separateness, while the opposite is true for men.

It is important to keep in mind that neither is better than the other. Our weaknesses are inseparable from our strengths as men and women. The difficulties women typically have in *disengaging* from their children are no more problematic or pathological than the difficulties men are likely to have *engaging* with any intensity. So the mother naturally takes on the interpersonal jobs of parenthood, like nurturing and loving the child, while the father takes on the practical jobs of parenthood, like earning money and painting the nursery.

Marital problems arise not just because of these differences, however, but because of our inability to *tolerate* difference in the highly anxious setting of new parenthood. We confuse closeness with sameness, mothers wanting their partners to love the baby with the same single-mindedness that they feel, fathers wanting their mates to be able to detach from the baby with the same ease that they do.

As discussed earlier in the sections about the pursuer and distancer, or the hypo- and hyperparent, our loyalties to our past, in this case to the gender stereotypes promoted by our first family and our culture, come to the surface, and our anxiety-based expectations heighten the pressure we put on each other and, consequently, our reactivity to each other. The more *she* insists on his increasing his involvement with her and the baby, the more threatened he'll feel, and the more he'll pull out and focus on nonparental activities. The more *he* insists on her relinquishing her bond with their child, the more threatened she'll feel, and the more likely to throw herself into the tasks of motherhood with zeal.

And of course the ways in which they manage conflict may also be infiltrated by these gender distinctions. Women are sensitive to tension and seek to address and dissolve it by wanting to talk and make contact. While men, too, recognize tension, they prefer to defuse it by *not* talking about it, by *avoiding* contact. I'm reminded of a comic's line about the differences between men's and women's sensitivity to emotions. He said that women have the psychological equivalent of a satellite dish and pick up every conceivable feeling, while men have the equivalent of a wire coat hanger with a piece of foil twisted around it: They pick up only the "major stations," pain and orgasm.

It may look like women "care" more than men, but it's more that each gender *handles* the ways in which they care according to different guidelines.

My tendency, for example, is to deal with the more difficult aspects of parenthood by figuring them out for myself and shielding Karen from them. If one of the kids gets sick while she is off doing something on her own, I'm very reluctant to interrupt her. However, she is often offended that I didn't make the effort to come get her and include her in what was happening, and feels I'm being "insensitive."

Karen likes to involve me in every aspect of family life. If one of the kids gets sick while I am off doing something on my own, she is *sure* to come and get me. And I am sometimes offended that my privacy is not as well guarded by her as I think hers is by me and feel *she*'s being "insensitive."

Our conflict originates not from a lack of mutual consideration or respect, but from the different ways that we have been taught to manage these challenging child-rearing moments.

So designing and implementing a new model for shared parenting will require us first of all to reduce our reactivity to the differences between us. One of the best ways to do this is to *learn* more about these differences, rather than simply ignore, or fight about, them, so that we can thoughtfully respond, rather than impulsively react, to them.

This chapter is devoted to describing the view from the male side of the fence.

The New Man and Fatherhood

Without question, the process of becoming a parent is an extraordinary transition not just for a woman but also for a man. He may find himself filled with love and adoration toward his child, excited about the wonderful, charged moments that parenthood brings about, and delighted by having a chance to witness and participate in the miracle of human development. The transformation is a complex one, however, joyous and enriching, to be certain, but filled with experiences that challenge his self-esteem and confidence.

Michael Lamb, one of the first psychologists to study fathers and fathering intensively, once commented that fathers were the "forgotten contributors" to child rearing. While men may not be *forgotten* anymore, it is still not clear that they are actually *understood*.

There are many reasons why even those men who consciously decide to become fathers, and actively look forward to being fathers, still have difficulty taking hold in family life once their children are actually born. Here are some:

1. MIXED MESSAGES FOR THE NEW FATHER

Don't be too quickly deceived by that newly anointed masculine paragon, the actively nurturant American Father. The very fact that he is the darling of well-intentioned members of the media who want to be on the cutting edge of any emerging trend implies that there is *still* something novel about seeing a man who is regularly and capably involved with the care of children.

What else could we expect? After all, it was not too long ago that prestigious leaders in the field of human development were solemnly proclaiming, "Male physiology and that part of his psychology based on it are not geared to infant care" (Bruno Bettelheim), and "If a father engages in activities like feeding, diapering, and bathing a baby, there is a danger that the baby will end up with two mothers, rather than a mother and a father" (Haim Ginott).

Until recently, the only articles in professional journals that addressed the theme of early fatherhood carried titles like "Pregnancy as a Precipitant of Mental Illness in Men" and "Sexually Deviant Behavior in Expectant Fathers."

Psychologists believed that men became fathers only because they were either possessive or envious of women, because they wanted to preserve their genes, or because they wanted extra help hunting or gathering food. Rarely did anyone consider the possibility that men, like women, had a primal desire of their own to love and raise children.

Even today, "mothering a child" is associated with nurturing, while "fathering a child" is associated with depositing seed for conception. The essayist Andre Dubus, writing about the bias against American fathers when it comes to custody issues, wrote that the court system views fathers as "spermbanks with checkbooks." A renowned female psychologist recently wrote enthusiastically about how good it was to see that "fathers are doing more mothering than they have in the past." And another woman, a dear friend of mine, observing my conscientious attempts to get used to being a father, told me, without realizing how it would sound, "It's so cute to watch you . . . you're such a mother hen."

One father complained to me, "If I'm with the baby alone, and he starts to cry in a store or something, all of a sudden I'm surrounded by a bevy of women who act like they know what they're doing and I don't. What a crock! They've got no more right to tell me how to deal with my kid than I do telling them what to do with theirs . . . but can you imagine if I went running up to some woman with a crying baby and made some suggestions? I'd probably be arrested!"

Another patient confessed, "Nothing gets to me more than when I'm with my two kids, and someone walks by and says, 'Oh, so you're baby-sitting today' . . . like I'm not really a parent, I'm just a baby-sitter. You can bet they would never say that to my wife."

It is not surprising, then, that men enter parenthood beset by conflicting images of themselves, and feeling besieged by all of the contradictions between what they have been taught and what is now expected of them. With no cultural guidelines for the entry into modern fatherhood, and no socially sanctioned ways to rehearse for it (see section 6, this chapter), they are explicitly commanded to become "instant" fathers: Just add child, and presto! Yet their family, work, and peer culture may implicitly be working to prohibit this.

And their wives, the same women who may be so valiantly breaking the stereotypes that locked them into being seen as weak, overemotional, and illogical, may expect their husbands not only to be the new man, sensitive, emotional, involved, but the traditional man, too, ambitious, aggressive, powerful, self-reliant, and self-contained. So if men change too little, they are accused of being chauvinists; if they change too much, they are seen as ineffective.

No man violates the traditional norms of masculinity without facing a tremendous onslaught of reactivity, and this is exactly what happens when a father makes the commitment to become more involved in parenting.

A new father explained, "You know, it seems I can't win—my wife says she wants me more involved with the kids when I get home, and I do this, with pleasure, but then she wonders why I don't have the energy to ever finish the basement, or why I'm not as horny as I used to be. It's like she wants me to change *and* stay the same, and I really can't do both, although, frankly, I kind of wish I could, too, and still don't realize that I can't."

2. MOURNING SICKNESS

Although it is only a nine-month precursor, his wife's pregnancy is a man's first encounter with parenthood, and it is a strange one, indeed. While *her* expectancy is physically inescapable and biologically determined, *his* is invisible: There are no tangible reminders or displays for him or others to latch on to. So even though he appears to be able to choose, more than she can, how involved with pregnancy to be, he cannot choose to *not* feel worried about what is happening to her, and what is *going* to happen to him.

Psychologist Doris Entwistle's research came up with the surprising finding that men worry more about their wives' pregnancy than their wives do. Yet this makes sense when you realize that his experience is by definition a cognitive and indirect one, without the gradual and potentially reassuring sensations of fetal growth that his partner is privileged to experience.

Out of control of the situation, a state he and all men abhor, he is confronted with potentially runaway anxieties about how he'll function in the delivery room, whether the baby will be healthy, whether it will take over his life and marriage, what kind of father he'll be, how much his sex life will be altered, and whether they'll have enough money.

He is ambushed by old issues and conflicts that suddenly reappear, such as rivalries with siblings, his envy and awe of his mother, and his disappointment in, fear of, competition with, and love for his father.

His own disquieting feminine undercurrents, represented by his shameful desire to be pregnant, too, now begin to reemerge after having been buried for years. The somatic symptoms he is prone to display, like the constellation of "couvade"-type stomachaches and backaches, his weight gain or loss, and his mysterious injuries, are his way of identifying with his wife, getting some attention, and *subjectively* participating in what has hitherto been a primarily *objective* event for him.

He is supposed to be excited about beginning a family, and sometimes feels this way, but only when he's not busy feeling guilty about putting his partner through the discomfort of pregnancy and the pain of childbirth, and feeling scared of losing her to either of these processes.

Simultaneously, he wonders about his capacity to love a baby who may take her away from him. Knowing that it is partially his "fault" that he is going to be upstaged and displaced makes it even harder to acknowledge how upset he is about his wife's dissolving commitment to him as she begins her "unholy" alliance with their child.

In the backseat during pregnancy, he will soon be ejected from the car altogether. At the point when he is expected to be most supportive of his young family, he is actually *needing* support more than he ever has before, and is too embarrassed to admit this.

Distressed to find himself already competing with the child whom he was sure would make him feel wonderfully warm and complete, he begins, before the baby is even *born*, to be swamped by unacceptable feelings of rage, resentment, and revenge. Asked to be a beacon of hope and stability to his lumbering wife, he is instead mired in ambivalence, condemning himself for reacting with immaturity and fear at the time when mature sensibilities and courage seem to be most called for.

Yet his apprehension is not as out in the open as his wife's expanding belly, and thus is mostly ignored. Lonely and resentful, feeling bushwhacked by his surprisingly intense emotions and neglected due to everyone's interest in his spouse and unborn child, he strives to make some sense out of a situation that defies his capacity for understanding.

Expected and expecting to be delighted, strong, and free, he puts on an act while his worries and fears mount internally. Desperately wanting some of the solicitous concern directed toward his wife but unable to ask for it, he departs into an unapproachable exile, which makes him feel more excluded still.

It is at this point that he may seem most distant and insensitive, stubbornly unwilling to participate in the drama of preparation for family life. Yet it is not that his distance means that he has no feelings about parenthood or is not in love with his wife or child-to-be; *distance is the only way he knows of* managing *the feelings that he is uncomfortable with.*

Afraid that his neediness might be discovered, that his hostility toward his wife and unborn child might leak out, and that his unworthiness as a father might show through, he withdraws to protect himself and them from the menace of his turbulent emotions.

Retreats into work, depression, hobbies, affairs, addictions, sexual impotence, neediness, and childishness are all unconsciously calculated ways to fend off his fears, avoid his grief, and get his wife and others interested enough in him to find out why he's feeling so sad and confused.

One expectant father reported, "We're moving into the ninth month, and I'm really getting scared now. I go with my wife to her ob-gyn appointments, but I feel sick to my stomach, stiff and wooden, there. The doc asks me if I've got any questions, and usually I've had half a dozen or so in my head, but it's like I freeze up. Then my wife gets on me for not being very excited, for leafing through magazines in the waiting room rather than talking to her, but it's just that I don't know what to do with myself anymore, like I'm hiding out from something that's big and scary . . . and I can't seem to talk to anyone about it, because I just don't think anybody'd understand."

3. HELPLESSNESS

Anyone confronted with newborn babies is struck by their complete, abject helplessness. Following closely behind in the helplessness sweepstakes, however, are the parents of the newborn. Nothing can make a solid, confident adult feel more impotent than a wailing infant who does not respond to any of the techniques suggested by the experts (or by friends, family, and all the other *self-styled* experts).

The helplessness that new parents experience is hard on both the mother and the father, of course. But men tend to have more difficulty with feelings of helplessness than women do, because they have been taught that they are to be "in charge." This, in fact, is part of the basis of their definition of manhood: They're supposed to be problem solvers, but there are times when all babies seem like insoluble problems.

It is typical for a woman to respond to helplessness by seeking more help. It is typical for a man to respond to helplessness by withdrawing from the situation that is making him feel helpless. Thus, many fathers wind up withdrawing from contact with their newborns not because they are uninterested or unloving, but because coming to terms with how little impact they may have on relieving their baby's distress is so painful. They protect themselves from feeling impotent, or appearing so to others, by removing themselves from that which makes them feel that way.

I have also worked with a number of fathers who hold themselves aloof from their children for another reason, which is that they fear they'll react violently to their children's tears or distress. One father reported, "Sometimes I think I'll hurt or kill her, when she's crying like this, hour after hour, or always on the verge of it . . . and I really can't stay around, because I'm afraid I'll do something I regret. One time I was holding her and clearing the table, and I was literally afraid to take the knives and forks to the sink because I thought I'd actually stab her on the way just to get her to shut up. In reality, I know this would never happen, but it's a terrible feeling just to even consider it."

This situation can be exacerbated when a new mother chooses to nurse, for a new father may then wind up feeling even more helpless in comparison with his wife, who seems uniquely capable of soothing the baby. Acknowledging this disparity in "comforting ability" is difficult, and, again, many a father reacts by simply backing off from the baby and investing himself in activities that allow him to feel more in control, such as his work.

One new father confided to me, "I would be happy to go to his crib in the middle of the night and give my wife some extra sleep, but all this guy wants to do is nurse, and nothing I do satisfies him; so I just lie there while she gets him, and nurses him, and it feels lousy, you know. It makes me not want to do anything with him, I get so pissed off that I can't help out. I can't even get back to sleep, I'm so angry, and then I'm tired and irritable the next day and snapping at everybody."

4. THE ROLE OF WORK AND CAREER

A cartoon depicted a disconsolate man admitting, "I'm afraid if I fell in love I'd lose my competitive edge."

Psychologists have demonstrated that women and men are brought up to derive self-fulfillment in different ways. Women, for example, tend to be encouraged to care deeply about social connections and relationships, and to focus their energy on the development and maintenance of these connections and relationships. Men tend to be encouraged to find satisfaction not from interactions with others but instead from individual achievements.

Before a couple has a child, this major difference can be more easily negotiated, as there may be time and room for each partner to work at both. As we have seen, however, with the entry of a child into a couple's life, each parent tends to specialize, reverting to gender stereotypes because that enables them to do what they know best and are most comfortable with. Thus, motherhood provides a woman with a tremendous and nearly limitless opportunity to establish a close relationship with her baby, fulfilling many of her interactive needs. For the new father, however, it is more complicated.

On the one hand, he may long to spend time with his baby, but on the other, the new financial pressures he is probably feeling will draw him *away* from the baby. Many men, in fact, feel most certain that they are demonstrating caring by provisioning their kin, and how successful they are at doing so may be at the very root of their self-esteem.

Also, there is, in this culture, much more reinforcement for accomplishment than for caring. A cartoon depicted a man who had

WHAT MOTHERS SHOULD KNOW ABOUT FATHERS   145

brought his infant to work asking, "What d'ya think, Boss?" and his bespectacled superior stuffily responding, "Adorable, Dobson, but baby pictures will suffice from now on."

Few are the accolades bestowed by their peers and mentors upon men who give up stature, prestige, or income to invest their energies in their families. There are luncheons and plaques for the Salesman of the Month, but nothing you can eat or frame for having hung in there with your trying and contentious toddler every night. The beckoning lights of ambition and achievement are sometimes so incandescent that everything else is blotted out.

It becomes natural, then, for a man to react to the birth of his child not by involving himself more deeply with that child, but in fact by involving himself more deeply at work. This becomes a way that he can feel useful to his new family, as well as negate his anxieties and uncertainties about fatherhood and child rearing.

The temptation to escape into work may be especially intense if a man becomes a father at the same time as he is establishing his career, which is quite often the case. Many of the men I work with, for example, have their first child just as they are completing the last component of training, such as their internship, residency, clerkship, or apprenticeship. So after years of preparation, at the point when they are ready to set up their own office, practice, or company and begin to reap the benefits of years of subservience and training, they are suddenly confronted with the needs of their wives and babies.

This spins them into a predicament of fiercely clashing expectations. Told that their twenties, thirties, and forties are their "prime money-making years," their chance to really establish themselves professionally and financially, which is indeed true, they are also warned that they will never again have a chance to bond with their children in the way that they can during the first years of life, which is just as true.

Some men are able to delay their self-fulfillment even longer, and shift a portion of their energy away from work for a time. Other men cannot do this. They may feel obligated to carry the financial load for a time, particularly if the new mother used to work and is now on leave, if they have taken out higher-education loans that now need to be paid back, or for other reasons. They may also find that their work life is more gratifying than the constant effort to satisfy the needs of a fretful infant.

Their wives may subtly persuade them to follow through on the male legacy, too. They may be reluctant to give up what they perceive as their "sole area of expertise" to their husbands. After all, they were raised with the same expectations regarding men and women that men were.

This explains why one study demonstrated that even though unemployed or underemployed men were more involved, playful, and creative with their children than their employed counterparts, there was still more marital conflict in these families. This was *not* just because there was less money, but because the wives resented their husbands' inability to be competent breadwinners. So men are not paranoid when they think that they really need to be out there making a living for their wives to approve of them.

One father, who had completed law school the month his first child was born, lamented, "Now I feel really caught. I wanted this baby, and I want to get to know him, but he doesn't do much right now, and I'm busy trying to make it in this law firm that hired me. So I'm lost, I don't know what's most important—we need to have money, since I'm the only one working, and I love finally *making* money after all these years of school, but I feel like I'm missing something when I'm away a lot . . . yet he's so hard to be with that no matter how hard work is, it always feels better than being with that baby."

Another new father observed, "It took me two years to design this computer system at work, and now I'm kind of the expert there, people are always coming to me for help, and it really builds me up . . . and then I go home and I'm not the expert at all, I'm some dumb amateur; I can't make the baby happy and I don't have any good advice for my wife, and she feels like I'm not there enough but, frankly, I feel too good at work and too bad at home to want to be home much of the time."

The work structures that are in place in this society don't help too much, either. Our policies still rest on the assumption that men have little investment in direct contact with their children, and still provide little "give" when it comes to men and women making important pledges to their families.

Unlike seventy-five other countries, and every other industrial-ized nation but South Africa, the United States has no comprehensive policy that enables parents to adapt to the demands of family life, such as through providing paid or unpaid parental leave or well-supervised day care. While there is some push for more flexible paternity-leave policies in the business community, men are still not encouraged to take advantage of these. And many of the companies that have paternity-leave policies in place don't publicize this very extensively to their employees.

In the three years that one large corporation has offered a three-month unpaid paternity-leave program, for example, it has never been used. This is not only because it is the rare family that can survive on one or no income for three months, but also because there is some evidence that men who exercise their paternity-leave options do, in fact, pay for this, by putting themselves at risk when it comes to competitively based promotions and raises. And of course there is also the question we are addressing now, which has to do with whether men really *want* paternity leave.

The possibility that frequently utilized paternity leave would create a *better* class of workers by giving men new and challenging opportunities to develop more self-confidence, better interpersonal skills, and freer and more creative thinking seems completely lost on us. This despite the fact that there is much evidence that since women have more forcefully entered the work world, their values and strengths have impacted positively on the way that people do business with each other.

Until we are able to change the values of the work world, rather than simply ask people to change to adjust to them, fathers will be caught in the slipstream of traditional manhood, and unable to make manifest their fatherly potential and desires.

5. LACK OF EXPERIENCE AND ROLE MODELS

A woman who wants to make child rearing a priority has many role models to choose from and many people to talk to for information. She may consult her own mother, her grandmother, or an aunt, neighbor, or friend, but somewhere, and probably in several different quarters, she will find someone who shares her commitment to motherhood.

Men do not have the same luxury. While there is an abundance of adult males who are models of devotion to their careers, it is harder to find men who have made child rearing a priority.

In fact, making nurturance of others a priority can be a source of embarrassment or humiliation for males. An adolescent patient commented to me, "I wanted to be a camp counselor this summer because I like working with little kids, but my dad sneered and asked me why I wanted to be a nursemaid, why I wasn't getting a *real* job: making more money, I guess he meant, or doing something physical."

This contempt may come not only from males but also from females. After Josh was born, I cut back on working so that I could be home with him most mornings and a couple of afternoons a week. During the long walks we would take each day, I would often pass a woman who was also walking her baby, and we would stop and chat for a bit, and compare notes on naps and feedings before moving on.

My son got sick at one point, which prevented us from taking walks for a couple of weeks. When he felt well enough for us to commence our strolls again, I ran into the same woman, who commented sympathetically when she saw me, "Oh, I was hoping you had finally found work."

She was embarrassed as soon as she said it, but the point was clear: The only way for her to imagine my making time with my son a priority was to assume that I had somehow failed in my "real life" and was unemployed. Being with my son was not really "work" at all.

There's also the simple matter of socialization and experience. Many adolescent girls and young women feel proud and comfortable earning money by baby-sitting, while older brothers may have other responsibilities, or more freedom to do as they choose.

This means that new fathers enter parenthood without having had any parental "internships," and with few role models to turn to for advice and assistance. I remember being amazed that I did not even know how to do that most natural of actions, which is to *hold* a baby. When I first held Josh, I felt dispiritingly uncomfortable, as this bundle of randomly firing neurons almost squirmed right out of my inexpert hands. Laying him down in the cradle that first night, I was convinced that I was going to smash and permanently disfigure his face. "What a klutz I am," I muttered to myself, wondering how I could play the piano and snag a baseball so well and yet not perform these most basic acts of coordination.

When my wife suggested that we shift to cloth rather than disposable diapers when Josh was around a year old, I balked at first. This was not because I didn't want to save some money and play a bit part in environmental consciousness, but because I was so exhausted and lacking in self-confidence by that stage of parenthood that I simply did not want to take on one more activity that would involve new skills. I felt that I had experienced enough incompetence in that first year to last me a lifetime, and I was not looking for any more.

6. ISOLATION

I once did an informal but interesting experiment in my free time. At the gym where I work out, I hung around the locker room, listening in on the conversations between the men who were there. In the space of forty-five minutes, I tracked thirteen different discussions. Of those thirteen discussions, only one focused even tangentially on a fathering issue, and that had to do with the fact that one man would not be able to join his racqetball buddy next week due to a doctor's appointment he had to take his son to.

Later, I did the same thing at a local playground, this time focusing on women instead of men. In the space of forty-five minutes, I tracked fifteen different discussions, *all of which* focused almost exclusively on mothering issues (nap times, feeding schedules, complaints about tedium, interesting anecdotes, etc.).

Granted, this was a biased experiment, for I was listening in on men in a nonchild-centered environment and listening in on women in a very child-centered environment. On the other hand, the data do point to the fact that women more naturally come together around parenting issues than do men, and that something about being with other men may lead a man *away from* interacting around family themes.

Until a man makes his transition into fatherhood, of course, this may not be a source of concern at all. However, with the onset of family life, fathers, whether they are aware of it or not, may need as much contact with other fathers as mothers need with other mothers, to process the profound changes in their lives.

Unfortunately, at the very time when men most need this contact with other men, they may find it most difficult to *establish* this contact, since connecting in this way feels so foreign. Men become consumed by their pride and their competitive striving with other men to the extent that they will withhold their problems from each other in an effort to display an unruffled mastery of the situation. They would rather maintain this facade than open up and admit to another man that they are having difficulty adjusting to fatherhood, even though this might be a tremendous relief. Or they're so busy trying to balance work and family commitments that they barely have enough time to keep gas in the car, let alone to make meaningful connections with other fathers.

It was interesting for me to note that during the first years of the Father Center, the program that I direct for expectant and new fathers, more than 80 percent of the telephone calls that came in were from mothers, not fathers. "He's too busy but asked me to call" would be a common remark, or "I think he would benefit from your workshops, but he'll never go unless I call first." Once again, it was women doing the legwork for their partners rather than men trying to establish a linkage with other men by themselves.

The net result of all of this is that a man can become very isolated at precisely the time in his life when this isolation is most damaging, and when intimacy with others around the transition into fatherhood is most necessary.

When a man does not discuss his feelings with others, he does not know if his feelings are typical or not. He may get a very distorted picture of what a "normal" father's experience is like if he has no one to compare and share experiences with.

One father observed, "I see all these other guys with their children, and it looks so easy, it's like they're gods, and their kids seem so pleasant and so devoted . . . and my son is so hard at times, so exhausting, and I'm embarrassed, and I'd like to talk about it, but

I feel sheepish, in a way, like I haven't succeeded at fatherhood because I'm not comfortable with it yet, and wonder if I ever will be."

When I asked him if he had attempted to share any of his concerns with his friends, he responded, "Well, sort of, but it's hard to bring up, in a way, and one of us will usually change the subject. They may feel the same way, but we'll never know for sure; one of us always winds up shifting to work or sports or something... so I have all these things I want to say, and no one to listen to me."

Another new father who had consulted me said, "Sometimes I'm scared by how much I dislike being with my daughter, but I can't tell anyone but you. If I told my wife, she'd be all upset and worried about me, and one time I tried to talk to my dad about it, ask him, you know, if he ever felt the same about us when we were little, and he didn't really know what to say, he just reassured me that I've got a great little girl... and I do, I know that, but I just don't want to hear that sometimes, I want to know that I'm not alone in feeling all this stuff, but I think, maybe, that I am. . . ."

7. FANTASIES

Any parent can tell you that no matter how much much you attempt to prepare for it, parenthood will always catch you off guard. Some aspects may be easier than imagined, some may be harder, some may simply be different, but the actual texture of parenthood simply cannot be anticipated.

Men probably fantasize less about family life than women because they are encouraged from an early age to focus their energies on other aspects of life, such as their careers. But because they have usually had so little contact with babies, what fantasies they do have are likely to be much more remote from the realities of life with a newborn than women's are.

So when men stroll into parenthood with their notions about what fatherhood will be like, they may get some big surprises—and the disturbing ones are likely to exceed the pleasant ones. Because of this, even though many men become parents very optimistically, which is one of the ways they cope with the tremendous uncertainties of expectancy, they often find within months that their confidence has begun to erode.

When I ran track, my teammates and I on the "J. Dawkins Speedboys" created an imaginary entity called "Uncle Riggy," short for rigor mortis, which was the feeling that seemed to take over at the end of a difficult race, when our energy and will was spent, leaving us with almost no capacity to finish. "I was doing fine until that last turn, when Uncle Riggy tapped me on the shoulder" was the shared lament we could all identify with.

Uncle Riggy seems to tap many new fathers on the shoulder, too. During the first study of expectant fathers that I did, I was sometimes shocked to see that the generative and creative energy they had been running on during their wives' pregnancy had often completely dissipated at some point around one year postpartum.

The man who had lost weight and started running four miles daily because he wanted to be around a long time for his children now barely got up to two miles a couple of times a week and had gained almost all of his weight back. The father who had excitedly planned a three-week paternity leave for himself right after childbirth was now working sixty hours a week and sweating his family's financial future.

The man who had lovingly and laboriously built all of the furniture for his baby's nursery hadn't even entered his workshop since the baby had been born. The man who had begun connecting with several long-lost family members as he enthusiastically wrote a family history in anticipation of the new generation had lost the time and energy to write, visit, or stay in touch.

One new father, an elementary school teacher, remarked, "I thought I was ready for a new baby, and bragged to everybody and was told that I would be such a good father, because I'm used to working with kids and think I understand them... and yet my son has a way of getting to me that no student has ever done; I get angrier with him than I ever get at anyone else. He whines and whimpers and takes such a toll on us, and then my wife and I begin fighting, and it's really awful, so different than I imagined. ..."

"I guess my preconceived notions about what babies are like was based on TV," another new father noted. "I'd see these cute little babies on diaper commercials strutting back and forth smiling, or I'd see a sleeping baby in a laundry detergent commercial, or I'd see all these babies playing contentedly in the corner on some other TV show, and I figured that's what it's like; then I come to find out that my baby took months before she smiled, never sits *anywhere* and plays by herself, and sleeps calmly only after rocking her and singing to her and talking to her for hours. I read once that some actress took her *twins,* for God's sake, on the set with her, and I can't even get the goddamn laundry done or the checkbook balanced. I wish that someone had told me what it was really going to be like, although, to be honest, I probably wouldn't have believed it, because I could never have understood how it could be this hard."

And then, of course, there are children who may be easier to raise and be with than one's own, "fantasy offspring" that stir up painful feelings of envy and longing as you see them and their parents effortlessly and joyously interacting with each other at the playground or in the store.

Thus, many new fathers find fathering difficult not only because it is, in fact, difficult, but also because of the contrast with their fantasies about what fatherhood would actually be like. One response to this difficulty is to retreat some from the realities of fatherhood, and to attempt to re-create a fantasylike family life, one that is free from the jolts and bumps that feel so uncomfortable. As one new mother complained, "My husband was great at first, really involved with diapering and middle-of-the-night feedings, but after a few weeks, something began to wear off, and he stopped helping out . . . so now, it's annoying, he's always there to play when Jessie's in a good mood, but once she starts to deteriorate, he finds something else 'important' that needs to be done, and I'm left alone with her. It's like she's his daughter only if she's happy, and otherwise, he wants nothing to do with us."

How Mothers Can Help Fathers

1. GIVE HIM A CHANCE

What are the best ways for you to implement your understanding of what new fathers wrestle with so that a more equitable home environment is created?

Perhaps the simplest, but most powerful, way is to create opportunities for your partner to be alone with children, *whether or not he appears willing to do this.*

You need to remember that because men have little experience and few role models, how they father is very susceptible to your influence. If fathers sense that their involvement is not only desired but also *expected* and *endorsed* by their wives, they'll be more involved. If not, they won't.

You may *explicitly* support your husband's increased participation in family life but *implicitly* undermine it, either by providing few chances for him to be alone with your child, setting him up to fail by angrily or suddenly turning over complete responsibility without any discussion or preparation, and/or by being very quick to criticize and take over.

Gina came to a workshop for couples at the Father Center because she was so frustrated with her inability to "get" her husband, Bobby, more involved with child care. She related a typical scene, in which instead of working out a more equitable arrangement with him in a dignified and thoughtful manner, and planning a gradual transfer of power, she threw a tantrum one Saturday, handed their ten-month-old over to him, and said, "Here, you take over."

Of course Bobby felt confused and belittled, but tried to do his best. His first move was to take the baby out for a walk, but as he was getting him dressed, Gina showed up from out of nowhere and snapped, "I hope you're not going to take him out in the stroller— he'll fall asleep, and that'll ruin his nap."

Bobby dutifully took their coats off, distractedly played with the baby in the living room for a bit, and then tried to put him down for a nap, not knowing that the baby needed his special blanket to sleep with. He left the room with the baby sobbing to find Gina standing in the hallway glaring, holding the blanket out and superciliously asking, "Need *this?*"

Bobby went back into the room, dumped the blanket in the crib, and started to walk out, producing yet more howling from the baby. Gina strode in to take charge, shaking her head and grumbling about how incompetent he was. Bobby, relieved of duty, put on his sweat-suit and trotted out to the gym.

This, obviously, is no way to create an opportunity for shared parenting. While it is certainly half Bobby's responsibility to have been more involved in the first place, and not to have agreed to such a haphazard plan, Gina, too, needs to draw her bottom line from a less blaming and enraged position. Otherwise, while she gets to feel justifiably frustrated with her husband's lax approach to fathering, she loses out on the possibility of catalyzing any change.

As a solution, I suggested that Gina tell Bobby that she would like him to start helping out more, and asking him where he thought he'd like to begin. This automatically invited him to feel more trusted, and more self-confident. At first, of course, he chose some activities that already came naturally to him, such as playing with, bathing, and walking the baby.

Once he was regularly taking over some slots of time by engaging in these activities, additional tasks that he was less comfortable with, such as showing up for doctor's appointments, or emptying the diaper pail, were easier for both of them to build into the system.

Women have to help destroy the myth that fathers are incapable of being intimately involved with infants and children. Many studies have demonstrated that fathers *can* be just as "interested, nurturant, and stimulating" with newborns as are mothers, that they're just as likely to vocalize, kiss, touch, look at, and be sensitive to distress cues like coughing or spitting up.

But it is not just a matter of fathers parenting like good, sub-stitute mothers, but men displaying their own unique, built-in par-enting talents. Child psychiatrist Kyle Pruett has written about the "biorhythmic synchrony" that fathers in primary caregiving roles dis-play with their children, and psychiatrist Martin Greenberg has ex-plored "engrossment," the male preoccupation with children that goes beyond involvement and enables men to feel enlarged, rather than burdened, by their offspring.

Plus, we all need to remember that the absent father of recent generations is a cultural aberration. In many other cultures, and up until the Industrial Revolution in our own culture, men have traditionally been *closely* involved with the raising of children, and have taken on many of the most important tasks, such as academic and vocational training, and moral and spiritual education. But this was much easier when a father's work was at home, and he was there all day, as opposed to at the factory or office.

In any case, it is not surprising, then, that most mothers find that when they *are* able to authentically cede some child-rearing authority, their husbands bloom, and are quite willing and able to help out. One woman reported, "I was reluctant to give my husband the responsibility to get the baby in the middle of the night, because the first few months he slept right through those cries, and I pictured my poor baby just lying in the crib sobbing for hours before his daddy finally was aroused.

"But the funny thing is that once he knew it was his job to get the baby, he kind of grew the antennae, and now, he gets up as soon as I do—it's like all that had to happen was him becoming the One, and then things were fine."

Some mothers may have to simply declare that they will be out of the house for a certain period of time if their husbands do not seem very willing to go along with this idea. Rare is the father who will refuse to care for his child if they are left alone together. These opportunities, even if created under stressful circumstances, are likely to benefit every member of the family.

One woman I worked with, for example, had to be extremely resourceful when it came to setting up some fathering time for her husband. The first two evenings he was supposed to be home from work on time so that she could go to a book club that she had recently joined, he called a half an hour before he was due home, saying something had come up and he'd be very late. Each time, she gloomily gave up on getting to her club at all.

She came to me feeling disappointed and stuck. She knew she couldn't "make" her husband come home promptly, but was determined to effect a more equal division of child-care responsibilities. I asked her to think about the things that annoyed her husband the most, and after only a moment's thought she responded, "Wasting money, and having to deal with my mother."

With this data in mind, we worked out a plan in which she told her husband that on her next night out she would be leaving on time whether he was there or not, and that she would be paying for a sitter, or inviting her mother over to watch the kids, as backup.

He hit the ceiling, as predicted, aware that he'd have to either spend money on a sitter who wasn't really necessary, or spend the evening with his mother-in-law without his wife to buffer him. Not surprisingly, he showed up on time from then on, and eventually came to enjoy these evenings of unadulterated parenthood.

One other fact for you to keep in mind when creating opportunities for paternal involvement is that the surest way to undercut a man's motivation to be a father is to be critical of that involvement. Time and time again, a new mother will complain in a workshop I am leading, "But why can't he learn how to diaper better?" or "You can always tell when he has dressed the baby: Nothing matches," or "Is it so hard to wash *all* of the shampoo out of the baby's hair?"

Yet further questioning invariably reveals a situation that is not as simple as it first appears. Sometimes a new mother's criticism of her husband's care for a baby is a symbol of her competitiveness and her insecurity. By highlighting her partner's inadequacies, she helps to obscure those areas of child care in which he is, in fact, as competent, or *more* competent, than she is. She may be trying to reassure herself that she is crucial to the well-being of their child. It may be hard to give up her "expert" role at home, particularly if she is on maternity leave from a job that gave her a feeling of competence at work. Moreover, her complaint about how the diaper fits or the clothes match could simply be a mask for a deeper complaint, such as that he is not around enough, or that he has become uninterested in her sexually.

Of course, it may be true that her husband is so far not very good at the practical aspects of parenting. But she may be giving him so few opportunities to practice that he never gets much of a chance to *become* competent. Or, because he is sensitive to her constant criticisms, he may respond either with nervousness, which makes him all the more awkward and fumbling, or rebelliousness, which makes him determined to screw up simply to provoke her and thus get out of having to do anything at all.

In either case, criticism rarely does any good, and obviously causes harm. When a couple is working together to raise a family, it is not necessarily desirable or efficient that each partner have the same strengths, but more important that their strengths complement each other, so that there are relatively few gaps. So aside from situations in which a father's less-than-perfect child care might endanger the child (such as inattentiveness in supervising a toddler), the more tolerance you can exhibit and praise you can express when he's got the "job done," the more likely he'll continue to do these jobs. If you don't like the baby's pink shirt with orange pants, maybe that's something you could learn to live with in exchange for a husband who participates willingly and actively in the raising of his child. *To get fathers who are more positively involved and empathic, you've got to be more positively involved and empathic with fathers.*

2. SLOW DOWN

One of the most challenging aspects of being a parent is recognizing that children grow and develop at different rates. It becomes difficult not to worry and compare your child to other children, particularly when you are envious of the level that another child has already achieved. Yet accepting, and helping your child to accept, his/her own rate of development is crucial to the growth of self-esteem and a positive self-concept.

What is just as crucial is accepting your *own* rate of development as a parent. When we look back on our childhoods, we may imagine that our parents were always very sure of themselves, very "parental," even if we didn't particularly like the way they were parenting us. Yet in talking with our parents, we often find that they were much more unsure of themselves than they appeared, and for whatever reasons, did not convey this to us.

New parents often feel that they have to be instantly "parental," that they have to be just as sure of themselves as they imagine that their parents were, and other parents seem to be. And the expectations that we have as parents are often applied not only to ourselves, but to our partners. We look to them to be good parents to confirm our wisdom in choosing them as spouses, and to assuage our own inadequacies or insecurities as parents.

Problems arise when such expectations are unrealistic and don't leave much room for growth and learning to take place, either in ourselves or in our partners. The fact is that fathers and mothers grow into parenting at their own, individualized pace.

That this pace may at first be slow, particularly for men, can be very frustrating for the new mother, particularly if she is wanting or needing more from her husband, and/or if her peers' husbands seem on the surface to be more "advanced."

Some fathers take a long time connecting with their children, having little idea how to relate at the preverbal stage, but once they do connect, the bond is strong and deep. Other fathers connect instantly with a newborn but may become less willing to be available as the child becomes more willful and less malleable. And of course there are infinite variations on both themes, based on all of the idiosyncrasies inherent in family and personal development.

Dorothy, for example, explained to me on the phone why she wanted to set up an appointment for herself and her husband, Mike: "He just doesn't seem into fathering like the other fathers are. They all seem excited to come home and be with their children, but he acts kind of weird, like he's not sure what to do. I get on him, and try to make him like it more, but he just doesn't seem to respond."

Mike, naturally, was reluctant to come for their first appointment, expecting that he was going to be ganged up on by Dorothy and myself for not being much of a father. Instead, I tried to understand the origin of Mike's timidity as a father, as well as why it was having the impact it was having on Dorothy.

As we spoke, a number of issues became more clear. One, Mike was baffled by infancy. Although he had a younger brother, there were only a couple of years separating the two of them, so there were no meaningful memories of or experiences with an infant, and his older sister was expected to do any of the spillover child care. He, like many fathers, was caught off guard by how difficult it was to connect with an infant:

"I had lots of fantasies of what it would be like having a son, but none of them have come true," he reported glumly. "I pictured taking him to work with me, conversing with him, going to a ball game, building models together—all kinds of things—but right now he doesn't *do* anything, and I guess, in a funny way, I'm disappointed in him. I thought there'd be more going on . . . he doesn't even notice me yet, let alone talk or do things."

Also, I learned that when Mike was six, he had a younger brother who was only a few months old when he died of SIDS. So it was clear that being close with his infant son would inevitably remind him of the sense of fear and loss that had overtaken him as he and his family had tried to make sense of this tragedy long ago.

Another issue that became clear was the importance Dorothy was placing on Mike's being a good father, for a number of different reasons: "My parents like Mike, but they were never really crazy about him, and I always figured, you guys just wait, wait until we have kids and you see what a good father he'll be—because they just didn't think he was that great a guy, they still don't . . . and now, it's like I don't have any proof for them that I made the right choice."

She added later on, "You know, my father left us for about a year when I was little, although no one ever talked about why—they still don't—and I always felt like it was my fault, somehow, that he and my mom could have worked it out better or been closer if I wasn't there."

The combination of Mike's fantasies about what infancy was like, and Dorothy's fears that Mike was not the kind of father she had fantasized about and that he might someday leave as her father did because of the challenges of fatherhood, were making it hard for Mike to simply grow into fatherhood at his own pace, and for her to be patient while he did.

Another complicating factor was Dorothy's fantasy about what other fathers were like. As she stated initially, her assumption was that "all the other fathers" had mostly positive feelings about being fathers, something that clearly had not been checked out and arose more likely from her own insecurities.

When I asked her, in fact, to do a more careful evaluation of this assumption, she came back with more realistic data: "You know, after talking with some of my friends, I found out that their husbands can be the same way sometimes, that it's not as easy as it appears to be for some of them."

Mike, also, responded quickly to some normalizing of what he was experiencing. I asked him to leaf through a couple of books on child development, and he came back somewhat relieved: "All of these books say it *does* get better as they grow . . . harder in some ways, because you have to watch them more, but it's like they actually become people at a certain point, and I guess I was just wondering if this was ever going to happen . . . knowing that it will makes me feel a little better about what a nothing he is right now."

I suggested that the two of them spend some time with Mike's older sister, who now had three kids, all of them older, for further confirmation that there was an end in sight to some of the typical unresponsiveness of infancy.

As Dorothy learned more about why she was so impatient with Mike's development as a father, and as Mike grew more confident that some of his fantasies about fatherhood might, indeed, eventually become a reality, they both relaxed and were able to enjoy each other and the baby more.

We have examined in this chapter the personal and societal challenges that face men as they become fathers, and how when women understand these challenges they find themselves better able to enhance their husbands' participation in family life. In the following chapter, we'll reverse polarities and look at the challenges that women face as they make the transition into motherhood, and how men's appreciation of these challenges can help them to create a more well-rounded marital and parental team.

CHAPTER SEVEN

What Fathers Should Know About Mothers

"**O**h, if my husband only knew what this was really like," Helaine, the mother of a one-year-old, sobbed in one of our therapy sessions. "All he sees is this beautiful girl of ours, and she really is beautiful, I love her to death, but he just doesn't understand why I feel the way I do all the time, and the horror is that I don't really understand it either. . . .

" 'What's wrong, honey, what could it be?' he asks, and he means well, but there's no way to explain to him how bizarre this all is for me. I know I'm very lucky, my husband loves me, our daughter's healthy, we have enough money to get by, I don't have to work more than a couple days a week . . . but since she was born, I've been in a terrible funk, and to make it worse, I feel awful that I'm not more appreciative of what I've got. What *is* wrong with me?" she pleaded.

Every new mother, like Helaine, has to undergo a complete and startlingly pervasive shake-up of her identity once she has children. She must grieve for the abrupt ending of her pregnancy, a perfectly private nine-month relationship with her idealized unborn child; become attuned to the enormous demands of her real-life infant while tolerating less fulfillment of her own; deal with her ambivalence about her new role and her new baby; learn to live without some of the gratifications of her pre-parenthood marital, social, and professional life; acknowledge her shortcomings as a less-than-perfect mother; and, in thinking back on her relationship with her own mother, which almost always happens on becoming a mother oneself, relive some of the inadequacies of that relationship. All of this has to be done against the physiological backdrop of hormonal storms catalyzed by the end of pregnancy and the inception of nursing.

There are many specific realities about becoming a mother that most men, especially those who have taken childbirth-education classes, are indeed aware of. But childbirth-education classes prepare men mostly for understanding the stages of pregnancy and labor, and leave husbands underprepared for supporting their wives when actual parenthood has commenced. Here are some issues, rarely discussed in these classes, that almost every new mother wrestles with and that every new father should know something about.

1. NEW MOTHERS, SAME OLD WORLD

In one episode of the cartoon strip "Marvin," which focuses on the adventures of a diaper-clad child who tries to make sense of a non-sensical world, his little female playmate crawls up and innocently suggests, "Let's play house... I'll be the principal wage earner and you be the primary caregiver." Marvin puzzles for a moment in front of his blocks and comments, "I forget... Does that mean I'm the Mommy or the Daddy?"

Perhaps the current generation of children will in fact be that gender-blind when they enter parenthood, but for those of us who are becoming parents now, there may not be as much gender flex-ibility as we'd like to think there is. What *could* be, and what's highlighted in the media as newsworthy, has far outpaced what ac-tually *is* when it comes to our attempted liberalization of sex-role stereotypes.

And even in "modern" marriages that were more symmetrical or egalitarian prior to childbirth, starting a family seems almost always to "traditionalize" the roles of men and women. Parents find them-selves inexorably pulled toward divisions of labor that they may pre-viously have rebelled against.

When Betty Friedan suggested decades ago that the average middle-class household was a "comfortable concentration camp for women," she may have envisioned that much would have changed by now. Yet one study showed that women still do as much as 75 percent of the household tasks and 80 percent of the general domestic management (scheduling, menu planning, etc.) when there are chil-dren at home, and another one concluded that *working* mothers spent over three hours daily on housework, while working fathers averaged less than twenty *minutes* of housework.

When it comes to child care, the divergence between mothers and fathers is just as striking. The second study listed above discovered that working mothers averaged fifty minutes of "exclusive" time with their children, while working fathers averaged seventeen minutes. One survey determined that no more than 20 percent of men fully share in the "responsibilities and chores" of child rearing, while another one concluded that women have "twice as much responsibility" for child care as do fathers. Yet only 12 percent of these women anticipated, during pregnancy, that they'd be saddled with "significantly more child rearing tasks" than their husbands.

What needs to be kept in mind, too, is that the tasks men, in fact, *choose* to do are often just that, "choices," jobs that they have some interest in doing and that leave them with some sense of control or freedom in their lives, such as play or exercise with their children. This of course abandons wives to sweat through everything that is left over, and that is, most likely, less pleasant and more constricting.

Also, many of the tasks that men do are not initiated *by* them, but are "thought out" by their wives, who do all of the orchestration and organization, and then "assign" responsibilities. So even when men are doing "the work" and women do not have to be or are not "supposed" to be responsible, they really are.

Furthermore, women are generally responsible for the "invisible" care that is entailed with raising children, the less tangible activities that don't show up in these kinds of studies. For example, they are the ones who can be counted on to maintain contact with the extended family by sending cards, writing letters, and making phone calls.

So when it comes to active domestic involvement, men usually resist it, sometimes begrudgingly cooperate with it, but rarely ask for, insist on, and orchestrate it. When they *do* join in, they often refuse instruction, even if their wives have more experience with a task. This is because they're sure they can do it themselves, and because they don't want to be placed in a dependent position vis-à-vis their wives.

And of course no matter how little a man does as a husband and father, it is often more than his own father did, so he insists on being indulged and praised for his efforts, and gets to revel in the self-congratulatory glow of "being better" than his own father, which puts a limit on any further motivation and initiative. If he is involved for a while and then backs off, nobody questions him about this. If the living room is messy, guests don't wonder what *he's* been doing all day; they point the finger at you-know-who.

Finally, when both men and women work, it is generally the woman who is asked to balance her commitment to home and work life, who takes off from work when the child is sick or rearranges her schedule to arrange transportation. We don't ask whether working fathers harm children, only whether working mothers do. This is often the case *even when the necessity of their being at work, or their compensation for that work, is equal to that of their husband.*

When we realize that working women generally come home to work what sociologist Arlie Hochschild describes as "the Second Shift," an unpaid eight hours of employment on top of their paid employment, we become aware that while we have fought for equality for *women,* this equality may not always apply to *mothers.* In the words of a bumper sticker I saw recently, *Of course I'm a working mother . . . what other kind is there?* No wonder many feminists believe it is the home, not the office, where women are truly most vulnerable to exploitation.

It is also no wonder that all of these inequalities lead to discord. Doris Entwistle's research concluded that 92 percent of the hundreds of couples she interviewed experienced heightened conflict after the birth of their first child. What is significant is that her study found that "most conflict was around the division of labor." Other studies have also concluded that unequal distribution of family labor is the most salient reason for marital conflict.

Dr. Hochschild writes that a woman who perceives and lives this imbalance will respond to it in a number of ways, including anger, resentment, irritability, loss of interest in sex, and an undermining of her husband when it comes to child rearing. With this in mind, a man's options are simple. He can either write her off as hysterical and perpetually dissatisfied while smugly ignoring his own contribution to this state of affairs, or conscientiously address this imbalance and courageously attempt to redefine what it means to be a man.

2. Mother Guilt

A family therapist once said, "Show me a woman who doesn't feel guilt, and I'll show you a man." While I think this is a bit extreme, and that men are vulnerable to guilty feelings, too, there is an important point embedded in this wry observation.

Men tend to feel guilty about specific aspects of fathering, what they did or didn't do at a particular moment in time. But a woman's guilt about motherhood is more universal, encompassing, and pervasive: It irrigates every channel of her being, and cannot easily be turned off or neglected.

This is partially due, of course, to the biology of pregnancy, in which how a woman takes care of her body directly influences the health of her baby. It is natural, then, that she feel responsible for how the baby turns out, since at least some of the variables are tied in with how responsible her own behavior was. But dozens of problems that arise during pregnancy and childhood have *nothing* to do with whether or not a woman was vigilantly healthy, yet she'll still be prone to feel guilty about their presence.

This overarching guilt is rooted not so much in physiology, but instead in a culture that blames Mom for everything that goes wrong in the lives of her children. After all, a man who takes his breadwinning too seriously is still seen as successful, valuable, and even heroic. A woman who takes her mothering role too seriously is seen as smothering. As feminist thinkers have been pointing out for years, you cannot divorce the personality characteristics of men and women from the social and political narratives of which they are a part.

When news reports focus on the tortured, crack-addicted babies who are born to crack-addicted mothers without also examining the context in which these addictions occur, *and men's responsibility, as partners and public policymakers in creating and sustaining this context,* guilt will surely arise.

We consider prosecuting the women, as if their addictions arose in a vacuum, while letting their equally responsible partners off the hook. In fact, it is interesting to note a recent study that showed that male exposure to alcohol, nicotine, and other drugs is related to a matrix of reproductive problems, including miscarriage, childhood cancer, and birth defects. Yet I don't hear anybody suggesting that men's self-abusive behaviors are criminal acts, and I'll bet that we never do.

Nowhere is our culture's tendency toward mother-blaming more apparent than in the disapproval directed against mothers who seek professional satisfaction, supposedly at the expense of their children. Psychologist Harriet Lerner has astutely pointed out that child-development theories that focused on the exclusive importance of the mother-infant bond began to abound at the very time when women began working more and experiencing greater freedom.

Psychologist Louise Silverstein has written insightfully about how we have subtly glorified motherhood in a way that ensures that women will feel guilty should they choose to do anything else but make motherhood a full-time "profession." She points out that all of the studies that examine the impact of day care on children start with the assumption that children's bonds with their mothers are "the" crucial foundations for their development, ignoring all of the other profound influences that have been noted to exist.

Rather than responding to the vast increase in the number of mothers working outside of the home (90 percent of whom feel that they have no choice when it comes to whether or not to work because of harsh economic realities) with realistic, thoughtful, and constructive political action, we have instead created the mythological image of a "Supermom" who can have a career, consistently be available for her children, remain sexually attractive and interested, stay in top physical condition, and host a party or two on the weekends.

Because men until recently have so deftly excused themselves from parenting, and few have ever offered to share the burdens of family life with them, it remains easy for women both to be given *and* to assume the blame for when family life or their children's development goes awry in some way.

It is not, by the way, that guilt in itself is such a bad thing. In the right dosage, it is a feeling that can prevent us from doing or repeating things that could cause us or others some harm. I remember the first time I worked with a patient who had abused her children, and how hard I was working to relieve her of her guilt, feeling that would free her to parent less violently.

My supervisor, watching my work through a one-way mirror, and in touch with me through a telephone, buzzed me immediately. "Don't relieve her of her guilt too completely" were her unforgettable words. "At first it'll be her guilt that will keep her kids from landing in the hospital again."

On the other hand, guilt, in megadoses, quickly outlives its purposefulness, and cripples our attempts to move forward in our relationships. Robert Beavers has half-jokingly suggested that "about five minutes of guilt" for every regrettable act is all that is necessary for us to get the message that we need to get, and reform. Anything more than that is useless overkill, and actually gets in the way of our functioning.

Because women in this society are so strongly encouraged to feel responsible for so many aspects of family life, it makes it very difficult to tease out the guilty feelings that are useful and instructive from those that are obstacles to their capacities for nurturance and fulfillment.

So, a woman winds up traversing a never-ending Möbius strip of guilt in which she feels bad no matter what she does. If she *lets* her baby cry, this means he will grow up without being able to trust and love; but if she *never* lets her baby cry, this means that his opportunities to learn on his own are being impeded.

If she *can* put her baby down to sleep without protest, this means that he must not be very bonded to her; if she *can't* put her baby down to sleep without protest, this means that he has never truly been comforted by her. If she shows too much emotion, she's hysterical and obsessive; but if she shows too little emotion, she's a coldhearted, withholding bitch. Who could possibly fail to be tortured by such invalidating dilemmas?

If she is not around enough, she is told that her children are suffering. In the professional literature, the situation in which men are unavailable to their families is dryly called "father absence." But when women are unavailable, it's denoted by the melodramatic and heart-wrenching phrase "maternal deprivation." Choosing to work outside the home means that she is betraying her "biological imperative" and abandoning her offspring. Her own mother, feeling threatened by professional achievements that she herself had limited access to, may try to minimize, compete with, or, most likely, undermine them by suggesting that she is hurting her children.

But if she is around "too much," she is also told that her children are suffering. Many early family and child-therapy approaches (developed, of course, by men) were centered around displacing the mother from a position of expertise and authority, so that the father could come in and handle things more appropriately. The implication was not that family problems had resulted from his lethargic underparenting, but from her cloying overparenting, and it "took a man" to calmly undo the damage. Today, the woman who chooses to stay home and mother full time may also be accused of betraying the freedoms that her predecessors strove so hard to obtain for her.

It was interesting, and difficult, for Karen and me to note that when we decided that she would be home full time for an indefinite period of time after the birth of our second son, it was sometimes her *female* colleagues, fellow clinicians, who seemed least sympathetic and supportive.

Temporarily delaying her career advancement during her children's most needy and vulnerable times was seen by some who were supposedly sensitive to the importance of child development *not* as a thoughtful and courageous decision, but as a "waste" of her training and a deadly surrender of the political advances that had already been made. Thus, just as men are given mixed messages about how to balance career and parenthood, so are women.

Meanwhile, while women are feeling this burdensome and dual-edged sense of ultimate responsibility, the facts are that, for better or for worse, fathers really can and do disengage from parenthood more readily than mothers do. Perhaps because of their freedom from the biological and sociological pressures that shape women's attitudes toward parenthood, men find it easier to absent themselves, both emotionally and physically, from their relationships with their children. For example, a man may choose to ignore his baby's cries by clicking on the television or distracting himself with other activities. To a woman whose breasts are leaking milk at the sound of these same cries, and who is walking a tightrope strung above the expectations that her work, peer, and family culture volley up at her, disengagement is not such an easy option.

3. MOTHERS HAVE TO LEARN, TOO

One of the many outcomes of the fact that men were mostly raised by their mothers rather than their fathers is that they incorrectly tend to assume that women have an intuitive knack for motherhood and that men don't.

This belief is reinforced in two additional ways. One is their observations of their wives during pregnancy, which may have an effortless, natural look to it, even when there is some physical discomfort. The second is their general sense of confusion and incompetence compared to their wives during early parenthood, which they may attribute to "instinctual deficits" rather than their relative lack of experience with small children.

The reality is, however, that even if there is such a thing as an intuitive "mother love" that has genetic, evolutionary roots, this will not in itself provide a woman with the insight, ideas, and strength to know what to do with her child at any moment in time. Just because the baby grew in and emerges from her womb doesn't mean that she is suddenly privy to an ancient wisdom that unerringly guides her down the fragrant pathways of maternal serenity. Even nursing, the parenting behavior with the most significant biological basis, has to be learned and worked at.

Men's image of women as all-loving, all-giving earth mothers is often their defense against seeing their wives more clearly, and acknowledging their own fear and envy of genuine feminine power. With this exalting but poorly founded belief in "instinctive motherhood" firmly in place, however, men are less liable to support their wives during motherhood, and less willing to share in the work, since they may have conveniently decided that they are only second best anyway, so why bother trying.

One mother observed, "My husband says he's willing to help, but whenever I ask him for anything, he backs out by saying that I do it better. He tells me the baby takes the bottle better from me, goes down to sleep better with me, even *dresses* better for me—it's getting a little absurd. I mean, I don't really think I'm instinctively a better baby dresser, for God's sake; in a way, it's kind of insulting, and I think he's just looking for a way out."

A passive new father spoke on the same theme from his perspective: "I think she's just terrific with the kids, and I think I cause nothing but trouble when I get in there, so I've basically abandoned ship to her."

When I asked him how he thought she felt about this, he said, "Pretty pleased, I'm sure. I mean, she knows that if I take over, the kitchen'll be a mess and the kids'll get to bed late and be cranky the next morning."

When I suggested that sometimes people will intentionally do a job halfheartedly or poorly so that they aren't asked to do it again, he responded innocently, "Well, I don't think that's what's going on here. I mean, *she's* better at some things, and *I'm* better at some things—I don't ask her to work on the car, because it would be a big mess. So she stays out of that . . . so why shouldn't I stay out of this?"

This father is so bent on absolving himself of the child-rearing responsibilities that make him nervous that his unwieldy analogy between working on a car and parenting children has actually begun to make sense to him. Unfortunately, the security that his circuitous inner logic gives him will deprive his wife and children of his support and presence, while robbing him of an opportunity to grow.

4. THE LONELIEST OCCUPATION

A cartoon depicted a little girl and her father staring at some animals who were penned in an open yard at the zoo. Her comment: "Mommy says she's lived in a cage without bars for years."

As we already know, what happens in most new families is that the woman becomes the primary caregiver, *whether or not she continues her work outside of the home.* What happens to the new mother who begins to sacrifice the fulfillment of her own needs and interests to meet the needs of her family is intimidating, indeed. First, when women have finally given birth, they are abruptly dismissed as the center of attention, which is now suddenly occupied by their beloved but insatiable baby. The questions that used to be directed at them about how they were doing now evolve into questions about how the baby is doing.

If she goes back to her work relatively soon, she has to contend with the aforementioned guilt that she is depriving her child of nurturance, as well as handle the aforementioned double shot of work and home responsibilities that loom in front of her like a mountain range.

If she goes on maternity leave and/or cuts back on her work, she finds herself faced with greatly diminished status, intellectual and social stimulation, and income. She may find herself yearning for her extended family, who may or may not be geographically or emotionally close enough to nourish her during this isolated time.

The kind of thinking and acting that led to successful problem solving in her work life may have limited applicability to the dilemmas and demands presented by her nonverbal and ferociously insistent baby. Her time and space are intruded upon as never before, and even her basic needs, like eating and sleeping, must often be overlooked. Unable to call in sick, she is, on the contrary, on call twenty-four hours a day with no control over the situation and no tangible end in sight.

Because, unlike at work or school, there is no objective standard by which to measure her accomplishments, she is left vulnerable to a roller coaster of emotions. The moment-to-moment vicissitudes of her child's routine, such as how long the nap was, how well the feeding went, how long the crying lasted, circumstances that may in fact be completely outside of her control, are now the determinants of her emotional life, making her feel great one moment and like a total failure the next.

Her social life is precarious, too. There is an initial increase in social supports shortly after childbirth, but this typically drops off after a time. Bonds with friends who don't have children begin to fray. Bonds with other new mothers are vulnerable to the competition that arises as they all try to evaluate their competency through an anxious comparison of their children's strengths and weaknesses. The play group that is designed to be a source of camaraderie and support often turns into a schoolish nightmare in which each mother is constantly being judged, and judging herself, according to how well her child is doing vis-à-vis the others.

Filled with self-doubt, her days have a disorienting loneliness to them, and she is more reliant than ever before on her husband, both financially as well as socially. Yet she'll have more difficulty interesting him in her life, since it's so out of his realm of conception and awareness.

So starved by that time of the day when he reenters her life that she is like, in Virginia Woolf's words, a "sponge sopped full of human emotions," she'll be unable to calmly wait for him to make his own transition and may tear after him in a way that can inadvertently alienate him.

And even if they do eventually make contact, she'll believe that she's less compelling than she was before motherhood because all she seems to have to talk about is child-related issues that seem to wear thin after just a few minutes of conversation. His thinly veiled impatience or boredom will stir doubts in her as she desperately tries to envision new ways to connect with this man who used to be the person closest to her in all the world.

She'll begin to resent his involvement in work, which will put him off even more, but it's really not his involvement that's the issue. Instead, it's the way he *uses* his involvement to avoid joining her in parenthood, and her wish that she, too, felt free enough to lose herself in something, like work, that made her feel less fragmented and more competent.

She turns *on* or *to* her children not because she has nothing better to do, or because she thinks this is healthy, but because she's feeling abandoned by her husband and by the world at large. Her contact with her offspring, however overdone, may be the only way of feeling connected to life.

"You've got to live this to believe this," a frustrated wife tried to explain to her husband, who couldn't understand why her days were so difficult.

"I don't know, my mother never made a big deal of it, and she had three kids, we've only got one, what could possibly be so hard?" was his brittle reply.

"Your mother had her mother and her mother-in-law in the same neighborhood, a sister and a dozen friends on the same block who also had little kids, and never was expected to do anything else with her life but raise you guys. I'm completely by myself all day, and even though I wasn't crazy about my job, I miss it, because at least I could talk with some adults there, pick up a paycheck every couple of weeks and feel good about myself, and take a walk at lunchtime just to clear my head. Now I'm home all day, I never know whether I'm doing anything right, I can't complete a conversation with you or anybody else, let alone know how to start one, and I feel like I'm going to crack. And you wonder why it's so hard. . . . "

Her lowered self-esteem and increased feelings of depression are the inevitable sequelae of an oppressive existence that leaves her little freedom to feel all right about who she is and what she's doing.

5. WEIGHT FOR ME

Because our culture discourages women from feeling good about themselves unless they are sexually attractive, which by contemporary standards means being thin, the aftereffects of pregnancy may precipitate or exacerbate an obsessive concern with weight and eating.

After nine months of being encouraged by her doctor, husband, friends, and parents to "eat for two," it's suddenly back to the Diet, in an attempt to recapture her pre-pregnancy self. This is often difficult, both because it's hard to break the eating habits of the last nine months and because of postpregnancy hormonal and metabolic changes in her body. If she chooses to nurse, a diet may be just about impossible, because the maintenance of body fat is the body's natural way of sustaining an adequate milk supply. So she constantly stares at herself in the mirror, wondering why she's not as slender as the radiant women in the baby-food ads, while clothes that she wore nine months ago beckon and taunt her from the back of the closet.

Making things even more difficult is the fact that the cycle of food cravings and aversions that began during pregnancy may continue after the baby is born. Also, if she's nursing, she will find that because the baby's needs are not consistent from one day to the next, she, too, is irregular in her eating habits, experiencing periods of mild hunger followed by days of voracious appetite. And all of these other factors aside, she may turn to food for the same reasons that many people who feel depressed and overwhelmed do, for solace, and because it's one of the few things in her strange new life over which she has control. Food comforts her in her isolation, nourishes her in her moments of feeling deprived, gives pleasure to her at a time when she has access to few other pleasures. It becomes a new mother's most reliable mother.

Barely able to stand up to the cascade of responsibilities that are crashing down upon her, she turns to eating as one of the few irresponsible acts that are left to her that won't harm, and in fact may help, the baby. Pacing back and forth with a colicky newborn for night after night, unable to count on sleep, or quiet, or time to herself, she finds that the gulped snacks and furtive gobbles serve to keep her going when there's nothing left to give.

And unlike a husband, who may have demands of his own, food is a perfect companion. It provides a sense of fullness and satiety, without asking for anything in return, and temporarily distracts her from the more elemental feelings of depletion and loneliness that may beset her.

However, at the same time as it is providing all of this for her, she is being asked to give it up. Her doctor or husband may inform her that she has a Weight Problem, if she hasn't already convinced herself that this is the case, and subtly or overtly suggest that she cut back. This may provoke a diet-binge cycle, and further feelings of incompetence, hopelessness, and depression.

How Fathers Can Help Mothers

How can fathers best support their wives as they enter the turbulence of motherhood? The obvious answer, as you probably already know, is to participate more actively in the child-rearing process.

Men who are more involved with their families have happier and more satisfied spouses. Just as a father's emotional support for his wife during her pregnancy predicts an easier labor and less need for pain medication, his physical involvement in child rearing facilitates better mothering on his wife's part, less depression and anxiety in both her and the children, and a smoother relinquishing of her attachment to the children when it is time for this to happen. It will also benefit both of you in ways that are profound and manifold.

1. BE THERE

You may have very little idea of what being a father entails, but it's time to abandon the excuses, roll up your sleeves, get in there, and start pitching. When men enter the no-man's-land of family life, and vault the towering barriers to paternal intimacy that our culture has erected, *everybody* is a beneficiary.

Fathers may be right when they complain that their wives *do* typically pay more attention to their babies than they do to them, but the best way of getting more love and affection from your wife is by becoming more of a father to your children. Instead of whining about being neglected or belittling her for talking to you only about the children, use your shared investment in parenting to draw her closer to you.

Now is the time to stop counting on your wife to anticipate your own and everyone else's needs. Instead, think about how you can actively plan and participate in the rhythms of family life. You'll have to figure out how to do more than "take it like a man, and blame it on a woman" when things don't run smoothly, and you must grow beyond the kind of *quid pro quo* mentality in which you expect everything you do to be paid back or rewarded to a more generous and altruistic attitude.

You must also learn to lift your sights beyond a "making ends meet until we meet the end" philosophy, and learn to find a balance between work and home life. A richer family life may mean less prestige and less income, but may also mean that you live longer and love better.

One psychologist who works with men who are highly successful at their jobs demonstrated that fathers who are more involved with their children go just as far in their careers in the long run as do fathers who are not. Another study concluded that men who have satisfying family lives generally do better at work than men who don't. A third study of "successful professional men" found that 40 percent of them had "serious regrets about the cost of their success, and in retrospect would have given up some of their success to spend more time in the role of husband and father."

But just because men can and should take on more responsibilities at home doesn't mean that it will be easy. When a man spends lots of time with his children, and starts to share the Second Shift, he learns what women have known all along, that raising children and running a home are lonely, exhausting, and undervalued job. If you and your wife have thus far had a conventional division of responsibilities, you might want to try an experiment. Give your wife the weekend off. Tell her to go visit her folks or take a camping trip with her best friend, or whatever. Just two full days with your children in which you are completely responsible for meeting their every need will relieve you of many of your fantasies about parenthood, give you new respect for your wife, and, just possibly, teach you something about not just the difficulties but the joys of this experience from which you have absented yourself.

Whatever else it does, however, such a weekend will enable you to identify with your wife. I get annoyed at Karen when she assaults me with information and questions at the end of a difficult day with the kids, and find her obsessions about such "mundane" topics as the length of their naps or their refusal to share redundant and unnecessary. Until *I* have spent a difficult day at home, that is. Then *I* obsess and assault her the moment *she* walks through the door in the same way that she does with me, and I am fully aware of what she has been up against. On one occasion, I was condescendingly wondering to myself why Karen made such a big deal about not being able to keep the house neat when she was home. But that same week I found myself losing it after a long day of solo parenting when I discovered the kids jumping on the bed right after I had made it. A made bed was the only evidence of my having accomplished anything the entire day, and I was hurt and enraged that it could be so quickly erased.

The difficulties, of course, are easy to describe. The rewards are much more intangible, and much deeper. While the infant may seem like an incredible conundrum to you, if you hang in there and endure the inevitable feelings of incompetence, loneliness, and uncertainty, you'll eventually begin to feel the stirrings of a paternal instinct that is every bit as profound as the much-celebrated maternal instinct. The "gentling" of your masculinity that accompanies this confrontation with yourself, and your acknowledgment of your emotional vulnerability, will be one of the most extraordinary experiences you will ever have.

The men's movement in this country has inspired many men to go to conferences and workshops designed to help us get in touch with our inner selves, our inner warriors, our inner child. Yet the truest foundation and test of our manhood, our capacity to be there for our children in authentic and caring ways, somehow got left by the wayside.

Every religion teaches that holiness can best be found in what is ordinary. I can assure you that one year of ordinary child-rearing activities, changing your baby's diapers, playing hide-and-seek every night, or dropping him/her off at nursery school, will result in a more significant and lasting transformation of your manhood than will signing up for a dozen dramatic retreats and rituals, and will improve your marriage to boot.

2. Don't Compete . . . Too Much

Competition has developed a bad name in our culture because we are used to only one kind of competition, the kind that insists that our companions are our foes, and we must defeat them to succeed.

The competitive urge at its best, however, has little to do with *winning* and more to do with *excelling*. The striving between two people to "get there first" or to "see who's better" can be one of the highest of human endeavors, resulting not in feelings of dissolution or superiority, but in ones of connection and transcendence.

Just as women's entry into the sphere of work sparked competitive issues between the sexes that may have been dormant for some time, so will men's entry into the sphere of the family. The urge to compete, built into both males and females, will always be amplified whenever somebody enters into what was previously our exclusive area of expertise.

Mothers and fathers begin to compete for their baby's affections and attention even before it is born. This is both a natural and essential component of evolving parental identity and commitment, but it can be a source of tension.

Men may throw themselves into parenting as if it is a contest to be "won." If they can view fatherhood as another notch in their belt, another series of accomplishments in which they can take pride, it may be easier for them to buck the cultural imperatives and share fully in the responsibilities of child care. You'll know this is what's happening in your home if you find yourself trying to accumulate and get attention for the paternal "firsts"—first man in your family or peer group to participate in childbirth, to change a diaper, to make homemade baby food, to take paternity leave, etc.

But this can be hard on your wife, who does not receive any comparable accolades for her parenting. She may feel particularly undermined if she's quit or taken leave from her job in order to be a full-time mother. "If he can do well at work and at home, what is special about me?" she may find herself wondering.

While the modern mother is constantly told by her forebears how fortunate she is to raise children in an era in which men help out so willingly, she still tends to feel threatened by this help rather than appreciative of it. She smiles weakly when her child calls for Daddy rather than Mommy at night, and her arms ache to hold the baby who may at times be more easily comforted by her husband.

So a father who wants to be more involved needs to be sensitive to the ambivalence with which his wife will meet his efforts, and not automatically assume that her lack of enthusiasm means that he's doing anything wrong, or that he should back off.

3. SPEAK UP AND LISTEN UP

Men have the responsibility not just to initiate an active participation in child rearing and to do their share of the work wholeheartedly, but to know when they feel unjustly criticized for their efforts. While you may be tempted to seek revenge on your wife for her comments by going on strike and refusing to do anything, what is a lot more useful is letting her know that you want a little more appreciation and a lot less evaluation.

"It got so I didn't feel like doing much of anything," acknowledged one father. "She didn't like how I fed the baby, she didn't like how I held the bottle, she didn't like how I laid her in the stroller—and of course I should have said something to her about this, but it was easier to just get angry and hang back, and think, You do it yourself, then, honey, I'm not doing a thing."

His wife admitted, "I was awful, I know, but so was he. I was so angry that he didn't make any time for me, he was so interested in having the baby feel loved and cared for, that I wound up angry myself at how neglected I was. He'd do anything for her and little for me, asked about her day but not mine, and the only way to get back at him was to nail him any time I could find anything wrong with what he did."

What helped this couple to change was learning how to be clearer with each other about what they wanted. He had to tell his wife what he was needing from her, which was some acknowledgment of all his efforts, and she had to be straightforward about what she needed from him, which was some affection and care. Soon they were both getting a lot more of what they wanted from each other, which made their parenting efforts much more enjoyable, too.

All this talk about standing up to criticism notwithstanding, you must be able to take instruction from women without feeling that your self-confidence and manhood are going down the drain. One of the reasons that women make suggestions to men is because they may indeed have a better way to do something, and given the likelihood that they have spent much more time with babies than their husbands have, there is every reason that this should be so. If men are so proud and brittle that they have to reject every comment outright, and figure everything out for themselves, they lose the opportunity to learn and to expand their competence.

One father whose wife was a full-time caregiver said, "I was always so pissy when my wife peered over my shoulder and gave me a tip on diapering or bathing, and sort of went out of my way to figure it out on my own, but then I realized, this is silly, so far she's spent more time on this than I have, so why fight it? Who the hell cares whether it was her suggestion or mine, when you really think about it? And just like I'd be peering over her shoulder if she was trying to fix the plumbing in the basement, and would have some time-saving ideas for her, I realized it's okay for her to do this with me."

On the other hand, men must also sometimes take the risk of doing the wrong thing, and not passively wait for instructions. One father said, "I'd do more, but she's got her way of doing things, and I don't want to offend her by putting away the wash wrong or putting the wrong clothes on the baby, because when I do, she gets really angry."

This may be so, and maybe his wife could learn to be a bit more tolerant. But he has a lot of other options, too, besides just giving up, including asking her more specifically how she wants things done so that he can learn to cooperate more effectively.

4. SLOW DOWN 2

Just as in the previous chapter I encouraged women to be patient with their husbands' parental evolution, I would urge you, too, to display tolerance. As we discussed a moment ago, motherhood does not arise like magic vapor at the moment of conception. A man's sense that his wife is not taking good enough care of their child will make her feel less supported and interfere with her capacity to bond with the child.

Because you are feeling so much uncertainty about your own ability to be a parent, you may be looking to your wife to make up for your deficiencies. If her mothering does not conform precisely to the contours of your fantasies or memories of what good mothering is all about, you may feel that something terrible will happen. Anything less than bonding ecstatically with the newborn, or being totally thrilled with nursing, or showing a willingness to put aside all the rest of her interests in order to focus completely on the baby, may cause you to put unendurable pressure on her.

Tony, for example, the father of a four-month-old, hovered over his wife, Michelle, like an umbrella. "I feel like I'm constantly letting him down," she wept during our first session. "If I'm not living, breathing, and talking mothering, he feels like something's wrong and gets on me for not taking this seriously enough."

"This is our son, for God's sake," insisted Tony. "How could you *not* take it seriously? I've read that you've got to stick with nursing, and then I see you staring at the free sample of formula that they gave us at the hospital like you're going to use it."

"I am!" she shrieked. "I'm sick of him wrenching and sobbing at my breasts, sick of him always wanting it, sick of not getting any sleep . . . it's enough already, I've had it."

"But you can't give up now. It's only been a few months. He'll get used to it."

"*He* may, but I won't. I just want to use some formula at night and get a break. Is that so horrible?"

I spent some time with Tony alone and got a clearer understanding as to why he was so intent on Michelle mothering in the "correct" way, which dated back to his own childhood, when his mother and father, in their single-minded effort to keep the family store in business, had neglected him. He had vowed then that his children would be given all the love and attention that he himself was missing during those lonely years, and now he was pushing Michelle to join him in making that promise come true, rather than addressing his own responsibilities to his wife and children.

Once he got some insight into the ways he was replaying a tape from childhood, I also helped him to understand that parenthood is a long *series* of choices, none of which is absolutely crucial by itself. What matters in the long run is the extent to which a couple can help and support each other in making and accepting these choices, rather than ensuring that we make the "right" choices.

As Tony exerted less pressure on Michelle's development as a parent and focused instead on his own involvement with their baby, he became a lot more successful at building her confidence, and their tension level dropped significantly.

*   *   *

In this chapter, and the previous one, I have provided men with perspective on motherhood, and women with perspective on fatherhood. To further facilitate our transition into parenthood, however, we need to revisit a theme discussed earlier in the book, which has to do with developing perspective not just on each other, but on our own parents and our family of origin. It is to this that we will now turn our attention.

CHAPTER EIGHT

The Way In Is the Way Out: Dealing with the Parents from Our Past

"You can, and should, go home again."
—*James Framo*

S hortly after becoming a parent, I had a dream in which I was taking a long and difficult run. What challenged me was not the length of the course, nor its steep inclines, but the fact that I was running through a forest and had to look out for the tree roots that would suddenly jut above the surface. The run required constant vigilance; I was ceaselessly shifting my sight from down below, so that I didn't trip on the exposed roots, to ahead of me, so that I could see where I was going.

At one point in the dream, I did trip, and had to be taken to an intensive-care unit. As I thought about the dream the next day, I remembered that intensive care units are known by their initials, ICU ("I see you"), which suggested that I needed to have looked more carefully at my "roots" if I wanted to avoid disaster.

In some ways, our journey through life is much like my dreamy jog. Paying attention both to what lies before us (where we are going) and what lies below us (where we have been) is the only way to keep moving, to keep progressing. Growth requires an ongoing balance between these two kinds of vision, which is why we all need to map out our psychological topography so that we are aware of the places where our heritage rises to the surface and threatens to trip us up.

You Can't Surpass What You Don't See

This chapter is about the look back at our roots. Until we recognize that looking back is an essential part of moving ahead, we are destined to live emotionally immobilized lives. As already discussed, the transition into parenthood assists us in this process because it reactivates much of what may hitherto have been dormant from our past and illuminates and rejuvenates relationships with our family of origin that we may have sought to diminish. And the influence goes both ways: While our marriages ostensibly involve two people, our dialogue with each other is actually like a large family dinner-table conversation, involving parents, in-laws, siblings, even aunts, uncles, cousins, and whoever else was significant in our childhood years. Our goal, then, is to identify the voices that fill the air between us so that we know whom they belong to and can then choose either to amplify or exorcise them. When this has been done, we become the true authors of a new, unchained, and more satisfying dialogue.

The best way to go about this is by examining and, if possible, nurturing our relationships with our first family. A conscious acceptance of our past infuses and transforms our capacity to love and be loved, and gives us the courage to persist during those times when we lose faith in our intimate contacts with others.

While staying connected, or reconnecting, with our family of origin during the transition into parenthood may seem irrelevant or even counter to the process of improving our marriage, that's a shortsighted view. The connecting is important as another step in the process of differentiating from that first family in order to avoid repeating its most destructive patterns in the present.

Unfinished business with our parents and other first family members must be worked at and finished. If not, it is my belief that the stalemates in our marriage will always echo the stalemates from our past. The fights we have with our spouses will have as much to do with what happened twenty years ago as they do with what happened twenty minutes ago. We are sometimes fighting with our spouses the same fight that we fought, or should have fought, with our parents, or that our parents fought, or should have fought, with each other. As long as these ancient battles remain secret or invisible, they will get fought over and over again.

You can vow to be different with all of the fervor you can summon, but until you know better whom you're trying to be different from, and why they were the way they were, your vow will simply result in a very fervent similarity to them. As one poet wrote, "What is not known, returns and returns."

If we, as adults, learn more about our first family, we can liberate ourselves from the shadows and ghosts of our childhoods. The lessons we conscientiously learn about our multigenerational histories pay handsome dividends in our marriages, and contribute more to our being authentically "grown up" than any other experience or event. So it is paradoxically through facing and acknowledging the *hypnotic* power of our past that we derive the *creative* power to transcend it.

While we have been focusing on how the past directly influences our marriages, however, we cannot ignore the fact that our past influences our child rearing, too, which *in turn* affects our marriage.

We may imagine that our children are the sole product of *their* temperament and *our* parenting, but family research points with resounding clarity to the conclusion that children are products of a *multigenerational* parenting process. What that means is that *all* of an extended family's assumptions and themes, issues and dilemmas, are naturally passed, like genes, from generation to generation. Unlike with biological genes, however, which we can do little to alter, we can have an enormous effect on which of these psychological genes are in fact transmitted simply by addressing the nature of our attachments to our families of origin.

None of us wants to relive with our children the conflicts that we, as children, endured with our parents. But unless we know more about who our parents were and are and continue to work on these conflicts in the present, our future with our children will also be invaded by them.

Individuals who have honest, committed relationships with their parents and extended family generally enjoy and succeed at parenting more than those who don't. Individuals who *refuse* to explore and resolve the unhealed wounds and the hidden resentments that exist between them and their first family will provide their children with the exact same inheritance of wounds and resentment.

This is because they will be obsessed with subconsciously seeking revenge for their pain, and their children will be a logical, and undefended, target. Being cut off from our past severely limits our skill and resilience when it comes to raising our children well. The unhealed wounds fester, and the parenting we do remains embedded in our past. When parents are aware of their past, however, this awareness frees them from its chains. They are no longer imitating or rebelling against anyone else; they are bringing Selfhood to their relationships and enacting their own sense of what marriage and parenthood should be.

Now that we know the *advantages* of remaining in contact with our extended family, we need to approach the more daunting topic of how to sculpt and maintain a contact with them that is rich and meaningful without sacrificing ourselves or our marriage in the bargain.

1. A PART VERSUS APART

The most common solution to extended-family problems is some form of avoidance, the various forms of "cutoff" that people orchestrate to deal with difficult family members. There is no question that it is easier to shun people that we have a hard time dealing with than to remain in touch with them. However, when these "people" we have a hard time with are family, this avoidance perpetuates the very problems we are seeking to escape.

We can always find ways to justify our cutoffs: a need to limit the impact of our family's "toxicity," to establish our independence, to protect our children, to simplify our lives, etc. And cutoffs do often provide a short-term payoff, a temporary decrease in anxiety or respite from ongoing conflict.

But while the creation of some distance may temporarily calm things down a bit, it is also the option that will most certainly limit our emotional maneuverability over the long haul. *When we avoid real contact with our family of origin, we ensure that we will carry its problems with us, and pass them along to our offspring.*

When I talk about being in contact with one's first family, I don't want to minimize how difficult and challenging encounters with relatives can be, and suggest that they will or should always be enjoyed. It is fine to limit your time with family members from whom you feel you get very little, or to pull back for a while to let tempers cool and perspective return.

We will always have some degree of unresolved business with our first family: Nobody is a completely differentiated Self. But differentiation relies on our understanding of our extended family and of what our role in our family is and has been, and this can never come about unless we are in some kind of direct contact with them.

This is much easier said than done, however. Many of the changes in the individuals you will be reading about in this chapter took place over the course of months and years, rather than in days and weeks, and often within the context of ongoing therapy. Family patterns do not reconfigure at the mere touch of a verbal or behavioral wand. Moments of insight don't lead automatically or instantly to change. Nor should you expect to engage in major emotional confrontations with your family in the hope of some catharsis to follow. While moments of melodrama can be wonderfully healing, it is usually the smaller, steadier shifts in perspective arising out of regular contact with our family of origin that, in the long run, catalyze the greatest growth in our marriages.

2. LEARNING THE STORIES

After having worked with hundreds of families over the years, and examined my own very carefully, I still never cease to be amazed that there are as many stories and interpretations of events as there are family members. What your childhood was like will sound very different depending on whether you ask a parent, a sibling, an aunt or uncle, or a grandparent.

None of these "stories" is more or less valid: There is no objective accuracy when it comes to family life. But piecing all of them together will give you a better-limned picture of your family's emotional process, and its past and current impact on you.

Once I had children, it became particularly important for me to learn more about my father's side of the family, the side that I knew least about and that had the most secrets. I knew that my father's grandfather had died in an accident as a young man, but did not know the details, and so I began asking around. It was startling for me to discover that no two people had the same version of the story: One said that he was hit by a trolley while walking to work, another said that he accidentally rode his bicycle into a storm drain in a drunken stupor, a third said that he was hit by a car while on his bike. My widowed great-grandmother, who was left with four young sons to care for by herself, was described, depending on whom you spoke to, as brave, insane, protective, foolish, remarkable, impossible, and loving. To this day, I cannot get two relatives to agree on whether or not she did the right thing by keeping her boys at home rather than letting them go to a school for fatherless children that they were eligible for.

Getting at your family's multigenerational process is different from simply doing a genealogical history or family tree. We can collect tons of family "data" and still not alter any of our preconceptions as to how our family operates, or liberate ourselves from its stifling myths, legends, rules, and secrets. An enriched sense of family history is not just food for thought but fuel for action.

So when we embark on such an undertaking, we should be less like a neutral transcriber or transmitter of family facts, and more like a very curious investigative journalist who wants to hear about everybody's version of events and the emotional atmosphere in which they took place.

The purpose is not to reach a conclusion or end point, for there is no such thing. Nor is it to "dig up dirt": If we approach the family mythology in an adversarial way, we'll get repulsed, and then self-righteously report, "See, I knew nobody would talk about this."

Instead, as with any good investigation, we should go at the process thoughtfully and respectfully, and try to come up not only with *answers*, but with an imaginative array of important *questions* that have yet to be asked.

As we discussed in an earlier chapter, starting a family is a perfect opportunity for such a project, because the presence of children brings family members together and causes them to reminisce about the past.

Songs that our grandparents sang to our parents are now sung by all of us to our children. Stories and anecdotes that have been sewn into the family's historical quilt are now carefully unfolded and retold. Techniques and remedies, strategies and recipes, are all passed back and forth as everybody responds to the hope that the new baby represents. Never is an extended family more malleable than when they extend themselves in time and space by spawning the next generation.

On the other hand, going beyond and behind the family mythology to get at deeper, and perhaps darker, "truths" will not be easy. Historian of science Thomas Kuhn has discussed the resistance of scientific communities to data that contradicts the reigning theoretical paradigm. Likewise, we never challenge our family's self-flattering paradigm without incurring the resistance and possible wrath of its loyal defenders and conservators. The censorship that all families to some extent enact needs to be peacefully overthrown if we are to paint a more useful and accurate portrait.

All of us are fearful of peering into the family closets and taking everything in. Those topics that were designated as off-limits when we were children may still seem scary. Years of being told not to ask my father how his day was when he came home from work looking angry or beleaguered make it hard for me to ask how his work is going even to this day. And this message infiltrates my marriage, too: I sometimes hesitate to ask Karen how *her* day was when she enters the house with a certain look on her face, even when she's made it clear that she would like me to ask no matter how threatening her visage may be.

Surely the simplest way to relearn your family history is to talk to anyone you can find, and by anyone, I mean *anyone*. Our sense of family history is powerfully biased by our parents' intentional and unintentional editing. All experiences and interpretations first passed through *their* lens before they got down to *us*. A clearer, more fortified understanding can best come from viewing our heritage through a multitude of alternative viewpoints. So check in with various family members, even relatively distant ones, who congregate around child-oriented rituals, such as birthday parties, christenings, and naming parties. Siblings are especially valuable sources of information about your childhood, while aunts and uncles are invaluable sources of information about your parents and *their* childhoods.

Nonfamily members can be useful, too. Connecting with your parents' colleagues or friends can often be enlightening and instructive when it comes to gaining more objectivity about their lives and their impact on ours.

Eagerly anticipating such gatherings and contacts as opportunities to accumulate more perspective, rather than as ordeals to be dreaded and endured, makes it more likely that you'll enjoy and get something out of them.

Sometimes just making the effort to enlarge your perspective and get an "aerial view" of your past, regardless of any specific insights that emerge from the view, has a salutary impact on your marriage.

3. Ending the Blame Game

No matter how many people we talk to or how impressive an armada of stories we are able to assemble, if we filter our information through the assumption that our parents and extended family need to be held accountable for their "deficiencies," we will not succeed in our differentiation mission.

With all of the emphasis on getting to know and heal our "inner child," it wouldn't be such a bad idea for us to take a look at our parents and try to understand *their* inner child. One way to do this, particularly if you know or knew your grandparents well, is to try to picture each of your parents as a child in his or her parents' home, and to imagine what this must have been like. If we can stop insisting that our parents apologize for what they did to us when we were children, and recognize what they were up against when *they* were children, we can better appreciate them. This shift in viewpoint enables us to accept, rather than revile, our parents' flaws and imperfections, and to value, rather than minimize, their strengths.

Accepting our parents' imperfections *does* mean giving up the fantasy that they could have made our own lives perfect if only they had tried harder, but it must be done. When we can make this shift, we will not only be more open to loving and being loved by our parents, but more open to loving and being loved by our partners and offspring. As Nancy Friday wrote, "When I stopped seeing my mother with the eyes of a child, I saw the woman who helped me give birth to myself."

Getting away from blame may be particularly challenging if we feel or know that our parents have abused us in some way. We may feel that they are at fault for not having treated us better and need to be punished for having inflicted such pain on us. This is particularly so in cases of sexual, emotional, or physical abuse.

In absolutely no way should a violent or abusive parent be excused. There can be no condoning, minimizing, or ignoring such acts of violation. However, it should be remembered that these behaviors do not occur in isolation, but emerge out of the *parent's* developmental history, too. The most obvious demonstration of this is the well-supported fact that well over 90 percent of abusive parents have been found to have been abused themselves when they were children. The process of managing unacceptable feelings through inflicting pain on somebody else almost *always* has a multigenerational history to it.

What can be just as damaging to children who have endured abuse is not the traumatic event itself, but the process by which the family *deals* with the event. Abuse is a horrible enough betrayal of a child's sense of trust. But it is also the terrible sense of secretiveness that may accompany this event that creates the legacy of self-hatred, humiliation, fearfulness, and shame that survivors carry with them. In many ways, the covering up becomes more deadly than the actual violation itself, and although the trauma can never be "taken back," sometimes it is only when the family begins to confront their dark reality that the survivor's pain begins to lessen.

Becoming preoccupied with the abuse itself, and with apprehending the victimizer and holding him/her responsible, limits the survivor's ability to grow beyond it. This is because the preoccupation is rooted in the assumption that someone is to blame, and that there is no underlying process that is worth taking note of. Getting at *the process of which the abuse is a symptom* is not meant to let anybody off the hook but is instead intended to broaden our focus and understanding so that such events can be prevented from occurring again.

My feeling is that, whenever possible, it is best to deal with painful events such as these in person. We may feel perfectly justified in never again wanting to see our parents or any other extended-family member who has done serious harm to us. But without contact, there is little opportunity to make sense of something so overwhelming and inconceivable. When we can take the "demon" on and deal with him or her face-to-face, not only we, but our children, reap the benefits.

Nadine, for example, came to see me because of conflicts she was having with her husband, Art. These usually revolved around two themes, her lashing out at the children in a way that invited Art to lash out at *her*, and her difficulty enjoying lovemaking, a problem that had always been there but that had got worse shortly after her first daughter had been born (she and Art already had two sons, who were three and five years old).

In one of our first sessions, Nadine mentioned that in the six months since her daughter had been born, she had begun to be haunted by some fleeting but disturbing images, all of which took place in her childhood bedroom at night and involved her father and oldest brother. She said that she would dismiss them as quickly as they arose, but felt that she was more vulnerable to "losing it" with the kids for the next day or two, and wouldn't want to make love for another week or two. She also complained about a vague sense of anxiety and tearfulness that hung over her like a cloud.

Over the next year, very slowly and very gradually, she began to piece these and other images and memories together and uncover the fact that she had been sexually abused by both males. For the year or so after that, she found herself avoiding visits with her parents and with her brother, who was also married and had three children, as she found being with them while sitting on this family secret more and more intolerable. Finally, however, the pressure got to be too much, and during one unavoidable gathering, her niece's birthday party, she blurted it out to her mother. Her mother gave her a stricken look, then responded by calling her a liar, vowing never to talk with her again, and walking out.

At first this was fine with Nadine, who was so consumed with anger at her father and brother for having taken advantage of her, and at her mother for not having protected her, that she thought she would "murder" them if she saw them. She *certainly* did not feel like extending to her parents the "privilege" of seeing their grandchildren, nor did she feel at all trusting that they weren't colluding with her brother to make sure they supported each other in keeping the family secret a secret.

After a number of months, however, she began to notice, with some distress, that she missed her parents. Holidays and birthdays stirred an ache for her as she winced at the thought of not getting, or being able to send, a card or gift. Her children's questions about "When are we going to see Grandmom and Grandpop again?" also made her uneasy. While she had never much turned to either parent with issues of importance in childhood or adulthood, she still acknowledged a gap in her life and a desire to reconnect with her mother.

Over the next year, she summoned the courage to get back in touch with her mother, through a letter, and to let her know that she wanted to come up and visit so that they could talk. She was surprised to hear her mother's voice on the phone a week later, hesitantly agreeing to this. During that visit, she filled her mother in, in more detail, about what she remembered.

Her mother, to her credit, said that she had, in fact, been worried that something was going on at the time, but that she was too frightened to ask or say anything about it, and had hoped silently that "it never got too bad." She then talked about her own explosive father, whom she had witnessed hitting her mother, and how she had learned to become meek and paralyzed in the face of scary men. "I figured your father would react just like mine if I wondered what was up, so I just sat tight, like a little mouse, and prayed that nothing terrible was happening."

With her mother's support, and in her mother's presence, Nadine then tried to speak to her father about what she remembered. He left abruptly, then came back several hours later and sorrowfully acknowledged what he had done. Later on, in a letter, he told Nadine for the first time about his own experiences growing up, which included having been sexually abused in a foster home that he had been placed in when his parents had split up.

Together, the three of them talked with her older brother, who denied everything, called Nadine "a nut," and promptly cut off contact with her.

This is a necessarily abbreviated summary of a very complicated case. On the down or "unresolved" side, the disclosure of the family secret has thrust Nadine's brother into an even more acute, and possibly dangerous, denial of what has happened, leaving him at risk to be abusive with his own children. Furthermore, Nadine's courageous acknowledgment of this betrayal from her past threw her parents' marriage into disarray. What will happen in their lives is still unclear.

On the up side, several months after having talked with her parents, Nadine admitted to feeling closer to both her mother and her father, and was able to re-commence more regular visits and open the lines of contact between her parents and her children. Instead of embarking on a witch-hunt to establish why her parents were culpable for her marital distress, she had approached them firmly and intently, but with an open mind, and they had eventually been able to hear her pain and acknowledge their responsibility. And as she learned more about the family process that, like an iceberg, lay under the brutality that she had absorbed, Nadine was able to begin sorting out the sources of her anxiety and irritability, and begin to make plans for the abusive "buck" to stop right here.

Even more important, the next year of therapy involved her making the connection between having been abused as a child and having difficulty staying in control with her kids and enjoying sex. The tremendous amount of energy that had needed to be summoned to repress the trauma from her past was now liberated, free to be redirected into an increased sensitivity to the needs of her children, as well as to her own needs. Finally able to understand why she had felt so frightened when making love, Nadine and her husband used the therapy to begin learning how to create a safe sexual environment that allowed for both erotic and nonerotic contact. Her husband, much more sensitive to her now that he had a clearer sense of the origin of what had seemed so inexplicable, supported her as she made important changes, and in doing so changed, too.

Nadine cannot rewrite her past, and will always, to some extent, be beset by her childhood anguish. But instead of simply blaming her parents for victimizing her, and viewing herself as "damaged goods" and her first family as mere criminals, she has grown beyond the powerlessness of being a child to become an empowered adult, one who bravely opened up new possibilities for connection and understanding with her husband and children, as well as her parents.

By commending Nadine's efforts at understanding and forgiveness, I do not mean to underestimate the difficulties. Nor do I want to encourage skipping over the hard parts to an instant reconciliation. Too strong a desire to forgive can be just as immobilizing as too automatic an impulse to blame. If forgiveness grows out of fear of seeing our first family clearly, and a desire to whitewash the darker parts of our childhood and "make nice" without any true resolution taking place, then it is not true forgiveness, and it has no healing power.

Forgiveness that grows out of a sensitive understanding of our parents' heritage and obstacles, and that relinquishes the belief that they were supposed to have raised us "correctly," on the other hand, can greatly enhance our resourcefulness both with our first, and our new, families, and help us to better appreciate and take on the marital and parenting challenges that await us.

4. TALKING TO THE GHOSTS

We have been focusing on situations in which parents and other members of our first family are still alive and involved with us. Death, however, does not put an end to the relationship we had with these people. In fact, our parents' influence on us can even be *amplified* once they are dead. This happens in a number of different ways.

We might feel some unprocessed guilt about all that we didn't do for them and devote ourselves to making reparations. Or their death might increase our loyalty toward them and what they stood for, which might or might not fit in with what *we* stand for. Or, we might become more susceptible to deifying them now that we can no longer interact with them in a skin-on-skin way.

On the other hand, their death may free us to locate and express some of the mixed feelings we have been harboring about them. This experience can be unsettling when they are still around, but it can be even more complicated if they are dead, because we do not get the opportunity to share with them our new insights, and to let our new discoveries create new pathways for our relationship to grow in.

The two processes that are most important when it comes to reconnecting with deceased members of our family of origin are *completing the mourning process* and *deidealizing*.

Regarding the former, the ultimate purpose of mourning is to allow us to carry with us the strengths and lessons that inhered in our relationship with the deceased, and to apply these strengths and lessons to all of the tasks and relationships that we take on after they have left us.

Mourning stirs up painful feelings of loss for all of us, however, and because of this we sometimes cut short the grieving process to protect ourselves from these feelings. Although we may have spared ourselves some short-term distress, the price we pay is substantial. Without a completed grieving process, we often remain stuck in some important way, enslaved to some image of or connection with the person who has died, and unable to move on.

Ilona, for example, a thirty-eight-year-old accountant, came to my office several months after she and her husband had adopted their first child. Her concerns had to do with the increasing number of fights that she and her husband were having about parenthood. The constant bickering about child-rearing decisions related to feeding, limit-setting, and schedules was leading her to doubt whether they should have become parents in the first place, and whether their marriage would survive parenthood.

I learned that Ilona's mother, Carolyn, had died of cancer only a few months before the adoption had come through, and that Ilona had chosen to have a child by adoption after years of being unable to conceive due to medical problems. I also learned that shortly before her mother's actual death, Ilona and her mother had had a stinging fight, having to do with whether Ilona should adopt if she continued to experience infertility, a fight that never got resolved. Ilona had said that she probably would adopt, while her mother had said that having a child by adoption simply because she had not been able to have a child by birth was selfish and unwise, and would lead her to always treat this child as "second best," particularly if she was one day able to have a child by birth.

While some of the marital skirmishes that Ilona was experiencing probably had to do with the natural increase in tension that goes hand-in-hand with early parenthood, their persistence seemed to me to be related to the unresolved fight with her mother, and the sadness she felt at never having had the opportunity to share her beloved child with her mother.

Ilona and I worked together to facilitate her mourning process so that she might come to terms with the complexity of her relationship with her mother. Among other things, I asked her to visit her mother's gravesite with her now six-month-old son and to introduce her mother to the grandson she had never met. She reported back to me that she had filled up with tears when doing so, and had come away convinced that, despite their disagreement, her mother would have been delighted to have seen and got to know her grandson.

Ilona and her husband were Jewish, and shortly after this visit it came time for them to schedule the ritual circumcision of their son, the *bris milah,* which had been delayed because of the adoption. I asked her to invite the friends and relatives who would be attending this ceremony to bring along a memory or anecdote that would relate to what her mother would have been like as a grandmother.

The material was of course heavily weighted toward the positive, which helped to temper the negativity that Ilona was carrying toward her mother because of their last, bitter fight. One of her old girlfriends remembered that Ilona's mother had always made wonderful coffee cake, and suggested that the baby would certainly have had his fill of such delicacies if Carolyn were still around to feed him.

One of her mother's friends, whom Ilona still kept in touch with, recalled that Carolyn had always enjoyed traveling, and would probably have insisted on taking her grandson to visit his original South American homeland at some point.

Ilona's brother reminded her that their mother had always loved animals, particularly birds, and that it would have only been a matter of time before a discussion of what kind of parakeet her grandson should have would have been initiated.

The process of reconnecting with her mother through a communal recollection helped Ilona to put to rest the incomplete battle she had had with Carolyn even though she was no longer alive. The frequency of her marital battles dropped dramatically because the sense of completion she now felt in her relationship with her absent mother diminished her need to do battle with her husband. The root of their conflicts had finally been addressed.

In another example, Ned scheduled an appointment with me at his wife's request. He said that the two of them had been locked in a bitter dispute for almost a year about whether he would continue working for the architectural firm he had been with for years, and had long since felt he had outgrown, or would take the risk of leaving and starting his own firm. For most of that time, his wife had urged him not to give up the security of a good job, but now, he reported, she no longer cared which decision he made, so long as he made one and stopped complaining about his life. The problem was, without his wife's opposition, he no longer knew what he wanted to do.

In exploring his family of origin, I learned that Ned's father, Hiram, had died around the time that Ned and his wife had conceived for the first time. While Ned and Hiram had been somewhat close for most of Ned's life, as Hiram aged, he became more and more sour, and more and more reclusive. He focused obsessively on how much he regretted some of the choices he had made in life, and kept insisting, perhaps because misery loves company, that Ned, too, would one day live to regret all that *he* chose to do.

Ned had dealt with his father's acrid attitude by withdrawing from him. By the time he died, Ned was visiting him only once or twice a year, and they spent little time talking or doing anything together. He did not cry when he heard the news of his father's death, at the funeral, or at any point afterward.

My thought was that because he had neither commenced, nor completed, his mourning for his father, he had inadvertently been maintaining loyalty to him by making good on his father's dour prophecy. If he could get the flow of grief going again, perhaps he might be free to transcend this bleak loyalty and resolve his career dilemma. But at this point Ned was uninterested in discussing his father, so we stayed away from that subject.

Meanwhile, however, his father's prescient comment was ringing true, as Ned went on and on in sessions about how impossible it was to stay with this firm that was, in his eyes, so stodgy and conservative. Though he seemed sincere, I could not ignore how resourcefully he orchestrated ways to subvert his possible success as an independent architect by refraining from any conscientious networking and follow-up with colleagues and prospective clients. Now, with two young children at home, he halfheartedly rationalized, was not the time to be an entrepreneur. And yet it was obvious that he could not resign himself much longer to his present circumstances.

A couple of months into our work together, he mentioned that his oldest, now five, had asked him why he had only one grandfather. I suggested that Ned take the opportunity to do a little family history for his son. Ned went home, got an old photo album down from the shelf, and, for the first time in years, began talking and thinking about his father. When he did so, a flood of powerful memories washed over him, some fond, some troubling. The next several sessions were devoted to exploring the feelings that these memories evoked.

One day, I asked Ned to imagine that he was his father, and to go shopping for a present for him (Ned) that would in some way speak to this stuck point in his life. Ned came to my office for his next session and wept when he showed me the gift that he had bought. It was a gold paperweight inscribed with his name, and followed by the words "Founder and Director," in front of the proposed name of his new business.

The next months were tense but exciting ones for him, as he bravely went ahead with plans to start his own company. Not surprisingly, once he resolved his inner conflicts by giving himself permission to live a life different from his father's, his conflicts with his wife evaporated. They had never been the real issue.

What is just as paralyzing for us as abortive grief is the idealization of a dead parent. Individuals who have died sometimes acquire the warm glow of godliness in our eyes, partially because we miss them and view them through rose-colored glasses, and partially because we don't feel comfortable thinking or speaking critically about someone who is no longer around.

Yet unless we arrive at a more balanced vision of our missing parents, we are doomed to feelings of discouragement and hopelessness. This will be the inevitable consequence of trying to live up to the standards of perfection that we have projected onto them.

Perhaps the best antidote to idealization is, as stated above, getting as much good and varied information as we can from as many possible sources.

Joanne, for example, came to me because she felt that she had little interest in any kind of physical or emotional intimacy with her husband. She wasn't sure whether she had "fallen out of love" or was "just depressed." The mother of a six-year-old daughter and a four-year-old son, she spoke adoringly but achingly of the former, Deborah, and of all of her varied talents, although she also mentioned in passing that her daughter could be kind of "bitchy" and had trouble getting along with people.

I discovered that Deborah had been named after Joanne's mother, who had died in a car accident when Joanne was seventeen. Joanne's description of her mother bordered on the hagiographic: "I'll never meet anyone like her," she murmured poignantly, after enthusiastically listing her many attributes, "she's irreplaceable."

My guess was that Joanne felt so maritally lethargic because she was using up all of her energy sustaining her idealized image of her mother, idealizing her own daughter (who, being named for her mother, symbolized her), and criticizing herself for not being able to be like either.

Over the course of a number of months, I asked her to get a clearer picture of her mother from the relatives and friends who were available and interested in talking. Eventually, she came to establish a more complete depiction that included some notable flaws that she hadn't been aware of before. One person in particular, her father's sister, emphasized that from *her* perspective Joanne's mother was a selfish woman who was known to cut friends out of her life if they didn't do her bidding, and whose marriage was fraught with frequent fights and threatened separations. This was at first quite painful for Joanne to hear about, as she was forced to incorporate some unattractive features into the reigning, and holy, portrait.

But these insights helped her in a couple of different ways. For one thing, her ability to deal with her daughter improved. The fact that she had identified Deborah with her idealized mother had made it all but impossible for her to discipline her own daughter. Where formerly she had agreed to be bossed around by Deborah and buffeted by her moodiness, Joanne now decided, completely of her own volition, that it was time to set firmer limits regarding what she would and wouldn't do for her daughter. She talked with me about how to put some of these limits into action, but that was my only contribution. A situation that she had not even identified as a problem when she came into therapy was now well on the way to being resolved.

Her husband, Eric, who had been somewhat baffled by Deborah's extremes of temperament, noticed this shift, and enthusiastically joined with Joanne in helping to modulate their daughter by joining her for a couple of therapy sessions to discuss this further. They found themselves feeling like a team for the first time since having become parents, and with this feeling of being teammates, Joanne noticed that she had more interest in her husband, and vice versa.

Realizing that one of the ways in which she could outgrow and surpass her mother was through having a satisfying marriage, she began to focus more on her and her husband's strengths, rather than on those of her mother. Her status as a wife and mother was now elevated, rather than "depressed," as it had been up until now. By deidealizing her dead mother, she no longer had a sainted maternal image to wither in comparison to, and could watch her marriage and family life blossom as she finally owned up to her own substantial attributes.

5. ONE-ON-ONE

Another important consideration when you're trying to deepen your connection with your family of origin is making sure you get some time alone with family members with whom you have unfinished business. Particularly if your family interaction style is characterized by what, in an earlier chapter, we termed "ritualized cutoff," your only opportunities to see relatives may be at large family gatherings, meaning that the opportunity for meaningful engagement is slim, at best.

With parents, it is sometimes the case that while we see "them" often, we rarely see one of them (usually the opposite sex one) alone. This may be our wish, their wish, or mutual, but either way it prevents any kind of real relational growth from taking place.

We may wind up dealing with our more "challenging" parent indirectly, asking our mother how our father's business has been going, or our father how our mother's health has been. The problems with this approach are not only that it places very low ceilings on the kind of relationship we can reestablish, but also that it does nothing to question the foundation of certain family myths and assumptions, the very process we are trying to jump-start.

This division of interest in our parents may feel justifiable if we see one of them as having victimized the other or us, and we may believe that we have to continue to side with the victim, and/or avoid the victimizer. Yet until we see each of them not as "blamed" and "blameless" but, like ourselves, as part of a unit jointly responsible for the course taken by their marriage, we will be prone to repeating a similar pattern in our own marriage.

Jenna and Jim contacted me because of fights they had been having about how to handle their five-year-old daughter Alexis, who continued to attach herself to her mother and shun her father. Jenna felt that because Alexis was a girl, it was only natural that she feel more connected with her mother than her father, while Jim felt that the situation was extreme, and that Jenna was at fault for allowing Alexis to get away with this kind of splitting.

I explored with Jenna her extended family, and noticed that she displayed the same pattern with her parents as her daughter did with her and her husband: During visits, Jenna tended to spend time with her mother and ignore her father. Her reason for this was the anger she still felt toward her father, an alcoholic who had been sober for ten years now but had made her mother's life horrible in his pre-sobriety years.

One of the first steps in the treatment was for her to take the risk of broaching more direct contact with her father. Even to arrange such contact was amazingly problematic. When she would call her father on the phone to set a time, her mother would find reasons not to get him ("He's a little busy right now, honey" or "He's taking a nap"), "forget" to relay the message to him, or offer to set it up *for* him, so that Jenna didn't have the chance to talk to him directly.

With some persistence, however, Jenna was finally able to arrange a time when both she and her father were free, and her mother was unavailable.

In talking with her father, she right away gained a much greater awareness of the family history of alcoholism, which went back several generations, and which was useful to know more about now that she was a parent. She also learned for the first time about the Twelve Step program that her father had committed himself to, and that she had previously been very wary about, since her mother spoke so negatively about "those meetings for drunks that your father is always going to."

Her father added that her mother had been very reluctant to take their pastor's advice that he be hospitalized at a point when his drinking was out of control a number of years ago.

Jenna told me that at first she thought that her dad was trying to shift the responsibility of his drinking onto somebody else, which he had been prone to do in the past and which instantly put her on guard. However, she reported to me that as she listened, it became clear that he was not accusing her mother of having victimized him or abandoned him, for he knew that getting treatment was ultimately his responsibility. He *did* tell Jenna that he thought her mother was so invested in avoiding the embarrassment of his being in a detox unit that she contributed to prolonging his descent into addiction by helping him to avoid what turned out to be a necessary step in his healing. And he suspected that she didn't want to deal with the volcano of emotions that would, and did, explode once he refrained from anesthetizing himself with regular doses of alcohol. That her mother's mother was also an alcoholic, which Jenna hadn't known, had perhaps complicated the issues even further.

It was only when a couple of old drinking friends who had attained sobriety came for him one night and physically escorted him to an inpatient addictions unit that he began taking his recovery seriously. Her father also commented that her mother continued adamantly to refuse to go to Al-Anon meetings, even though he and their pastor had both recommended this.

When Jenna began to reconsider her mother's enabling role in her father's alcoholism, she achieved a more balanced view of her parents' relationship, and, practically speaking, could begin to engage more fully with her father. She began talking in earnest with both her father and her mother, the former about his recovery, and the latter about the rage she still felt and sat on. She also attended an Adult Children of Alcoholics meeting, and offered to attend an Al-Anon meeting with her mother, an offer that was eventually accepted.

These changes slowly began to filter down to Jenna's new family. Once Jenna felt better about daughter-father contact due to the intensified contact with her own father, she was more willing to hear Jim out and work to facilitate his contact with their daughter. Not coincidentally, Alexis began displaying more interest in her father: It was almost as if she sensed that daughter-father relations were now approved of.

Also, the insights that Jenna gleaned from her ACOA and Al-Anon meetings stimulated some important discussions between her and her husband, who also was the child of an alcoholic, and left them feeling more connected with each other. All of this combined to reduce the tension among the three of them and give their marriage more buoyancy.

Let me conclude this chapter with a case study about a couple who utilized a number of these different strategies for reconnecting with their past. The result was personal growth for both of them, a much closer bond between them, and a greater ability to care for their child by learning how to set healthy limits for him.

Amy and Lorne consulted with me because of their difficulties getting along with each other since the birth of their two-and-a-half-year-old son, Corey. Each parent had a different understanding of these difficulties, of course. Lorne complained that Amy was increasingly unavailable to both him and Corey, and that she spent most of her time and energy at her job, which was a high-level administrative position in a community-wide senior citizens program.

Amy spoke of feeling troubled by Lorne's "bossiness": "He's always telling me what to do and how to do it, he's the authority on everything, the checkbook, the cleaning, Corey, you name it—I just don't think I need that kind of directing in my life at this time." It appeared that her current solution to this attempted domination was to withdraw into those activities where she felt more sure of herself, and more in control, such as work: "I used to take him on, but I really don't have the energy anymore, it's not worth it."

This approach naturally provoked Lorne to pursue her even more, and request more time for him and Corey, resulting in her creating more distance, and an increasingly intense cycle of polarization.

I asked them to bring Corey to our next meeting, and sat back to watch the three of them play with a toy garage and cars that occupied the corner of my office. Corey was a dashingly handsome toddler, with fiery green eyes and a bustling, take-charge attitude. Within seconds he was assigning tasks to both parents, insisting that his father drive this car through this entrance, that his mother place that sign there, and so forth. The two parents dutifully followed his master plan for an eventual three-car crack-up that seemed to me to symbolize his fears about where the family's tension level was leading them.

Lorne went along with the demands somewhat playfully, but Amy became more and more irritable with each command, several times sighing with exasperation as Corey relentlessly admonished and corrected her for not fulfilling his requests with complete accuracy and obedience. It was clear that her husband was not the only "boss" whom Amy had to contend with.

In a follow-up meeting, I asked Amy about her extended family. She described a background that was extremely female-centered, which included being raised in a household occupied by her mother, her mother's mother, her mother's unmarried sister, her own sister, and her father.

When I asked her who in her life most exuberantly displayed feminine power, she spoke excitedly about her grandmother, who was one of the few women in her generation to have started her own business, a small dry-cleaning shop. When I asked her who in her life represented masculine power, she drew a blank: She knew none of her grandfathers, had no uncles who were important to her, didn't have a brother, and spoke of her father as a "gentle but weak man" who had died shortly before Corey's birth of chronic heart disease that had seriously diminished his vitality over the last decade of his life.

My hypothesis was that the reason she had so little idea of how to deal with her son's and her husband's attempts at male domination was because she had little acquaintance with masculine power, and thus found herself so much at a loss that she simply withdrew.

If she could reconnect with those sources of male power in her life that she had, in fact, been touched by, she would feel less vulnerable, and better able to set limits, rather than have to retreat and distance herself. (It was interesting to consider the possibility that her choice to work with senior citizens was an intuitive, unspoken expression of her desire to know more about the family "seniors" who were still having impact on her life). A better balance between masculine and feminine power might lead her to feel more centered, and more sure of herself, as a wife and mother.

I asked her to do some thinking about her father's life before his illness set in, particularly whatever strengths she could recall, and to get in touch with any extended family members who could provide her with some anecdotes about him.

She came for the following session with a beautiful bird feeder that he had made. She then mentioned that although he had not enjoyed his job, he was a wonderful craftsman and a talented singer, and that she had a very happy memory of following him down to the basement so that she could listen to him singing to himself while he whittled away in his workshop.

She had called her uncle, too, and learned from him that when he and her father were children, her father was the only one in the family who had been able to train the family dog, and that neighbors often asked him for advice when it came to controlling their pets. Her uncle also told her that one time her father got a commendation from the police department for scaring away a gang of youths who were threatening a woman with harm.

As she relayed these memories to me, she appeared different somehow, less hesitant, more forward. It was as if a new conduit was allowing her to connect with an old energy source, and she was already feeling rejuvenated by the power that could now flow freely. I instructed her in some straightforward ways to set limits with Corey when he became overly bossy with her, and the success of these experiments gave her the confidence to begin setting limits with her other boss, Lorne. Surprisingly (from her perspective), he not only responded well to her limits but began pursuing her less, now that her ability to draw on inner strengths made her less inclined to retreat so much.

However, after a couple of months of living with his newly self-possessed wife, Lorne began to have some troubles of his own, centering around his job, which involved selling medical supplies to hospitals. He got in a verbal altercation with his boss, lost a fairly large account under circumstances he was unaware of, and talked aimlessly of leaving this company without coming up with any alternative plans.

In obtaining *his* family history, I came across several notable pieces of data, including information about his father's frequent job changes and his parents' sequence of marital separations and reconciliations during his adolescence and early adulthood, ostensibly due to financial problems and moves made necessary by his father's work. His father, he told me, seemed always to be struggling to live up to the high expectations of his wife but was never able to satisfy her. They had remained together, however, in part because his mother had never been able to make it on her own.

It seemed probable that Lorne's reaction to Amy's focus on work, which was what had brought them to treatment in the first place, was rooted in his envy of her success. Specifically, his fear might be that her continued success and his underachievement would enable her to abandon him, as he remembered his mother threatening to do because of his father's repeated failures. Up until now, he had been able to hide this fear behind the rationalization of her not being "available" enough to their son, which freed him from having to confront this fear, as well as from confronting his own sense of being a disappointment as a provider, as his father was.

When I asked about his current relationship with his folks, Lorne mentioned that his father had a habit of criticizing his mother to him behind her back, something that had always made him uncomfortable. He would find subtle ways to discredit her, portray himself as a victim of her "flightiness," and interpret Lorne's nodding silence as agreement. Lorne did acknowledge that he wished his father wouldn't do this, but also admitted that he did not make it clear that he wanted his father to stop manipulating him in this way, possibly because it was one of the few things they communicated about.

Although he had never done so, and expressed much unease at the idea, I asked him to arrange a time when he and his mother could be together without his father around. My suggestion was rooted in the hope that a better understanding of his parents' relationship might enable him to see the differences between his own marriage and theirs. If he could stop identifying so completely with his father's fears of abandonment, he would be less likely to assume that Amy's doing well might result in her abandoning him.

The meeting, over lunch, was a tentative and awkward one for both of them, filled with uneasy small talk, but they agreed to try it again a couple of months later. This time, Lorne reported, he learned more about his mother's perspective on the marriage, including the ways in which she had tried to support his father in adjusting to various jobs, support that she said he would firmly reject, and the resentment she still harbored that he hadn't stuck with a night-school program in heating and air-conditioning that might have improved his job opportunities.

Instead of being forced to view his mother through the lens of his father's resentment and fear, Lorne began reconstructing a new image of her, one that took into account the origins of her supposedly "flighty" behavior and that helped him to understand her as a woman who was committed to bettering herself and her family.

With this shift in perspective, he was able to see Amy's commitment to her work not as a flight from the marriage and family, but rather as an effort on *her* part to better herself by finding balance between her work and home life. This alleviated some of his anxiety, which made his pursuit of her less frantic and her running from him less intense. In turn, this shift brought them into a closer orbit where they could begin to define a less threatening intimacy with each other. Furthermore, once he was able to outgrow his loyalty to his underachieving father and come to terms with surpassing him, he was able to refocus his energies on his own career and reconsider the prospect of pursuing a graduate degree in business that he had abandoned midway several years before.

Each obviously has more work to do. Lorne needs to get back to his father and find out more about the origins of his unease with women, as well as to find ways to limit his father's tendency to try to get him to join against his mother. Amy needs to get back to her mother and find out more about how such a matriarchal hierarchy came to be established in the first place, and what sustained some of the imbalance throughout the generations.

However, the impasse that was provoked by the birth of their child has led them to embark on a satisfying and functional resolution of issues that had always been there but had become problematic only once the tensions of parenthood forced them into the open. They achieved this resolution *not* by insisting with greater and greater force that the other change, but by thoughtfully and nonjudgmentally getting a clearer sense of the multigenerational family process in which they were each embedded.

In this chapter, we have been designing ways to make sense of our childhood vision of our parents. But we also have a relationship with our first family that exists solely in the present, despite its roots in the past. Resolving conflicts and developing a healthy bond with them when we are all adults in the here and now deserves a look, too.

CHAPTER NINE

Grandparents and In-Laws: Dealing with the Parents in Our Present

When we begin a family, its success, as well as the success of our marriage, requires the delicate, ongoing work of shifting our primary attachments *away* from our parents and *toward* our spouse and children, while continuing to honor and be nourished by the attachments that are part of our heritage. We must allow ourselves to be informed, but not ruled, by the past.

Sometimes, however, our loyalties to our first family start to crisscross with our loyalties to our new family, which causes a series of psychological *triangles* to be formed. This chapter is about the many kinds of triangles that we may find ourselves participating in, often without even being aware of what we are doing.

Trying Triangles

The triangles we will be focusing on are not just random arrangements of three people, but interactive situations in which a couple involves a third person, usually a child or grandparent, to reduce the intensity between the two of them. Analyzing and understanding the origin, structure, and functioning of the various triangles we are in goes a long way toward helping us sort out and resolve our marital conflicts. It is important to distinguish between triangles and other kinds of relationships with people outside of our marriage. Triangulation does not occur just because one of us has an important connection with an outsider. That happens all the time and is perfectly natural. Triangulation occurs when we *use* our relationship with a third party to defuse the combustibility of our marital relationship. It can serve to reduce anxiety by confusing, obscuring, or diluting the emotional issues between our partner and ourselves.

Relationships between two people are often in a state of flux. The inherent instability of a two-person system leads us at times to seek outsiders who contribute to our groundedness. Just as a bicycle is more likely to tip over than a tricycle, and requires much more skill to operate, a dyad is more likely to "tip over" than a triad, and also requires more skill to "operate."

When there is a triangle, tension is diffused among three people rather than two, which means that there are more pathways in place for anxiety to be handled, reducing the risk of overload on any one circuit.

While we may think that the involvement of a third party makes things harder for us, such as when we complain about our in-laws invading our marriage, in reality it may make things easier at first, because some of our marital issues can then be detoured through the outsider, leaving us temporarily less vulnerable to distress. Instead of addressing the issues that divide us from our partners, for example, we decide to smugly blame our in-laws for being "too involved" or "too judgmental," and avoid the marital conflict altogether.

Ultimately, however, when a relationship is in crisis, the triangles in which we find ourselves are at best a diversion from the real problems, and at worst a system that feeds the crisis and keeps it going. But if we examine these triangles thoughtfully, they may be an important source of information about whatever it is we're trying to avoid.

Triangles create balance without anyone having to change, and thus are both appealing and deadly. The more we use a parent, in-law, or child as a focus for or distraction from conflicts, the more entombed in these conflicts we will be.

There are several other important things we need to remember about triangles:

1. TRIANGLES ARE FOREVER

Even if the original third person is no longer around or alive, the circuitry of the triangle may remain in place. The memory of the third person, or a substitute third person, will be invoked to supply the missing energy. A mother and father who were able to ignore their own marital tension by focusing on their son's underachievement will always be tempted to do so, even if their son grows up and leaves, or refuses to underachieve anymore. They will simply imagine he continues to underachieve and need their focus, or they'll find a replacement underachiever (another child, a friend, an aging parent) to focus on.

A mother and daughter may override their conflicts with each other through their mutual anger at their absent husband/father, even though he left more than twenty years ago. This ongoing collaboration unites them and thereby obscures the very real issues that divide them. The fact that the focus of their anger is no longer in their lives does not matter.

2. TRIANGLES TEND TO GENERATE OTHER TRIANGLES

Just as no twosome exists in isolation from other influences, no triangle does either. A father who backs off when his wife asks him for help in dealing with their dictatorial son greases the wheels for her to communicate her frustration to their daughter, who is now triangled into the mother-son and mother-father relationship.

Meanwhile, the good friend the father turns to to complain about his wife's demandingness supports him by aggravating his feeling of being victimized. This friend is now triangled into the husband-wife relationship. The fluctuation of interlocking triangles is one of the characteristic ways that couples remain in conflict with each other, despite their best intentions.

3. EACH PARTICIPANT IN THE TRIANGLE HAS A DIFFERENT ROLE

As discussed earlier, triangles are formed when anxiety becomes excessive. All of the participants have their own effect on the anxiety that is circulating. Some family therapists distinguish between the anxiety *generator,* the anxiety *amplifier,* and the anxiety *dampener.*

The generator is not the cause of the anxiety, but the one who is responsible for noticing it and bringing it to life. The amplifier responds anxiously to the presence of anxiety, either by trying to ignore it or by becoming overly reactive, thereby increasing the amplitude of the anxious energy that is already present.

Dampeners address the source of the anxiety, rather than just avoiding or reacting to the anxiety itself, and in this way facilitate a detriangulation, a process we'll explore later on in this chapter. Unfortunately, not every triangle has a dampener, which means that the triangle will last a long time since there is nothing to prevent the generation and amplification processes from running amok.

What does all of this have to do with the transition into parenthood? We have learned that the main reason that having a child is so difficult for couples is because it precipitates a "reverberating journey" that stirs up unresolved, long-buried feelings from our childhood. One of the outcomes of this reverberating journey is the almost instantaneous activation of new triangles, and the *re*activation of old triangles, that inevitably occurs between and within all of the generations once a child is born.

For example, at the same time that a hitherto forgotten triangle involving our mother and father and ourselves comes alive as we become parents, a similar triangle involving our spouse and his/her parents may be re-forming. Meanwhile, we are contending with the formation of our own nuclear mother-father-child triangle while our parents may be contending with our in-laws for influence and control over us and our offspring, creating more triangles still.

Then consider the possibility that one or more of our siblings is experiencing this same concatenating triangulation process, involving many of the same players, or that one or more of our grandparents are still alive, and we're watching old business erupt between us and them, or our parents and them. This gives you a sense of why a seven-pound lump of infant can engender such chaos in our marriages and extended families.

There are two *major* sets of triangles that are likely to accompany the birth of our child, the ones with our offspring and the ones with the new grandparents. Because the former often crystallize *in reaction to* the latter, however, we will examine those triangles that involve our first family, the grandparents. To start, let's take a closer look at what grandparenthood is all about.

What's Grand about Grandparents

With the birth of our parenthood come the sudden births of as many as four grandparents, or more in families where divorces and deaths have resulted in remarriage. Whether they are near or far, grandparents will exert a remarkably salient influence on the formation of our new family: They may become the most durable and dependable backup caretaking unit we have, an invaluable source of help and support, or they may create enough havoc that we feel like we have just participated in a multiple birth of chaotic, demanding older "babies."

Over 70 percent of people over sixty-five in this country are grandparents, and more than half of them will live long enough to become great-grandparents. Because of our increasing longevity and mobility, at no other point in our culture has grandparenthood occurred with the frequency that it does now.

As we have been discussing in many different contexts, we tend to minimize the importance of intergenerational relationships in this culture, imagining that the goal and definition of adulthood is the severance of the connection between ourselves and our parents. Yet there is much evidence to suggest that a loving and vigorous bond between the grandparent and grandchild is not just related to, but *essential* to, the emotional health and stability of *all three* generations.

Many clinicians and researchers in fact hypothesize that one of the main reasons that the incidence of child and adolescent depression, suicidality, and drug abuse has risen so sharply in the past two decades is not because of the increase in single-parent families (since there were many single-parent households during wartimes in our history, without a corresponding increase in these problems), but because the alliance between the oldest and youngest generations has gradually eroded.

What is it about the bond between grandparent and grandchild that is so unique and endearing? Psychiatrist Stanley Cath has written that grandparenthood is the "least ambivalent, most easily achieved, and most readily accepted of all family relationships."

Anyone who has witnessed grandparents spending time with their grandchildren can immediately see that this is the case. Because they are unfettered by clearly delineated responsibility or accountability for this new generation, it is often characterized by a special kind of freedom and harmony quite unlike anything they experienced with their own children.

Just as marriage gives us a "second chance" to rework and resolve old conflicts in more satisfying ways, grandparenthood provides a second chance to participate in both the giving and receiving ends of a richer, more fulfilling parent-child engagement.

The strict, authoritarian father may become, as a grandfather, astonishingly tolerant and indulgent. The bustling, efficient mother may become, as a grandmother, more relaxed and patient. One father commented to me, "We could never touch my father when I was a child because he was always afraid we'd pull at his beard. So imagine my surprise when he's leaning over my daughter's crib *inviting* her to pull it. He was actually putting her hands into his beard, *hoping* she'd do what we were never allowed to do!"

While the transition into grandparenthood has been underexamined by the psychological community, there is little doubt that it is indeed a remarkably significant stage in adult development. Grandchildren enter the scene at a point when their grandparents are likely to be particularly vulnerable. They are often in the process of experiencing the decline and death of their own parents and other members of their extended family and peer group, a diminution of physical stature and health, and an actual or "pre"-retirement from their paid, or unpaid, profession.

The losses and regrets as they experience this last phase of life, the increasing sense of expendability that this society promotes among its elders, as well as their growing concerns about mortality, combine to call into question their sense of achievement, purpose, and meaning. But such feelings, in combination with the physiological and psychological mellowing that occurs as men and women proceed past middle age, may make them all the more open and available to loving connections with others.

Joyriding into this maelstrom of yearning, fear, and ambivalence comes the grandchild, full of freshness, innocence, and hope, and pumping gallons of meaning and vitality into their grandparents' emptying psychic tanks. Free to love this child without the restrictions inherent in parenthood, grandparents find solace in this new kind of relationship, compensation for old losses, hope for the future, and an unending source of delight in the present. As one grandparent said, "It takes only one grandchild to feel loved a whole life long."

Grandparenthood re-stirs the old desire to have been, and to have had, a perfect child and a perfect parent. This desire fuels the intensity of their enthusiasm and altruism, the same enthusiasm and altruism that mystifies us, the middle generation, as we seek to understand the discrepancies between who they were for us and who they are for our children. Why couldn't they have been more like that when they were raising us? we wonder. For it soon becomes almost unbearably clear that their aspirations for and acceptance of their grandchildren are different than they were for us.

Grandchildren, of course, are more than happy to take the stage in this optimistic drama. They sense immediately that the burdens and tensions that are an inextricable part of their relationship with their parents do not apply to their relationship with their grands. And they know this can only mean fun. As Jean-Paul Sartre wrote, "I could drive my grandmother into raptures of joy just by being hungry."

While this may be wonderful for the grandparent and grandchild, it can be a mixed bag for new parents, for a number of different reasons. For one thing, children propel us into more proximity with our parents than we may be comfortable with. We may find ourselves seeing our parents more, talking to them more, and relying on them more than we ever have since having inched our way into self-sufficiency years before.

A carefully worked-out formula for spending time in a satisfying way with our extended family may have been one of our first conjoint marital accomplishments and a real source of pride. Unfortunately, no matter how neatly the system worked before children are here, you can forget about it working now.

Most new parents discover that the kinds of limits that were easy to set before quickly disintegrate when there are grandchildren in the picture. In-laws who were content to visit every week now clamor for extra allotments and find excuses to stop by. Phone calls that rolled in only on weekends now start coming in midweek, too.

It took Karen and me several years to master the complexities of our out-of-town visits to my first family, but we had gradually cobbled a routine for those one or two day trips that had a reassuring rhythm to them. Once we had children, however, everything was shot. The simple overnight or weekend visit became undoable, because it seemed to take one full night just to get everything loaded into the car, let alone allow enough time for close and distant relatives to take a gander at the little ones. We suddenly had to balance our needs with those of our kids, and it was another several years before we were able to reestablish some kind of equilibrium.

So in addition to being parents, we have suddenly taken on another new role, what Dr. Cath calls the "vertical gatekeeper," the linchpin between the first and third generations. We are the ones who can sanction or prohibit contact, and the ones who decide, to a certain extent, on the nature and texture of that contact.

It is not just an issue of time together, however. When children become parents, and parents become grandparents, the power alignments in a family necessarily and dramatically shift. The easy or uneasy truce between generations that may have been worked out during the years between adolescence and child rearing is jeopardized, and a new homeostasis must evolve.

We parents must relinquish whatever remains of our wish to be parented as we start to raise our own children. The grandparents must relinquish whatever authority and control they were holding on to, so that their child can come into his/her own as a parent.

As with any far-reaching and formidable alteration, it can take quite some time for this realignment to become comfortably established, and there will be much jockeying for position as a new hierarchy is shaped. Parents may fight with their parents to become the "real" parents, or become frightened of the responsibility and emotional intensity of parenthood and fight to become their parents' children again.

Grandparents may fight to be parental, either with us and/or with our children, or become frightened of the responsibility and emotional intensity of grandparenthood and avoid dealing with aspects of their relationship with their children and grandchildren. And in-laws may fight with each other to assume a predominantly special place in their grandchildren's lives.

However it goes, this shift will inevitably be accompanied by complicated interpersonal machinations that will strain everyone's capacity for tolerance and create periods of tense infighting.

For what parenthood usually does at first is rekindle the competition with our parents that may have been dormant since the turmoil of adolescence. The advice or criticism that we receive at our parents' hands may be their thinly disguised attempt to convey to us that they haven't yet grown to accept our autonomy. The bristling withdrawal or criticism that *they* receive at *our* hands may be our thinly disguised attempt to regain the autonomy we thought we'd won years ago. If we're not feeling very securely parental ourselves, we may think that the only way we can be autonomous is by overthrowing them. Sometimes we become bent on insisting that we're "the boss," and that the grandparents have to treat the children the exact same way that we do (the chance to finally boss our own parents around instead of vice versa expresses some of our unresolved competition with them).

Alternately, however, in the moment of profound weakness that all new parents feel, we may turn to our parents, the original sources of support during our weakest childhood moments, in the hope of finding expertise and reassurance. This may work out fine so that both parent and grandparent feel allied and victorious. Sometimes, however, it backfires; the support we long for was never really there for us in our childhoods, and we're trying to re-create something that didn't exist; or the process of asking is so fraught with confusion and anxiety that no matter what kind of help is forthcoming, we can't accept it without feeling condescended to. Rather than hearing the measured voice of our parents' calm support, we feel haunted by their criticism, by the ghoulish echoes of their pessimistic "voice of doom." The insidious effect of all of their cumulative warnings to us about what we should or shouldn't do take on the power of hypnotic suggestions, and we may find ourselves in a queerly resentful and childlike trance.

We sometimes fantasize that having a child will bring us closer to our parents, and will reignite some of the love and connectedness that we have (maybe always) been missing. But just as children by their presence alone do not improve marriages, they also don't, by their presence alone, improve their parents' intergenerational affiliations. They cannot heal all wounds, or speak to all needs.

Grandparents may have some issues of their own that get in the way of attaching to their grandchildren. They may be paying their son or daughter back for some past transgression (especially if it involves the choice of spouse or career). They may be communicating their dissatisfaction over an unresolved conflict with their child. They may be so intent on remaining psychologically "in the saddle" that they can't bear to witness such tangible evidence of their child's maturity and power.

Or they may be facing dilemmas that are strictly internal. They may be overly preoccupied with avoiding their sense of mortality, and see contact with grandchildren as too painful a reminder of their aging, of their waning activity and vitality. They may be struggling with conscious or subconscious memories and issues from their own childhood or parenthood that are troubling ones. They may simply be making a desperate, last-ditch effort to remain in control in the best or only way they know how.

All of these various situations create stress for us as individuals, but they also can be a direct line into marital discord when they lead to conflict-promoting triangles. To understand why this is so, we need to take a closer look at the unique relationships we have not only with our *own* first family, but also with our *partner's* first family.

In-Laws

Family therapist Jay Haley wrote, "What distinguishes man from the animals is having in-laws." When you think about it, it *is* hard to imagine any other species being even tangentially invested in its connection with its love object's mother and father.

In-laws get bad press in this society. The butt of jokes and satire, they are often avoided, fought with, or relegated to subordinate status without being fully appreciated or understood, often at a tremendous cost to the newly formed couple. But as we just learned, when children arrive on the scene, parents are usually forced to encounter their in-laws, the grandparents, more frequently and more intensely than they ever have before.

For many individuals, relationships with in-laws present a tremendous opportunity to rework and re-solve issues and conflicts that originated long before. The chance to deal with a "new" mother and father, but this time getting to start out *with* the resources and capabilities of adulthood, and *without* an injurious, turbulent history looming just offstage, can be an exciting and instructive one.

As discussed above, however, in-laws also present us with opportunities to avoid issues. Sometimes we triangle in our in-laws and use them as scapegoats for our conflicts with our spouse, while they triangle us in and use us as scapegoats for their conflicts with their child, our partner.

For example, it is easier for a man to blame his mother-in-law for meddling in his marriage than to find out more about why his wife is unhappy with him. It is easier for grandparents to condemn their daughter-in-law for not getting the grandchildren over to their house for visits often enough than to deal directly with their son about their psychological estrangement from each other. It is easier for us to set up our spouses to fight with our overcontrolling parents *for* us than to carry the banner of that fight ourselves, easier to use them to fulfill kinship-sustaining activities like gift-giving and letter-writing than negotiate a relationship with our family that is all our own.

Many fights between husbands and wives appear to have to do with the influence of their respective in-laws. But the foundation of these fights usually harks back to their relationship with their own parents. If we're jealous of our partner's ties with his/her parents, for example, we may be feeling insecure and wishing that we had closer ties with our own. If we're overly sensitive to our in-laws' involvement in or distance from our lives, we may have incompletely differentiated from our family of origin and be uncomfortable setting different kinds of limits with *them*.

These conflicts can and will occur at any point in a couple's development, but they are *more likely* to come about when a couple have children because our in-laws are then no longer just our in-laws, but also our children's grandparents, with all of the intensity that goes along with this.

Let's take a look at two different situations to see how starting a family can lead to the formation of a kaleidoscope of tension-producing triangles involving grandparents.

Keith and Jean were the parents of a two-year-old daughter, Megan. They came to see me because of an unresolved dispute that had to do with Jean's parents' involvement in their lives.

Keith was always annoyed at how often his in-laws were stopping by to see Megan, and how often Jean insisted that they go visit her parents. The "last straw" had taken place during the most recent visit. Keith explained that he had told Jean that he was ready to leave several times, and when she didn't get moving, he had just got his coat, left the house, and gone to sit in the car until she and Megan finally joined him.

Jean's version was that she had heard him, but was in the middle of an important conversation with her father about the possibility that he might need hip-replacement surgery, and that she wasn't comfortable just walking out in the middle. Also, she said that he could have facilitated their departure if he had really wanted to by helping Megan gather the blocks she had strewn all over her grandparents' family room, rather than leaving the task to Jean and her parents.

She further defended herself by accusing Keith of never wanting to visit her folks, which put her in the position of wanting and having to stay "as long as possible" because she didn't know when she'd have the energy to "fight" for another visit. "They know that you can't stand being there, and sometimes they ask me why I even bother to bring you along. You're so unfair—I'd never put any pressure on *you* to leave if we were visiting *your* parents," she asserted.

Keith disagreed with this, but Jean countered by sarcastically pointing out that they rarely visited his parents anyway, even though they, like her parents, lived nearby, so she never had a chance to prove herself. This antagonistic triangle involving Keith, his wife, and his in-laws had begun to spin out of control, and to affect Megan, too. In response to all the tension surrounding these visits, she was now throwing tantrums before and afterward.

Keith and Jean acknowledged that this conflict started shortly before Megan was born, and that it had worsened considerably since her second birthday a couple of months ago.

At this point in time, there was no anxiety dampener, only a generator, Keith, who blamed his wife for his distress, and two sets of amplifiers, Jean and her parents, who both counterblamed him for causing theirs.

As I said a moment ago, my belief is that in-law-related fights with our spouse have their origins in the hurts and conflicts with our own family. So I began the detriangulation process by exploring with Keith his relationships with his first family, particularly why he appeared so cut off from them.

I learned that his father had been killed in the Korean War when he was two years old. While his mother had remarried, he had never felt particularly close with his stepfather, and had always felt secretly identified with the birth father he'd barely known.

My guess was that he was so reactive to Jean's closeness with her father because this was stirring up feelings about the closeness he couldn't have with his own. The fact that his daughter was now at the age *he* was at when he had lost his father had probably played a role in reopening this old wound.

Once we addressed this topic directly, he started to remember how hard it had been to adjust to his "new" father, and how he had always resented his stepfather's strict disciplinary code and his mother's refusal to back him against his stepfather. Feeling angry and betrayed throughout much of his childhood and adolescence, he had sustained his loyalty to his birth father by never fully accepting his mother's remarriage to another man. That was why his visits with them were so difficult and infrequent, even to this day: He had not fully come to terms with the loss of his father, and thus could not more fully differentiate from his first family.

Since his birth father had two sisters who were still alive, I encouraged Keith to contact them in an effort to learn more about his first father, which he did, and which led to the beginning of what turned out to be a very close relationship with one of his aunts. It was particularly touching for Keith to learn from her that his father had planned on going to college to study engineering when he returned from the war; Keith had never known this, and yet currently worked as an engineer himself. His loyalties to this long-dead man were expressed at many turns.

I also suggested that he make some time to get to know his stepfather, Anson, without using his mother as an intermediary. Amazingly, Keith told me in response to this that since leaving home to go to college, he and his stepfather had never *once* been alone in a room together. Nonetheless, he agreed to try.

In making contact with Anson, he learned that his stepfather had *also* lost his father at a young age, something Keith had not known, and they were able to talk more closely than they ever had before about how difficult their losses had been for them. Anson told him that unlike Keith's mother, his own mother had never remarried, and thus he was raised without any father, something he always regretted. I suggested to Keith that perhaps his stepfather's strict discipline had been an attempt to give Keith the fathering that *he* had never received as a young boy. This thought softened some of the hard feelings that Keith had felt about all the docked allowances and grounded weekends he had endured at Anson's behest.

As Keith stopped focusing on what he perceived as Jean's overinvolvement with *her* family, paid attention to his *own* upbringing, and found within his family sources of affection he had not known were there for him, he no longer felt so orphaned, and thus ceased to be so jealous of Jean's rich family life. So visits with his in-laws, whose good qualities he was now able to see, were not just tolerated but on occasion even welcomed, especially because he and Jean's father began to reach out to one another. Consequently, Jean was more amenable when Keith didn't want a visit or wanted to cut one short, because she no longer had to "fight" with him for time with her parents, so much pleasanter now that she did not have the tension of being caught between her husband and parents. Megan, too, sensed the pressure drop, and the tantrums disappeared because she no longer had the burden of carrying the extended family's circulating anxiety for them.

While learning more about Jean's attachment to her family of origin may be necessary at some point in the future, the leap in Keith's knowledge of and differentiation from *his* family of origin has defused the triangle enough that their fights about this subject almost disappeared.

Often, however, *both* parents have some work to do when it comes to breaking up destructive triangles with grandparents. Let's now turn our attention to a family in which this was the case.

Clay and Melissa's early months of parenthood had been rocky. Melissa, a thirty-year-old nurse, was highly anxious about her son, Dominick, who was born prematurely, and had to be "watched carefully," according to the pediatrician. Dominick was a bright but fussy little boy who was impossible to schedule because of his constantly shifting eating and sleeping patterns.

Clay, Dominick's thirty-two-year-old father, was a lawyer who was bent on becoming a partner in his firm, a position he felt would help to ensure their financial future, and get them out from under the debt that they owed to his parents, the government, and the bank for his schooling.

Melissa, who always worked hard to preserve harmony in her relationships, was trying to keep her worries about Dominick under wraps because she knew Clay was preoccupied with his job. Sometimes this was impossible, however, and she'd find herself interrupting him while he was doing the mounds of paperwork he was always bringing home. Clay would listen patiently for a few minutes to her concerns about Dominick's raspy throat or lagging appetite, then listen *im*patiently for a few more minutes, and then toss up his hands and remark distractedly that he trusted Melissa and was sure she could "deal with it." This left her feeling unheard and alone.

Meanwhile, Clay, who also valued harmony and didn't want Melissa worrying about anything else on top of Dominick, hid from her his fears that he wouldn't be invited to be a partner in the firm, as well as his nagging sense of panic that their finances were in disarray unless either he got the partnership or she went from part-time to full-time work. So he said little about his work or hers, especially during the times when he really had a lot to worry about.

Communication between the two of them grew more and more stilted, Melissa pursuing Clay with her anxieties about motherhood, Clay distancing and hiding his anxieties about money. When they did broach either of these subjects, the exchanges were usually unproductive because they were each so careful with each other.

Eventually, Melissa's distress began to overwhelm her. Tired of pursuing her husband, she began making more regular calls to her mother, who lived a couple of hours away. At times she used these calls to complain about the distance and lack of support she felt from Clay.

Here is where an old triangle with new participants began to develop. Her mother could have avoided this simply by hearing Melissa out but encouraging her to find other ways to talk to her husband, or perhaps suggesting a neutral source of sustenance, such as a new mothers' group or counseling. Instead, she took the bait and sided with Melissa against Clay. This initially felt supportive to her daughter, but since what was really being supported was not Melissa but Melissa's negative feelings toward Clay, these feelings intensified.

So Melissa began to think angrier thoughts about Clay and approach him with a little more hostility and demandingness than usual, which of course jacked up his own hostility and defensiveness. Describing Clay's responses to her mother led them both to conclude that Clay was, in fact, "not being a very good father." The pursuer-distancer cycle worsened. By encouraging Melissa to air her anger with Clay to her, Melissa's mother had now become triangled into their marital conflict.

It was notable that Melissa's father, who had died several years before of pneumonia, had workaholic tendencies that had always been a source of tension between him and her mother. Little Melissa and her mother had banded together for companionship in the face of the father's absentee relationship with his family.

Both were *primed* for the formation of this new triangle because they had for years been in a triangle with Melissa's father around a similar issue. And there's a way in which Dominick could also be said to be in a triangle with Melissa and her mother, for the dynamic of mother and daughter affirming their loyalty to each other by uniting against Impossible Men had been set in motion once again by the birth of Melissa's own impossible, fussy little man (although it certainly was not his fault that his premature birth had made him so "impossible").

Clay, of course, sensed what was happening. He saw that his wife was turning to her mother, overheard the tone of these conversations, and started to become aroused.

He could have begun a detriangulation process by understanding that he and his wife were both using her mother to avoid facing their own issues. Instead, however, he simply came down on his overwhelmed wife for calling her mother all the time, and tried to intimidate her into stopping without offering any substitute sources of succor.

By leaping to the conclusion that the problem with his marriage was his mother-in-law, he didn't have to own up to his anger at his wife for having been so preoccupied with their child that he felt estranged from her, a state of affairs that he had exacerbated by withdrawing from her in order not to burden her with his own worries. All this unacknowledged anger led to his distancing himself even more belligerently from Melissa, working longer hours than ever. This in turn simply fueled Melissa's and her mother's anger with him.

Meanwhile, the anger that Melissa felt over Clay's lack of support was so intense that it blunted her awareness of the anger she was also feeling toward her mother for being so ready to complicate Melissa's marriage, and for having used her all of those years to help her deal with her *own* unhappy marriage. More comfortable being a daughter than a wife, she found it easier to betray Clay and be loyal to her mother than the other way around.

Clay mentioned his frustration with Melissa to *his* parents during a phone conversation, which brought them into the action, too. They, like Melissa's mother, could have played a dampening role by hearing their son out and encouraging him to discover new avenues of marital communication, or more neutral sources of support. Instead, they took advantage of this opening to belittle his mother-in-law, whom they "never trusted" anyway because of some promises she had made about wedding arrangements five years before that they felt she had reneged on.

To complicate matters further, Clay had a younger sister, Kate, who had acted out their family's tensions by drinking heavily and dating dangerously throughout her adolescence and early adulthood, and who had been estranged from the family for a number of years. His parents had always rallied around Clay's accomplishments and compared his sister unfavorably to him, another old triangle. So it was no big stretch for them to invite their daughter-in-law into this old triangle to take their unavailable daughter's place. All of the anger and frustration they felt toward Kate got dumped on Melissa, and once again Clay got to play the familiar role of Good and Innocent Son, absolved by his parents from any responsibility to be the Involved and Supportive Husband.

His parents' defense of Clay incited his feelings of being victimized by his wife and mother-in-law, which led him to retreat even more from his wife, exacerbating her fears of being ignored as her own mother had been and leading to even more volatile pursuit, distancing, and fighting.

Meanwhile, Clay's parents and Melissa's mother began to vie for primacy in little Dominick's life, creating still another triangle. Melissa's mother offered to baby-sit for Dominick overnight so that Melissa and Clay could go away together, which confused Melissa since she thought that her mother didn't really think that much of her marriage to Clay anyway. Clay's parents offered to come down for a full weekend to "help out," which made Melissa uneasy because on the basis of what she could overhear of Clay's conversations with them, she did not feel very secure about what her in-laws thought of her.

The baby's frequent colds and persistent cough provided *all* of the grandparents with further opportunities to exert their influence by recommending conflicting cures and preventions that Melissa and Clay then fought over. The unspoken question that the parents and grandparents were all battling to answer was "Who has the most influence over this new family?"

Melissa's mother began commenting on how much Dominick was beginning to remind her of various people in her family, which made Clay feel shut out. And she seemed to derive special pleasure from watching Clay fail in his efforts to comfort Dominick and have to turn him over to Melissa to be nursed. It was impossible for him to ignore her delighted smirk as he stomped out of the room, shut out from the Melissa/Dominick/mother-in-law triangle once again.

Clay would retaliate by making sure that the toys his mother-in-law bought for Dominick somehow never found their way into his room, leading her to wonder why she never saw him playing with them while Clay enjoyed a quiet smirk or two of his own. In this case, little Dominick is now invited into a triangle that includes Clay and his mother-in-law, his presence allowing them to avoid any direct confrontations with each other, and instead to do so indirectly, through their reciprocal preemptive strikes.

In this one family, then, we can easily see how the birth of a child precipitates the concomitant formation of a number of intergenerational and interlocking triangles, all of which are rooted in the new parents' unexamined and unresolved loyalties to their first families.

What was particularly troublesome, by the time that Clay and Melissa arrived in my office after months of this kind of infighting, was that not a single person had stood up to play a dampening role in any of these triangles. There were plenty of generators and amplifiers: For example, every time Melissa turned to her parents or Clay turned to his parents with their marital concerns, they were without even being aware of it reactivating old triangles, and every time any of the grandparents reacted with criticism of their son-in-law or daughter-in-law, they were amplifying the anxiety that was getting circulated. The detriangulation needed to start immediately.

Because Clay and Melissa seemed equally fed up with the situation, and thus equally motivated to change, I decided to put both of them to work on the primary triangles, those dating back to relations in their families of origin.

When I asked Clay to contact his estranged sister, Kate, he was shocked and perturbed. His first question was, "Do I have to tell my parents about this, or should I keep it a secret?" It was not difficult to infer from this that Clay, despite being a highly functional adult, did not have sufficient Selfhood when it came to dealing with his first family.

When I asked why he would want to keep his contact with his sister a secret, he said, "Well, they'll get very upset. I think Kate's really hurt them a lot, and just hearing about her pains them."

"You have a child of your own now, Clay," I replied. "Can you imagine ever being at a point where you would not want to hear from him or about him, no matter how badly he may have hurt you?"

"I guess not," Clay answered. "It's just that I don't even know what to say to her, or how to explain it to them."

"To her, you could simply say that you haven't heard from her for a while, and that she is your son's only aunt and you want him to have the opportunity to get to know her. To your parents, you could explain that you may want other children some day, and you think it's time that you modeled good sibling relationships in your own life so that your child will feel better about having a sibling himself. Your parents are probably going to be upset, but the sense that this may benefit their grandchild, and that you may have others one day, can help to mollify them a bit."

Clay went ahead and told his parents he'd be contacting Kate, and they reacted even more angrily than he thought they would; there was a great deal of cold silence on the phone that made him very nervous. Even the line about this being ultimately beneficial to their grandchild seemed, at first, to have fallen on deaf ears.

However, he recovered enough to contact Kate, who was at first wary at hearing from him. Once reassured that he was not spying on her, as his parents had asked him to do when she was a wild teenager, she was quite open to hearing from him. Within no time at all, she disclosed to Clay a family secret, which was that when she was in junior high, she had accidentally found out from her best friend that their father had been having an affair for a number of years . . . with her friend's mother.

This revelation, the subsequent rupture in her relationship with her best friend, and their father's continued secrecy even though he knew that she knew, had troubled Kate so much that she had found it impossible to live quietly at home, and instead funneled all of her rage and sense of betrayal into the self-destructive behaviors that had marked her teenage years.

Clay was furious when he heard about what his sister had gone through and what his parents had hid from him, and felt a wave of sympathy for Kate that he had never felt before. Amazingly, he also reported that while Kate still felt she had been made to play the family scapegoat and remained pretty angry at Clay for playing the role of Good Son, she felt sympathy for him, too. "After all, we both grew up with the secret... I just happened to have stumbled upon it," she had commented to him.

This new piece of important knowledge shocked Clay, but also helped to free him from some of the devout loyalty to his parents that was crimping his marital maneuverability. His increased sensitivity to his sister's lonely sojourn through adolescence and adulthood helped him to realize that his wife, too, was in the midst of a lonely sojourn, that of essentially being a single mother for a difficult baby.

We also talked about the possibility that his "hyperachievement," for which he had always received so much praise from his parents, was in fact the only thing that they could come together around. For a long time, he may have been overachieving both to distract himself from the deceit that had invaded his parents' marriage and to distract his parents from that deceit.

These twin realizations enabled him to move in a number of different directions. First, he decided to continue developing a relationship with Kate, who seemed equally glad to have him, and his son and wife, in her life. Two, he began moving closer to Melissa. To further this, I asked him to take two consecutive weekdays off from work. The first day would be spent with Melissa, finding out what she did on the days she was home, and learning about how to take care of Dominick. The second would be spent alone with Dominick, Clay fully responsible for his care for the entire day. Melissa was instructed to use the time as she saw fit, so long as she kept out of the house from morning until night.

Third, he decided, on my recommendation, to let his parents know that he intended to remain in touch with Kate, now that he had spoken to her. For the time being, we put on hold the option of bringing up the infidelity issue. It was probably obvious to them that the secret was bound to come out once their children resumed contact. Why else would they have reacted so badly when Clay told them he would be calling Kate? But the family system seemed to me to be too fragile and volatile for any direct acknowledgment at this stage.

And finally, without even having to discuss this in therapy, Clay announced that he had decided to stop bringing his complaints about Melissa and her mother to his parents. "I think I'm going to be very careful about what I tell them for quite some time," he told me. "After all, there's obviously been a lot going on that I haven't known about, and I surely can't trust them to hear about my marriage based on what I've learned about *theirs*."

Melissa, meanwhile, was busily working on her own unresolved issues. The reactivated triangle involving Melissa and her mother was the first to go. Melissa told me that she had stopped calling her mother as often as usual since things had got better between her and Clay, and that when she did call, she was not criticizing Clay anymore, since she had few complaints. In fact, she had made certain to let her mother know about Clay's taking time off to be with her and Dominick.

However, she reported that her mother had recently started calling *her* more often, and would ask leading and intrusive questions about her marriage that implied that she was looking for some material to "work with." Examples included "Is Clay still working late?" and "Do you think he really knows how to make sure Dominick takes his medications?"

"It's like she's disappointed that we don't share this dislike of Clay anymore," Melissa thoughtfully suggested.

"Maybe she is," I countered. "If so, what do you think about that?"

"It's kind of annoying, frankly. I mean, I don't want to have to have marital problems to be able to connect with my mother. It's like she needs me to be unhappy so that she can feel less lonely."

"Do you think that's a new pattern or an old one?" I wondered.

"I was going to say new, like only since Dominick was born . . . but now that I think about it, she was always much more involved with me when I was having problems with guys. And I always had a lot of problems with guys—I would fall in love, and then something would go wrong, and I'd be hysterical for days. It's not like she was mean to me when I wasn't hysterical, but when I *was,* she really rose to the occasion. We really bonded together then."

"It's been very loving and attentive of you to have offered to join with your mother by having relationship difficulties of your own all these years," I proposed, "particularly since it sounds like her own husband didn't do much joining with her himself, and she's always felt kind of alone. How much longer do you think you need to continue doing this before she'll be capable of finding other ways to feel joined?"

"I don't know," Melissa mused. "I mean, I've got my own kid to be loving and attentive to, and I sure don't want my marriage going down the drain, as it looked like it was until recently . . . I really don't know."

"Perhaps you could talk with your mother about some of your concerns, and your feeling that she seems lonely and unhappy these days. There are many things you could do *for* her or *with* her that wouldn't necessarily entail your giving up satisfaction in your own love relationships."

"Well, that's a good point," she acknowledged hopefully. "I mean, I don't want to just abandon her and go off with my own husband and child, but maybe there are some better ways for me to get her out of this rut she's always been in. It makes me sad when I think about her being that desperate. . . . "

Now that Melissa is seeing her mother differently, and considering other ways to support her without sacrificing her own happiness, she has more energy to focus on her marriage and new family. Clay feels that he can share some of his concerns with her without having to worry about whether this will be an overwhelming burden to her, and they've begun talking about the possibility that she could return to work on a full-time basis if their finances required that she do so. This freed him to take his work less seriously and be more involved with his wife and child.

Clay and Melissa were still involved in the triangles through which their in-laws were vying for power in their family life, but with the new strength of their marital dyad they were becoming ever more immune to being lured into these triangles, and they left therapy at this point, confident that they could proceed with the remaining detriangulation by themselves.

In this chapter, we have examined one of the most common stressors that affects new parents, that of their relationships with their child's grandparents. We have discussed how parenthood revivified old triangles with our first family that have been dormant, and how detriangulation, like any other conflict-resolution process within a marriage, relies on an increased knowledge of, and differentiation from, our family of origin.

We will now turn our attention to another common source of discord between new parents, and see how it, too, becomes less problematic when couples increase the Selfhood that they bring to their relationship.

Chapter Ten

The Marriage of Sex and Parenthood

D id you flip to this chapter first even though I placed it last? Don't feel embarrassed: Many other readers probably did, too. Who wouldn't, when you think about it? After all, if any one aspect of our life has been singled out for evaluation and equated with our individual and marital adequacy, it is sexuality.

This is not necessarily a good thing. While it is nice that sexuality can be discussed more freely than in other generations and that the cloak of enforced ignorance has been removed, once any activity becomes the focal point of an entire society, it is inevitably loaded up with all of that society's irrational pressures and beliefs.

Sex is then transformed from being a reproductive act that can also function as an intimate form of communication and contact between two people who care for each other into something that should be "good," with the automatic implication that it might also be "bad."

It becomes not an opportunity to rejoice and play, but a set of techniques to be worked at, mastered, and self-consciously displayed. It becomes not a vehicle for conveying our love throughout the course of an ongoing relationship, but a challenge that must be met, a "performance" with a lot of "anxiety" accruing to it, an activity that is supposedly better with someone new and younger rather than familiar and older. It becomes not one more way of touching, but supposedly the *best* and *only* way.

We dutifully read that if we simply possess the right ingredients, which may include (depending on the manual you read) tenderness, fearlessness, self-confidence, strength, assertiveness, intensity, passion, commitment, creativity, and, oh, maybe six or seven others, and stir them into the marital mixing bowl with a dash of exotic underwear and some fragrant massage oil, good sex will rise like an obedient bread.

And pity the poor person who is lacking in any of these ingredients: He or she is consigned to a marriage that labors under that most heinous of connubial stigmas, a Mediocre Sex Life.

New parents are particularly vulnerable to these pressures. If we weren't concerned about our sex lives before, we will be after discovering that what seems like every third article we read in our "Scriptures," the parenting magazines, tells us how bad sex is going to be in the early days of parenthood and how crucial it is that we head off these sexual problems at the pass, before they can bleed the vitality out of our relationship.

As if we're not *already* feeling incompetent enough as we listen helplessly while our children squall away in their cribs because their first teeth are erupting into their gums or their eardrums are pounding with infection, now we've also got to worry about the fact that we may once again have not made love that evening, that we may once again have not *wanted* to make love, and that we can't be absolutely sure we're ever *going* to want to make love again.

"Our marriage is dead," we glumly conclude. "Probably everyone in the entire world is making love tonight except for us," we sullenly imagine, or, if we *are* making love, "they're all having a dandier time at it than we are."

During one in a string of sleepless nights when everybody in my family got sick at the same time, I took stock of the complete absence of erotic potential in our bedroom. There was no "Bolero" to march us, panting, into a sweaty, lustful union, no candles to make our writhing shadows dance against the walls, no silk sheets to slide against or provocative garments to hungrily yank at and discard. Our chaste bed was instead covered by a years-old comforter splattered with the noted aphrodisiacs Amoxycillin and Tylenol from the latest medication battles. We wore bulky sweat clothes that would have taken several minutes to remove should we have had the energy or desire to do so. The only sound I could hear in between our own hacks and coughs was the vacant hum of the intercom that was the eternal, electric reminder of our new responsibilities. It occurred to me with depressing solemnity that our sexual intensity at this point in our marriage blazed with about the same wattage as did the tiny, dull red light that signaled to us that the receiver was indeed working, and that we would be the oh-so-fortunate first to know of our children's next screaming awakenings.

We have talked about how couples create big conflicts for themselves by becoming anxiously reactive to or avoidant of relatively small ones. There is no area in which this sequence takes place more frequently than in sexuality.

In a typical scenario, for example, a new mother is too ravaged from the hormonal upheaval of ending pregnancy and beginning nursing, and from the exhaustion of several months of sleep interruptions, to convey much sexual interest in her husband. He, embarrassed to admit to the reality that he, too, feels overwhelmed and exhausted, frightened and resentful of his new family's dependence on his breadwinning abilities, as well as excluded by his wife's absorption in this baby he's expected to adore, seeks affirmation the best way he knows how, which is to get her to make love. He, now, has become the pursuer, and she the distancer.

She is "affectioned out," however, emotionally and physically saturated after a full day with an infant clambering all over her. Much more in need of a brief, loving embrace, an attentive set of ears as she tries to make sense of this bewildering time, and maybe a back rub, she responds negatively to his entreaty. He, too, whether he can admit it or not, probably needs to be held, stroked, and listened to as much as he needs to have an orgasm.

Acknowledging this would mean enlarging his definition of masculinity, however, and he is not about to travel that path. Instead, he chooses to go the traditional route of *insisting* on intercourse as the best and only mode of connecting with her, without taking the time to join with her, or address their needs, in any other way.

Her next and inevitable rejection of his rough advances reinforces his conclusion that she "prefers" the baby to him. Humiliated by this realization but too embarrassed to check it out or say something about it, he buries it by pursuing her a little harder still, engendering more of the very rejection he fears, or withdrawing altogether.

She, already demoralized by her difficult-to-comfort child, reasons that she must simply not be a very good wife or mother, or she'd be more readily able to keep her husband and baby satisfied. So she may choose to distance even further to avoid a possible confirmation of this depressing realization, and the cycle of mutual withdrawal, hurt, and anger picks up steam, forcing both into a miserable standoff with each other.

Because neither feels comfortable acknowledging their basic needs for love, support, and nurturance during this unsettling time, they instead have canalized all of their emotional yearning into deciding whether or not they'll "do it." They feel that there is something wrong with them because sex is not proceeding in the way that it has in the past, or in the way that they are convinced it "should."

Their reciprocal disappointment in and bitterness with each other then distracts them from the more powerful themes that inhere in the transition into parenthood. It becomes easier to blame the other for their sexual "problem" ("You never want it!" and "You don't know how to ask for it!") than to address and talk about the real issues, the difficulties they're facing in the experience of being parents.

Most studies of the interaction between sexuality and marital satisfaction reach the exact same conclusion: While a positive sexual relationship is a very nice and important component of an enduring and happy marriage, it will not, by itself, ensure one, and many couples who feel fulfilled in their union admit that sex is not always good. Yet you would think, if you scanned the talk-show channels and perused the self-help shelves in bookstores, that sex was the sole and absolute determinant of psychological and marital health.

Our frenzied preoccupation with erotic success is hard on everyone, for it actually diverts us from "touching" each other in the most meaningful and loving ways. It is particularly hard on new parents, however, who, like the couple just described, are bedeviled by the conflicting passions and concerns that wash over them as they start a family.

There are lots of reasonable, well-documented ways to account for the change in sex life that appears to coincide with the transition into parenthood, as well as a veritable deluge of materials that propose solutions to every conceivable sexual problem. What we have not accounted for, however, is why so little of this helps couples feel comfortable with the inevitable sexual changes that accompany parenthood, and why they are so unable to implement these eminently sensible tips and techniques and arrive at the satisfying sex life that would seem only natural to expect for two loving, committed people.

The answer to this question is that our sexual patterns, just like any of the other patterns of marital life that we have been discussing, do not develop in a vacuum, but instead are an outgrowth of our upbringing and resonate to the loyalties we experience toward our family of origin. Liberating ourselves sexually, just like any other process of personal or marital liberation, will depend on seeing our first family more clearly, differentiating from them more fully, and bringing more Selfhood into the relationship.

Let's take a look at one couple who were experiencing sexual difficulties early in parenthood to see how it was an increase in Selfhood, rather than a change in technique, that heightened their satisfaction with their intimate life. While the difficulties, if any, that you may have been experiencing may be more mild or more severe than theirs, I will be focusing on them because the *process* by which they went about resolving their difficulties can be applied to any couple's sexual life.

Derek and Elaine consulted with me because they had ceased making love over the past several months. Both acknowledged that lovemaking had often been fraught with tension and anger during their initial years of marriage, although both also agreed that there were "more than a handful" of sweet or memorable encounters. They had twice before been to therapists about this issue, without having seen any lasting change. But things had apparently got much worse since they'd become parents for the first time four years ago, and they were currently in the middle of a sexual "desert" that appeared, to them, to have no end in sight. They thought that counseling was worth at least one more shot.

When they did take the risk of sexual contact, each from time to time experienced a specific problem that became a source of tension and discord. Derek would sometimes ejaculate prematurely, and Elaine would have difficulty reaching an orgasm. Both felt ashamed of these difficulties, and although each was fairly sensitive when it came to understanding the other's plight, each also subtly blamed the other for being the "real source" of their lack of sexual satisfaction. Either way, it sounded like the threat of encountering these problems, combined with the stresses of early parenthood, had demoralized them to the extent that they didn't even feel it was worth a try anymore.

As I said a moment ago, our pattern of sexual engagement is not something that emanates purely from within us and displays itself only in the context of our marriage, but is also something that reverberates to the lessons we learned about intimacy, gender, power, and sexuality in our childhoods. Not surprisingly, things that Derek and Elaine had seen, heard, and experienced long ago were now being stirred up by parenthood and impacting on them in profound ways they weren't even conscious of.

In speaking with Derek, I discovered that, in his eyes, the men in his family were very successful in their work lives, and less successful in their home lives. "They were kind of henpecked: I remember listening at the kitchen door during big family dinners and hearing all the women, my mom, my grandmothers, my aunts, putting down the men. And the guys probably knew what was going on, but they just kind of sat around in the living room playing cards or smoking, watching TV . . . it's like it didn't matter to them."

Derek continued by noting, "They did pretty well when it came to making a living, but their wives never sounded very satisfied."

When I asked him what it was that they were probably dissatisfied with, he hedged a bit: "I don't know. I mean, I really feel like I have a neat family, all of the men do interesting things, seem pretty healthy and all, but something must have been missing for them to have been bitched at all the time."

When I asked him whether he imagined the women in his family were sexually satisfied by their men, he laughed uncomfortably, saying, "I guess I knew you were going to get around to that and was kind of thinking about it already. If I had to answer directly, I'd say no. A lot of the jokes the women told had to do with this. I remember one joke, I was little so I'm sure I'm not getting it right, but it had something to do with a woman looking at her husband with his clothes off and seeing a 'dried flower arrangement.' All the women giggled, but the men got kind of fidgety, and nobody explained to me what it was about when I asked. Now that I'm older, I wonder if it had something to do with sex, like being impotent or uninterested or something."

As Derek spoke, it became clear that somewhere in his family there was a history of women criticizing their men, and men being unable to meet their wives' physical needs. When I asked him what he thought about this devaluing, emasculating atmosphere, he said, with some fire in his voice, "I didn't like it at all, partially because I'm a guy, too, and felt like I wanted to be one of the guys, but I thought, and still kind of think, that the women had it kind of good, really, their husbands were doing all the breadwinning, and nobody was living too badly, really, all of my relatives took vacations, had cars, some even had maids . . . I mean, nobody was wealthy, but sure as hell none of them were starving."

"How much of your anger at your ungrateful female relatives goes toward Elaine?"

"I never thought of that—what are you implying?" he asked worriedly.

"Well, you feel that these women were chronically dissatisfied, and perhaps Elaine, being the most important woman in your life, kind of symbolizes them, and becomes an unwitting repository of your resentment toward them."

"But I don't get angry with her much," Derek countered. "I never yell at her, and I've certainly never laid a hand on her."

"But when you come too quickly, you might inadvertently contribute to making her feel sexually cheated," I noted, "which could be your way of getting back at all those other women."

Elaine piped in, "I think there's something to that, because it's almost like the times I'm most into it, and the most hopeful that I'm going to come, are often the times when he comes too soon, and I'm left kind of hanging . . . and then *I* wind up pretty angry myself."

Derek, to his tremendous credit, hung in there with this possibility rather than defending himself or retreating. "So you mean I'm really playing out something old here with my wife. I'm getting revenge on the women in my family for not appreciating what they were given by their men?"

"Sounds like it's worth thinking about," I ventured, impressed with his crisp summary of what we had been working up to.

"Well, if that's the case," he went on, "what do I do about this?"

"From my perspective, I think you need to be gathering more information about your sexual heritage before you decide to make any changes."

"Gather information from whom exactly?" Derek asked.

"Any of the members of your family who will talk," I responded, knowing what the next question was going to be.

"Well, who the hell is going to talk to me about their sex life?"

"That's a good question, and maybe what you need to do is start by getting some information that is pretty general. Then you'll be able to gauge who is and who isn't willing to talk about sex, and how far they're willing to go," I suggested.

"Where can I start?"

"The best place with those relatives who are older than you, particularly your parents, is asking them how and what *they* learned about sexuality, and what *they* remember teaching *you*. You don't really need to, nor should you, ask them directly about their sex lives, as few people feel comfortable talking about this in anything but the most safe and trustworthy settings. And you can also ask other questions that will inevitably get around to sexuality, having to do with how the family defined being masculine and feminine, or which relatives had good marriages and which didn't, and why this was, or whether there were ever any 'secrets,' like affairs or pregnancies. The worst that can happen is you won't get much information, but most people are more than willing to think and talk about topics like these.

"And with those relatives who are age mates, like siblings or cousins, you can ask them what they know, as everybody usually has a story or anecdote that you never heard before, and ask them, maybe a little bit more personally, about *their* attitudes toward topics like intimacy, gender, and sexuality, and how they came to hold them."

"Well, I'm not crazy about the idea, but I'll give it a try," Derek offered. "But I've got a question for you: Why has all of this gotten worse for us since we became parents?"

"There are some obvious answers to that question that I'm sure you're already aware of, like how exhausting childrearing is, and how much less time the two of you probably have to cultivate your sexuality. But I wonder, also, if there have been any interactions between the two of you that may remind you of what you were just talking about."

Elaine folded her arms abruptly while Derek surged ahead. "I can sure think of something that's been going on since Scotty was born that might relate: I feel like Elaine gets real shrewish with me, like she's always *hocking* me about something that I haven't done right, and never thanking me for the things I do. The other day, when she had taken Scotty to a birthday party in the afternoon, and I spent a couple of hours going through his toys, like we had been meaning to do for months, and threw a bunch out and got the rest organized, I didn't get a word of thanks, just her harangue about the fact that I'd forgotten to put an extra outfit in the backpack before the party."

Elaine could sit still no longer: "I got angry with him about that because Scotty spilled water all over his shirt at the party and cried for a new shirt, but of course we didn't have one because Mr. Organization over there didn't do what I asked, so Scotty had to sit there in a wet shirt, miserable, for the rest of the party, sobbing, and I really let Derek have it when I got home. I really lit into him; I certainly was in no mood to pat him on the back for being a good cleaner-upper."

"But you never give me any credit!" Derek retorted.

"I asked you to pack the outfit, and you didn't—do you know what it's like to sit through a party with your son wailing the whole time?" Elaine countered, her voice rising.

I jumped in quickly so that we wouldn't lose focus: "You don't have to defend yourself, Elaine. You have every reason to be upset with Derek for not following through on something you asked for. But the theme here isn't who's right and who's wrong; it's that this feeling of being underappreciated that Derek experienced with you that day is an old and strangely familiar one and has complicated associations for him. Perhaps one of the reasons that sex has gotten harder for the two of you since you became parents is that there have been other interactions that take him back to the place where he first learned from his family what being a man was supposed to be about."

"Something else just came to mind, too," Derek added. "Since

we had Scotty, I've really thrown myself into work even more seriously than I did before, and I wonder if that's got something to do
with it."

"Probably does," I concurred. "All of us are confused and uncertain about parenthood at the beginning, and we naturally try to
act as our role models acted when they were parents to give us at
least a small sense of groundedness. Grown-up men in your family
acted grown up by working very hard, and perhaps you're doing the
same thing. How do you think that impacts on your sexual energy?"

"Negatively," Elaine laughed, and Derek joined in.

"She's right, I think, though," Derek went on. "I mean, it's
harder for me to shut my mind off even when I'm no longer at work.
I'm always thinking of a new marketing approach for the stuff I'm
selling, a new angle, and I just don't relax as much, I know that. I
don't have the luxury of having a bad quarter or a bad year now that
we've got Scotty and I'm trying to save for his education, and all
these other expenses roll in."

So there were other ways in which Derek's loyalty to the men
in his past was interfering with his pursuit of sexual pleasure, too.

As I had asked, he went ahead and explored some of his sexual
history and came back with much interesting information: "First of
all, you were right, almost everybody was happy to talk about one
aspect or another of this whole business. I was surprised at how
open-minded everyone was. And I found out a lot, too. One uncle,
for example, the youngest one, came right out and told me that he
and my aunt hadn't made love for years, and a cousin told me that
another uncle was, and maybe still is, screwing around on his wife."

"Sounds like you've got a lot to work with. What has it been
like to begin processing all of this data?"

"Well, at first, to be honest with you, I was kind of depressed,
like this is my history, and I've got this messy past to climb out from
under. I mean, I've got a son, now, I don't want him to grow up with
sexual problems haunting him. . . . "

"What about your anger at your female relatives?"

"It got rid of some of it, I think," he acknowledged. "I mean,
maybe the men *were* unappreciated, and I'm sure *some* of them were
decent lovers, or well treated, but, man, to have your husband just
shut down with half of your life left over? Or to have to deal with

infidelity all the time? That's pretty sad, and in a way, I don't blame some of them for being pissed off, or resentful."

At this point in the treatment, with Derek having arrived at a more hopeful perspective, I spent a couple of sessions instructing him in some techniques that have been found to be helpful in resolving premature ejaculation. He was skeptical at first, saying that one of the other therapists he had seen had suggested techniques identical to these, and they hadn't helped much.

However, the reason they probably hadn't had much impact before is that he wasn't aware of the ways in which his sexual difficulty was a way of maintaining his loyalty to the men in his first family. Now, having more fully differentiated from his family of origin by developing a richer understanding of the various components of his sexual heritage, he was ready to grow beyond the crippling aspects of this loyalty and use these techniques to find new, more dependable ways of satisfying himself and his wife.

Elaine, of course, had work to do, too. In getting a history of her problem, I learned that she would tense up as she began to get sexually aroused because she was fearful that someone was going to barge in on them, even if she was certain that she and Derek had the house to themselves and that Scotty was asleep. Suspicious, I asked her if she had ever been touched inappropriately as a child, or sexually abused. She hesitated a beat, then said that she hadn't, then added, "Not that I know of."

She answered uneasily enough to suggest to me that something *had* happened that was still unresolved, and was perhaps contributing to her current sexual frustration.

When I broadened my questions beyond sexual "abuse," and asked about her first sexual experiences, she shakily admitted that when she was four or five she used to go to a baby-sitter's house a couple of afternoons a week when her mother worked, and that sometimes the sitter's son, who was probably around thirteen, would come up to the bed she was napping in and fondle her genitals.

In response to my asking what her experience of this was like, she said, "It was terrifying. I was sure that somebody would come up and find us, and I'd be in big trouble."

"Did anyone ever find out?"

"No . . . in fact, that was the problem. One time I hinted to my mother what was happening, and she kind of tossed it aside, didn't seem to pick up on it or believe me."

"How did that feel?"

"I was furious, but mostly, I was kind of scared. It's all kind of a blur, I don't even remember when it stopped, or how it stopped, although at a certain point I know we just stopped using that baby-sitter, so it didn't happen anymore."

"Did you feel anything in addition to terror while he was there?"

"What do you mean?" she asked warily.

"Well, did he do anything that hurt you physically?"

"No, not really," she responded, hesitantly.

"Did he *threaten* to hurt you?"

"Not that I remember," she replied, still on edge. Finally, she blurted it out: "Actually, I'm embarrassed to admit this, but he was really very nice to me, nicer than anybody else that I remember. Everybody in my family kind of ignored me . . . hell, why else would my mother not rescue me? *He'd* bring me presents, and you're not gonna believe this, but sometimes he actually read to me."

"Sometimes children who have been overstimulated or molested have a hard time acknowledging that there may have been some pleasure associated with it, sexual or just emotional . . . as if acknowl-edging the pleasure would mean that it was their fault, or they should have put a stop to it," I said slowly.

"Well, that really wasn't the case with me," Elaine snapped.

"Maybe not," I agreed for now, realizing that I had brought this possibility up too quickly. Shifting gears, I commented, "In any case, you must have been left with a tremendous sense of having been betrayed by your mother for not believing you."

"Yeah, *that* was horrible. In fact, now that I think about it, I'm still furious at her."

"Have you brought it up with her since then?" I asked.

"No . . . what's the point?"

"The point," I suggested, "is for you to be freed of this rage that you carry with you from the past so that it doesn't interfere with your enjoyment of sexuality in the present. How much of your anger at your mother goes to Derek?"

"Why should it go to him?"

"Well, perhaps in some way he represents your mother, in that he doesn't always listen to what you're saying, like with the phantom outfit that you told him to pack for you."

"You mean that because he does things that remind me of how my mom dealt with me, he winds up bearing the brunt of my anger at *her*?" she asked incredulously, but grinning.

"Stranger things have happened," I replied.

With this in mind, I encouraged her to readdress this issue with her mother to see how she handled it. Elaine reported back to me that her mother reacted the same way as before, denying its having much validity. This time, however, Elaine had stuck to her guns, and let her mother know that she had really felt abandoned.

"How did all that feel to you?" I inquired.

"Awful, really . . . what kind of mother wouldn't believe her daughter when she said she was being molested? And what kind of mother would leave her daughter at the sitter's where she was *being* molested?"

"Tell me again how old were you when all this began?"

"Uh, four or five, I guess . . . " she figured, then looking shocked, she added, "My God, that's how old Scotty is now." It seemed clear that parenthood has sent Elaine, too, on a journey back to an ancient, painful place that accounts for a lot of her sexual tension. Her son's approaching the age that she was when she was first taken advantage of was agitating these memories, as was the sense that her husband, like her mother, wasn't listening to the urgent things she had to say. All of this was combining to make sexual contact with her husband even more precarious than usual.

I recommended a couple of books to Elaine that focus on recovering from sexual abuse, and she excitedly came back to our next meeting, commenting, "Boy, I feel so much more normal now; so many of the women in these books sound just like me!"

"What hit home in particular?" I asked.

"Well, a lot of it, but mostly the part about women sometimes not having orgasms so that they can stay in control, I think. I mean, one book said just what you said, that women feel guilty if they've enjoyed any of what happened to them, and so they put their sexual pleasure on hold as grown-ups to make up for their enjoyment as a child."

Obviously, Elaine, like her husband, was immobilized by a loyalty to her past, in this case a loyalty to "little Elaine" who, having little choice in the matter, had submitted to, and partially enjoyed, a highly inappropriate sexual incursion.

More fully differentiating from her first family, in particular from her mother, readied her to learn some helpful sexual techniques herself. At first she reacted the way that Derek had when I suggested some exercises to work with, quickly pointing out that she had tried some of these before. However, she, too, now had a different understanding of things. No longer feeling like a sexual "failure" who had to go in for "remedial" work, she saw herself instead as someone who had been wounded but who was strong enough to rise above the hurt and begin to heal.

The work that both Derek and Elaine had done to grow beyond their loyalties to their past had helped them to begin to address their specific sexual *problems,* but some additional work had to be done about their sexual *interactions* for their intimate life to truly grow.

For one thing, they had got into some bad habits over the years, through no fault of their own. The pressure for lovemaking to go "well" was enormous, and because both were afraid they would experience problems and "disappoint" the other, neither took much initiative. The stakes had simply gotten too high, especially because, like many couples, they equated good sex with achieving Simultaneous Mutual Orgasms (through intercourse only, of course), which placed inevitable limitations on how much pleasure and freedom they could experience in bed together.

With this in mind, I asked them to put a temporary ban on intercourse, and to begin doing some sensate-focus exercises that would enable them to cultivate different kinds of physical contact that were not laden with the anxiety of mutually achieving orgasms. These included, depending on the week, nonerotic touching and stroking, reciprocal massages, hand-holding, gentle kissing, etc. The exercises were particularly important for a couple of reasons. One, both had locked all of their sexuality away in their genitals, and were depriving themselves of the pleasure that comes with an all-body sexual engagement. Two, they had not only stopped making love with each other but, worse, had stopped *touching* each other, too, since a stroke or a hug might be misinterpreted as a signal for sex to begin, and both were highly ambivalent about becoming sexually involved with each other. Temporarily eliminating the possibility of intercourse enabled them to touch each other without worrying about what would come after.

Their communication about sexuality needed a tune-up, too. I have noticed that even couples who communicate exceedingly well on a wide range of difficult, personal topics may still stumble and falter when it comes to discussing sexuality. Our culture is more sexualized than it has ever been before, to be sure, but that doesn't mean that we have really been encouraged to speak about sex honestly and respectfully.

Men have a hard time talking about sex because they haven't had any role models to demonstrate for them how to do it. In this culture, they have usually been treated either to silence about sexual matters or to a pageant of exaggerated accounts of orgiastic escapades, with little in between.

Women have a hard time talking about sex because they are not supposed to want or enjoy it in the first place. That may be why research shows that lesbian couples have less sex than straight couples or gay male couples: There is often no initiator because neither woman wants to assert herself and be seen as needy or demanding.

Furthermore, talks about sex can be a more intimate affair than having sex, which is why couples devise all kinds of reasons to avoid them. They decide that "words will make sex less spontaneous," leaving out the possibility that words can be spontaneous, too, as well as the possibility that sex doesn't *have* to be spontaneous to be enjoyed in the first place. Or they decide that talking honestly about sex might lead to hurt feelings, and work to protect their partner by not saying anything about their desires or disappointments.

Whatever their reasons, the fact remains that a couple who deprive themselves of communication about sex inevitably deprive themselves of a certain amount of sexual pleasure. If a husband and wife are also wrestling with their adjustment to parenthood, it becomes that much more essential that they find a way to talk about sexuality, even if their initial attempts are bumbling ones.

One of the differences between men and women when it comes to communication is that for men, sexual contact is often a necessary precursor to verbal intimacy, while for women, verbal intimacy is a necessary precursor to sexual contact. This creates conflict because a man may want sex so that he can feel closer with his wife, while his wife may want sex only when she is already feeling close to her husband. They then get stuck in a "who goes first" battle that leaves them weary and disgusted with each other, exactly the place that Elaine and Derek had found themselves.

The way around this battle for them—and for any couple—was to make sure that there were opportunities for verbal *and* sexual intimacy in place, so that neither got short-circuited.

The first change in their sexual-communication pattern that we worked on was to help them to refrain from using their sexual encounters as an indirect way of communicating feelings that are better discussed directly.

Elaine's job was to learn to communicate directly two important feelings, anger and desire. I felt that she was doing a certain amount of sexual withholding from Derek as a way of getting back at him, expressing the anger she felt toward him for not sharing equally in the distribution of household labor and for escaping into work.

I asked her to practice making requests with a lot of Self behind them, in the way that we spoke of in an earlier chapter. The enhanced clarity of her requests, which were delivered with minimal complaining, got her the results that she wanted, although I was careful to make sure that Derek wasn't agreeing to things he would be unwilling or unable to actually do.

Conveying desire directly was challenging, too, because Elaine was still feeling guilty about having enjoyed her sexual encounters with her baby-sitter's son and felt some shame for having partially looked forward to them. Thus, any initiation of sexual interaction, even as an adult, was fraught with ambivalence.

With this in mind, I asked them simply to take turns initiating sex when they had worked their way back up to lovemaking, which removed for Elaine the pressure of having to own up to her sexual impulses too soon, but kept the two of them in sexual contact with each other. Also, they were both told that either could turn down the other's initiation, my thoughts being that once Elaine felt comfortable saying no in a way that she never could as a young girl, she would be more comfortable saying yes as a woman.

From Derek's side, once he was able to identify with his female relatives more clearly, he was no longer having difficulty sorting out which parts of his anger belonged in his marriage and which didn't. But there was another set of feelings associated with becoming a father that he had been sitting on for quite some time, and that needed, finally, to be aired out.

As already discussed, a significant majority of new fathers participate in the birth of their child these days. While childbirth-preparation classes are often successful at helping an expectant couple to anticipate and take an active role in labor and delivery, they often do not address the possibility that a man may see his wife's body differently after having witnessed childbirth.

Some men react positively to this experience, and use words like "wondrous," "miraculous," "unbelievable," and "a real high" to describe it. Other men find it to be a more troubling experience, and use words like "bloody," "gross," "too much," or "hard to take." Some men find themselves sexually stimulated by having participated in childbirth, while others are sexually turned off. Some men just feel squeamish after having watched their wives' bodies invaded so casually by both male and female childbirth practitioners.

Either way, it is not unusual for the participative childbirth experience to affect a father's subsequent sexual attraction to his wife. One new father gushed, "I had never seen my wife that physical before, and it made it exciting to imagine that we could be that physical together . . . so although we don't make love that often anymore, what with the baby and all, it has a certain power to it now that it didn't really have before."

Another new father, though, commented, "It's really hard to see her as sexual anymore. Once I saw the baby come through her like that, I couldn't really picture making love to her." And Derek, in an individual session, confessed, "It's not that I was put off or anything by having been there [for the birth]. I mean, I'm glad I was there to support her, but now when we're in bed, it's strange . . . I can't even touch her without remembering all of that blood. I guess it feels different now."

Generally, when men respond with this kind of anxiety, they are feeling either some *guilt* at having contributed to the labor-related pain or "disfigurement" of their wives by having impregnated them in the first place, and/or some *awe* and *fear* at witnessing perhaps the most vivid display of feminine power they have ever seen. Either way, they're likely to react to this anxiety by pulling away or tensing up sexually, which will in turn make their wives more anxious, too.

Derek explained, "I know it shook me up, seeing our baby born, but sometimes I think the problem is not what I saw, but that I'm so busy trying to shut out what I saw that I wind up in another world . . . and she knows this, picks up on it, I guess, and so it turns into a bad cycle."

I encouraged Derek to take the risk of being more up-front with Elaine about his feelings, and, as is often the case when we disclose what we think is a toxic or hideous secret to our spouse, she was touched and surprised.

"I certainly don't hold him accountable for my having been in labor, even though it was a pretty rough experience," she chuckled. "And to be honest, although I was in too much pain to care much about who was looking at my body, I can understand that it might have been a turnoff. I mean, that placenta, which I caught a glimpse of out of the corner of my eye as they were carting it away, was not exactly a pleasant sight, and that was a *part* of me, I'm supposed to love it, I guess . . . but I didn't." Her reaction almost instantly discharged the guilt that Derek had been burdened with, and made him feel much lighter.

With all these relatively serious, deep-seated obstacles to love-making on the way to being overcome, there remained one further challenge, this one common to most couples in the early years of parenthood—getting in the mood for love. The logistics of romance, from finding the time, money, energy (and baby-sitter) for it, to supplying some of the props (flowers, perfume, theater tickets, bottle of champagne, or whatever), may seem so complicated and daunting to exhausted new parents that they give up before they ever get started.

There hasn't yet been an article written on helping couples survive child rearing and improve their sex lives that doesn't encourage parents to make some time to get out without their children. Whether couples had active and flourishing social lives before they became parents or not, they will need some time to connect as adults without the presence of children.

Yet this is another one of those self-evident "tips" that sounds great but is hard to implement. Most couples intuitively know that they need to be dating again, but may find themselves mystified as to why it's so difficult to do so.

I have found that while both fathers and mothers experience this acutely, it is fathers who most frequently report some version of "I just can't seem to get her interested in going out with me." Yet if fathers pay attention to rather than just complain about their wives' resistance, they may begin to experience some success in getting things moving.

The first step is understanding the source of this resistance. A new mother may not be sensing enough of a connection with her husband to feel comfortable going out together, for example. After weeks or months of focusing exclusively on figuring out the baby, she may no longer be certain what she has to offer her husband, or what he has to offer her. She might be thinking she's less attractive or interesting, and/or that he is, and shy away from the possibility that this will be exposed.

She may be more comfortable interacting with a child than a partner because the child expects less of her, or she's become more familiar with the child than with her husband. Or she may be refusing because, as we discussed a moment ago, this is her indirect way of expressing her anger at the unequal distribution of responsibility and power in the relationship since children came on the scene.

Sometimes mothers have stored away so many of their own feelings and delayed so much of their own gratification in the interest of nurturing their offspring that they're intuitively afraid of how much has built up. They worry that, given the first opportunity, they'll vent all of this turbulence on their partner or lose control in some way.

I'll never forget going out with our friends Bob and Pat when we weren't parents yet and they were, and watching in shock as Pat started giggling at a joke her husband told her, and then burst into uncontrollable tears for minutes afterward. So much had been pent up that that small pinhole of release she had given herself quickly opened into a deluge.

Other times a woman may be feeling ambivalent about her maternal identity and feel instinctively afraid that if she gives in to a nonmothering activity, such as going out with her husband, she will suddenly feel the full weight of the exhaustion and depletion that chronically plague her. The sweet taste of "freedom" she'd experience from being asked just to be a wife rather than a mother might, she would fear, seduce her away from her commitment to her child, and feel more like torture than release.

If sexuality has become a source of tension, a woman might feel that being taken out by her husband is going to be bartered for being taken to bed afterward. If the sum total of a couple's romance, passion, recreation, and sexual interaction all has to occur in the course of the same one evening out, it'll be too difficult for her or her husband to really enjoy themselves and get what they need.

And of course it's always easy to imagine that a new mother doesn't have enough energy by the end of the week to sufficiently orchestrate by herself the requisite details of going out on a date, such as arranging a sitter, preparing meals, and coordinating phone numbers and backup.

When I asked Derek and Elaine how often the two of them got out without Scotty, both said about once a month. When I asked if this was enough for them, both said that it wasn't.

Derek then complained that he *had* brought this up with Elaine a number of times, but that she often backed out with an excuse; too tired, no sitter, etc. However, many times men who complain that their wives don't want to go out with them have limited their methods to simply asking over and over again, and then giving up because the response is not a positive one.

When asked to respond to Derek's complaint, Elaine said that she wasn't always turning him down, but that sometimes he "expects too much . . . it's like when we go out, we've got to do everything, dinner, a movie, drinks all in one night. I just don't have that kind of energy, I really don't."

Also, she felt that all of the responsibilities for going out, from calling the sitter to preparing Scotty's dinner ahead of time to laying out his bath toys and clothes, fell on her shoulders.

Finally, she said that she didn't feel that Derek was very seductive in his suggestions. "Usually I get a 'Wanna go out this weekend?' or 'Do we have a sitter Saturday night?' mumbled when we're both busy trying to get out the door in the morning, or as we're falling asleep. That really pisses me off; it's not the most romantic invite I've ever gotten—it's like I'm some slave six nights a week, and then I'm supposed to rise from the ashes and become his personal goddess. I mean, what does he expect?"

With these thoughts in mind, Derek agreed to limit their next few nights out to one activity, to take care of setting out Scotty's food and clothes before they left, and to make more creative requests.

Derek had a request of his own, too. He said, "You know, even when we go out, Elaine's gotta be talking about Scotty, and it gets kind of tiresome. I mean, we're either with him or talking about him so much of the time—I see dates as a chance to get away from this."

"Yeah, but I see dates as a chance to have some good, uninterrupted time to make some decisions, like whether we want to start him in nursery school, which we still haven't decided and never get around to. I mean, we do a lot of talking at home but never reach a conclusion, because we're always getting a phone call, or doing things with him, or something."

As I listened to them negotiate, I was reminded of the early days after Josh's birth. The first time we ever got a baby-sitter, Karen actually wanted to use our freedom to go to a mall and do some relaxed shopping for baby supplies. I thought that I would kill her: After weeks of doing nothing but focusing on the baby, I had stormed, I'll be *damned* if I'm going to spend our night out trying to find a mobile for his crib. Yet somehow that's what we wound up doing, and I remember sulking miserably as she strolled blithely down the aisles, thinking hateful thoughts about my son and wife and wondering why I wasn't happier.

In the case of Derek and Elaine, a reasonable compromise was quickly arrived at, which involved their agreeing that the ride *to* wherever they were going could be devoted to child-care issues that either wanted to bring up, but such topics were off-limits for the rest of their time away from home.

A little more than a year after first consulting with me, Derek and Elaine were feeling much more satisfied with their sex lives. "We still don't make love as often as I would like," Derek admitted, "but I have to say that we're a lot more comfortable in bed, and enjoying each other a lot more in general."

"Yeah, that's been the best part for me," Elaine commented. "It's that I feel able to touch him and be touched, so whether we're making love very often or not doesn't matter as much; we've found ways to simply be with each other and aren't blaming each other for being the Problem."

Sexuality, like any other pattern of marital interaction, has its roots in our connections with our family of origin. Just as the journey into the past that parenthood ignites affects how we communicate, how we get contact, how we get distance, how we parent, and a host of other relational tasks, it also affects our sexual identity. Only through exploring these roots can we grow beyond them and develop a sexual style that satisfies our needs during the uncertain and tempestuous stages of family life.

The Continuing Journey

"The secret of life is to devote yourself to one desire. Concentrate your life on achieving this desire, EVERYTHING, but remember: Choose something you can't do."

—*Henry Moore*

Tempting as it may be to think otherwise, there are no universally applicable answers to the question "How can we make sure our marriage survives and grows from parenthood?" Every couple I have worked with has their own strengths and weaknesses, their distinctive pattern of marital communication and interaction, their unique matrix of loyalties and histories, and therefore must arrive at their own answers.

In the words of the card my brother sent to me upon hearing that we were expecting: "There are three rules for surviving the arrival of a new baby. . . . Unfortunately, nobody knows what they are."

I have tremendous faith that people can change, and see and help them do so all the time. But I also know that change is effortful and comes about only when couples take the risk of being open to new ways of thinking, feeling, and acting.

I have provided in this book a theory that helps to explain what happens to our marriages as we make the transition into parenthood. While from time to time I have provided some specific suggestions or techniques that grow out of this theory, I have refrained from including a compendium of such "tips" and advice for several reasons.

One, as I stated above, each marriage is unique and distinct, and rare is the "do" or "don't" that applies across the board to everyone. One couple may need to curtail their fighting so that the intensity between the two of them is diminished, for example, while another couple may have to amplify their fighting so that the intensity between them is increased. One set of parents might be served well by increasing their attachment to their offspring, while another might do better by detaching some.

Second, sometimes a well-intended maneuver that eases tension in the short run creates bigger problems in the long run. As we learned earlier, for instance, cutting off contact with troublesome grandparents might temporarily reduce marital conflict, and thus sounds like good advice. But it will also simultaneously ensure that the marital partners don't differentiate fully enough from their first family, which will inevitably lead to new and worse troubles.

Third, I think that new parents often underestimate their own competencies and strengths. Although child-rearing experts in the media serve an often valuable purpose, mothers and fathers get the impression from the barrage of columns, books, and lectures that they need these "authorities" to tell them what to do.

I believe strongly that we are *all* quite creative and resilient when it comes to solving the problems of family life when we have some useful guiding principles in hand to explain the underlying mechanisms of our family relationships. With these principles, we usually find answers to even the most vexing dilemmas. Without them, we are a rudderless boat, constantly reliant on the latest winds of expert advice that blow over us.

Let me provide some closing thoughts that are worth keeping in mind as you use your new perspective on your relationship to go about creating healthy marital change.

1. REALISM

In our culture of having to have it all, and having to have it all *now,* we feel deficient if every single one of our goals is not met. Yet the reality is that we can't be committed spouses and parents without diminishing our capacity to perform some of the other roles that we are accustomed to filling.

Spending more time and energy with our family means having

less time and energy for our work, or hobbies, or friends, or some combination of the three. That is not to say that viable balances cannot be struck, just that we need to bring some realism to our expectations of ourselves.

We must be similarly realistic in our expectations of our partners, especially when it comes to the changes we hope they'll make in response to our needs. Part of making change come about is learning to accept the fact that change is not always possible. And sometimes the most meaningful change is not a change in our marital behaviors but a change in the way that we *think* about these behaviors.

Even when our partner changes, we can remain disgruntled if we feel it's not "genuine" or it's being done for the "wrong reasons." I remember one woman who was still angry at her husband even though he had finally begun sharing the diapering of their baby—because he still didn't seem to enjoy it. We must both accept the changes our partners are willing and able to make and understand the obstacles that may stand in the way of further change.

We also need to distinguish between acceptance and resignation. Resignation is when, in a spirit of defeat, we simply give up, lower our standards, raise our tolerance for dissatisfaction, and reframe this whole experience as "coming to terms with life" or being "well adjusted."

Acceptance is not just giving up, but actively surrendering our arrogant sense that we know what is best and that things should go the way we think they should go.

Finally, no matter how much change we are, in fact, able to catalyze in our marriage, no amount will bring about continuous delight. When it comes to our physical health, even when we diligently try to eat, sleep, and live right, we're probably going to get a cold or two, some cut fingers or banged knees, half a dozen headaches, and a few other ailments a year *at least*.

Likewise, when it comes to our relational and psychological health, no matter how much differentiation, Selfhood, and perspective we bring to our marriage, we'll still find ourselves feeling embattled, tense, anxious, and irritable at hundreds of different crossroads. But if we can envision the pathways of change as meandering roads that take us to closer and closer *approximations* of the ideal, rather than as highways that must immediately deliver us to a family utopia, we'll be more serene travelers who are better able to enjoy the journey.

2. PATIENCE

This book may make change look deceptively easy. After all, I am often condensing what may have taken individuals and couples several months, and sometimes several years, to accomplish into a few paragraphs or pages. Patients who have read self-help books before beginning therapy often anticipate that once our sessions begin, change will happen as it does in these books, quickly, dramatically, and straightforwardly.

The reality is quite different. After all, it often took us quite a while to get into our stuck, problematic places, so it's not surprising that it can take time to find a way out. Getting to a new and authentic understanding of our history and how it has influenced our marriage may not come quickly; nor, understandably, may the process of allowing that understanding to infiltrate our lives and influence our marital behavior.

And change may be actively resisted for a while. All of our behaviors were at some point ways of adapting, and in this sense served, and perhaps still serve, a protective function. Relinquishing these adaptations before we're certain that a better set is in place is something that we'll be understandably reluctant to do.

Also, all changes, even positive ones, are accompanied inevitably by a sense of loss. The loss of anything that is familiar, even unpleasantly so, must be mourned, and we may be sad to have to say good-bye to parts of ourselves or aspects of our marriage that seem like "home."

But the fear of betraying our loyalties to our family of origin is sometimes the most powerful immobilizer of all. Nobody walks against the family current without feeling pulled or tugged at in dozens of subtle and blatant ways. Taking a position that is different from the one that we were taught as children requires enormous courage.

Sometimes, when we are the ones making the change, our partners initially resist that change, making it harder still to stick to our guns. Just because they resist it, however, doesn't mean that they oppose it. They often resist because they want to test our resolve and see if we're really going to remain steadfast. One common sequence of events, which I've seen in my work with many couples, occurs when a father begins to display more involvement with his children. His wife may at first become even more critical of this involvement, even though she was the one who demanded it, or find ways to sabotage it. Alternately, when a mother begins to set reasonable limits on how much she is willing to do for everyone else in the family, her husband may sulk even more and do even less.

Such resistance to change is exasperating, of course, and the natural temptation is to give up after a small dose of these "early returns" in the data. However, if you're smart and invested in change, you'll see these responses as positive signs, signals that something is indeed happening, and that whatever changes you are implementing are significant enough to call forth real opposition.

When your "rebelling" spouses see that you are going to hold firm to your changes, they will be more likely to make positive changes of their own. Creative persistence is at the root of any enduring improvements that a marriage undergoes.

Finally, real change rarely occurs calmly and smoothly, but happens more typically in fits and starts. Our "beetling" toward a different conceptualization and configuration of our relationship is not a sequence of neatly paced forward steps, but a complex movement consisting of dozens of leaps ahead, side steps, and falls behind.

While this may be disappointing, it is important to keep in mind that, in general, the more slowly we move toward change, the more permanent that change tends to be. Just as the person who loses weight gradually is more likely to keep that weight off, the couples who diligently focus on a marital *evolution* rather than *revolution* find that the glacial speed of real change has its real rewards.

With this in mind, it's worth one more reminder that *any* movement toward us from our spouse is worth recognizing and validating, even if it seems negligible. We move in small steps because we're so fearful, and these steps will surely grind to a halt if they are ignored, diminished, or criticized. Building upon these small steps is what increases the likelihood of bigger and more frequent ones.

3. THERAPY

A couple in a cartoon asked their friends, "The work being done on your marriage—are you having it done, or are you doing it yourselves?"

As I mentioned above, many of the individuals referred to in these pages were making changes with the support of therapy.

Therapy can help to unstick us by encouraging us to look at ourselves, and at our present and past relationships, through a broader lens. This enables different information to enter, which leads ultimately to our capacity to remove the obstacles to intimacy that lie between us.

By noting, and examining the sources of, our reactivity, assisting us in further differentiating from our family of origin, and providing us with new experiences of closeness and separateness within our relationship, the therapist becomes the midwife of the marriage's rebirth, and reverses the trend toward resignation, alienation, and hopelessness that all couples will at times find themselves swept up in.

Women tend to be much more comfortable consulting with a therapist about marital or family matters than men. That is because women are socialized to attend to human relationships: They observe them as carefully as farmers observe the weather. Also, women tend to be the marital partners who are hyperparenting or pursuing, and thus the ones who are in greater discomfort, and more invested in taking the risk of making changes.

Men tend to be skeptical and reluctant about therapy. They are much less attentive to their own and their family's emotional states, feel like the admission of a problem and the process of seeking help for it is a weakness, may doubt that there is such a thing as a "relationship problem" or a "talking cure" in the first place, and are wary of anything that might challenge their perceived dominance in the family. But their resistance will not mean the end of any possibility for meaningful change.

As nice as it would be if this were the case, not everybody in a family has to be equally motivated to make changes for change to come about. When you think systemically, you realize that once *one* member of a family is in therapy, *everybody* in the family is automatically in therapy, too, whether they're actually present in the consultation room or not. If one person changes, nobody else in the family can possibly stay the same, because we are all reciprocally responsive to each other.

So individuals who complain that nothing can change because their partners won't join them in therapy are letting themselves and everybody else off the hook. Some of the most successful family therapy I have coordinated or witnessed has taken place with only one family member in the room—a member who was unafraid to examine his/her contribution to the family problem, and to commit himself/herself to changing.

Likewise, I have led and watched many therapy sessions in which every member of a family showed up and canceled everyone else out, and nothing of significance took place but a particularly loud and dissonant chorus of frustration and blame.

Change may be quicker and longer-lasting if everybody agrees to participate in treatment, *but it takes the energy and commitment of only one person to make it effectively happen.*

The difficulty of finding a good therapist may be another source of resistance to therapy. While there may be lots of therapists around, there are generally few superb ones. The best way to find one is by word of mouth. Knowing that somebody has been successful at helping someone you know and respect is the best bet that they'll help you, too.

Remember, though, that degrees, profession, and background rarely matter. The process of becoming a talented therapist is a long and arduous one that usually begins *after* one has completed one's official credentials. Just because someone has an advanced degree from a well-respected program does not mean he or she is a good therapist.

If you know of no one who can recommend a therapist, your second-best bet is to call the American Association for Marital and Family Therapists and get a listing of therapists in your area who specialize in these issues. With this list of names in hand, you can start shopping for a therapist who is not just well qualified, but is someone you feel personally comfortable with. Don't hesitate to keep looking until you find that person. You probably shopped around for your pediatrician, lawyer, or accountant; you'll want to bring the same attention to your search for a therapist with whom you feel a good chemistry. After all, you're entrusting not just your health or your finances, but your marriage and your family, to that person's care.

4. SELF-HELP

I have made the point over and over again that we can improve our marriages not by focusing on changing our partners, but simply by changing ourselves.

Still, it may be tempting for you to read this book and begin applying its principles not only to your life but to your partner's life, too. Becoming an expert on other people is a tantalizing, but ultimately self-defeating, business.

You'll get the most out of this book not by insisting that your spouse read it, or by consistently pointing out what he or she should be doing differently, but by doing your own work on your own life. This, more than anything else, will keep you growing, while exerting a positive influence on your partner.

Harriet Lerner has pointed out that the women's movement did not succeed by blaming men for sexism and demanding that they change, but instead by fearlessly examining what women wanted and how to go about getting it under the oppressive conditions that existed. Women changing themselves is what catalyzed change in men specifically and in society as a whole.

So when there are marital difficulties, we need to remember that these difficulties are not somebody's "fault," but an outcome of shared, bilateral responsibility.

Moreover, we have to remember that both of us interact in the way that we do because of our ongoing loyalties to our first family, and that sometimes it is hard to balance our loyalties to them with our loyalties to our spouse. Viewing our disagreements with this perspective in place, rather than blaming our partner or ourselves for being the cause of our distress, will increase the odds that relational change will come about.

5. PARENT REARING

From our first moment of parenthood, when we encounter the bloody, bawling, squishy-headed primate rather than the fragrant, rosy-cheeked newborn we've seen in the diaper commercials, our expectations of family bliss will be confounded.

Ellen Galinsky wrote, "Parenthood has become the romantic 'complex' of our day," and indeed, who could think otherwise? Advertisements display handsome, shirtless men cradling their silent babies while listening to a stack of CDs, and lovely, fresh-faced women picking fruit in the bright sunlight with their smiling, well-behaved toddlers. You could *die* for such experiences, yet how often do they really happen, and what about all of the grittier moments that bracket these scarce, airbrushed snapshots?

As you have learned by now, parenthood is generally a much more *un*settling than settling experience. Insisting that it be otherwise will lead us into the predicament that family therapist Monica McGoldrick warns us about when she says, "Trying to make things easy often results in great difficulties."

Yet one recent family development text by a well-known clinician described, as the ideal, new parents who "deal with the inevitable developmental strains and stresses without alteration in the basic structure of their relationship."

To me, this is absurd. If we experience parenthood without an "alteration in our basic structure," we are missing an important opportunity to grow and change, and our "structure" is at risk because of its inflexibility in the face of stress. It would be a great shame *not* to alter in response to this most earthshaking of changes in our personal lives. As psychiatrist Milton Erickson wrote, "Unless you're prepared to become more confused about something, you'll be unable to reach a better, bigger, or deeper understanding of it."

Just as there are "critical periods" in our childhoods when we are most teachable, parenthood is a critical period in our adulthood, a time when the constellation of our fantasies, fears, motives, and passions is most in flux, most susceptible to reconfiguring.

In this sense, it is akin to what psychiatrist D. W. Winnicott terms "the transitional state." This is a point when our everyday state of mind is seriously and frighteningly threatened, a sign that a hitherto unanticipated leap beyond our previous limitations is about to take place. Although such a leap is scary, it will result, if taken, in renewed energy and vigor, and a heightened sense of our purpose and potential in the world.

Carl Jung wrote that marriages do not "come to consciousness" without the experience of crisis. The inherent marital disequilibrium that parenthood engenders presents us with just such a crisis, a crisis that forces us to confront what is and is not between us as a couple, that unveils new feelings, skills, and competencies that we may not ever have known existed. If we maintain the courage necessary to support each other through this period, an enlarged capacity for connectedness and ripening will be unleashed, and a break*through,* rather than a break*down,* is in the offing.

Children challenge us to be an effective couple, and the achievement of this can be our greatest accomplishment, and our greatest contribution to their lives. They raise us as much as we raise them, and adapting our lives to meet their needs is not simply an altruistic response to an oppressive burden. Instead, it is a way to fill in the gaps in the poor or inadequate parenting that *we* received, and finally repair whatever damage we have inevitably, and unintentionally, wrought on each other. When this work is begun, the stage is set for all of us to love and grow as we participate in the remarkable experience of becoming a family.

Index

ABCD Analysis, 129
acceptance, resignation vs., 259
actions, specific focus on, 119,
        120, 122–125, 128–129
adolescence, 13, 21
alcoholism, 203, 204–205
American Association for Marital
        and Family Therapists, 263
anger, 205, 227
    genuine expression of, 114,
        116–118, 121–122, 131–132
    in marital fights, 111–132,
        241, 244, 247
    repressed, 109–110, 112–116,
        122, 125, 130
    see also blame
anxiety, 92
    dampening of, 214, 223, 226–
        229
    in marital relations, 30–31,
        35, 77, 83, 92, 135, 212
    in reexperiencing childhood,
        48–50, 54
    sex and, 235, 237–238, 248, 251
    stress and, 30, 35, 135
autonomy issues, 51, 64–65, 71,
        94, 205–210, 219

mutuality vs., 31, 34, 65, 72–
        73, 77–78
avoidance-fusion concept, 68–69

Beavers, Robert, 72, 168
Bettelheim, Bruno, 138
blame:
    change vs., 264
    differentiation vs., 68–75, 78–80
    family systems and, 191–196,
        203, 205, 221, 227
    as focus, 30–31, 41, 60, 67–68,
        77, 90–92
    parenting and, 18–23, 38–39,
        60, 156–158, 166–169
    about sexual issues, 238, 241
    see also anger; responsibility
boredom, fighting and, 113
Boszormenyi-Nagy, Ivan, 52
bottom-line position, 99–100,
        108–109
Bowen, Murray, 68
Bowen Theory, 68–69

case histories:
    of child's disability impact,
        45–47

case histories (*cont.*)
  of deidealizing, 197–200, 201–
    202
  of differentiation, 69–71, 74–
    75, 225–234
  of disciplining child, 55–58
  of fatherhood issues, 142–161,
    180–181
  of invisible loyalties impact,
    52–66, 222–225
  of marital communication, 89–
    90, 106–110
  of marital fighting, 116–118,
    120–121, 123–125, 126–128
  of marital imbalance, 25–44
  of marital sex problems, 239–
    255
  of motherhood issues, 59–65,
    162, 170–174, 182
  of mourning, 199–200
  of one-on-one relationships,
    203–205
  of reconnections with past,
    205–210
  of Selfhood achievement, 78–87
  of sexual abuse, 193–196
  of triangular relationships,
    222–233
Cath, Stanley, 216, 218
cause-and-effect thinking, 28–30
change, 67–88
  differentiation and, 68–75, 188
  guiding principles for, 257–266
  motivation for, 79, 84, 99,
    134, 229, 262–263
  for needs satisfaction, 89–100
  realism and, 259
  resistance and, 36, 84–85, 100,
    109–110, 140, 146, 147, 154,
    260–261
  risk in, 109, 257
  Self-centeredness and, 75–88
  small steps in, 261
  systems thinking and, 28–30,
    43–44
  therapy for, 262–264
charts, therapeutic use of, 42–43
childbirth, witnessing of, 251–
    252
child-care literature, 96, 138–
    139, 168, 236
children:
  abused, 54, 126–127, 192–196,
    245–248
  discipline of, 55, 56
  loss of, 60, 61
  needs of, *see* needs

  parents' fights and, 112, 113,
    122–125, 130–131
  perceived as "problem," 20–21,
    26–27
  rearing of, 265–266
  in triangular relationships,
    211, 214–215, 228–229
  see also parents, parenting
Chodorow, Nancy, 135
Coche, Judith, 16
commitments:
  equitable distribution of, 106
  honoring of, 104
communication, 21, 60, 91–92
  of angry feelings, 114, 116–
    118, 121–122, 131–132
  listening and, 179–181
  Self-focused, *see* Self-focused
    communication
  sex and, 235, 249–250
competitiveness, 41–42, 141, 157,
    178–179, 219
connectedness:
  within family systems, 71–75,
    185–188, 196, 199, 202, 205,
    210, 215, 220
  in males vs. females, 136, 144,
    150–151, 159, 173
  sex and, 237, 249–250, 253
  triangulation vs., 211–212,
    224, 232–233
cutoff, from family, 69, 71–75
cycles, disruptive marital, 25–44
  anxiety and, 30–31
  hyper- and hypoparents in, 37–
    44
  interpersonal relationship
    theories and, 27–28
  mutual contributions to, 28–29
  pursuer-distancer interactions
    in, 32–37
  systems thinking and, 28–29

defensiveness, *see* reciprocal
    influences
deidealizing, of parents, 196,
    197–202
dependence, *see* needs
differentiation, 68–88, 119–120,
    184–188, 219
  avoidance-fusion concept in,
    68–69
  rationalizations and, 69–70
  Selfhood achieved by, 68, 75–
    88, 110, 188, 223–225, 229–
    234, 239
  sexual issues and, 239, 245, 248

style vs. degree of, 69–70
  see also loyalties, invisible
divorce, 13–14
domination issues, 205–210
Dubus, Andre, 139

Entwistle, Doris, 140, 165
equilibrium, in marriage, 25–44,
    87
Erickson, Milton, 265
expectations, realism and, 20,
    22, 30, 46, 104, 145–146,
    151–153, 158–161, 258–
    259
extended family:
  cutoff from, 71–75
  support from, 72, 172, 219–220
  see also family systems;
    parents of parents

family systems, 50–66, 68–69,
    184–234
  acceptance in, 185–187
  blame and, *see* blame
  censorship and, 190
  connectedness in, 71–75, 185–
    188, 196, 199, 202, 205, 210,
    215, 220
  differentiation and, 68–87,
    219, 223–225, 229–234, 239
  family history and, 188–191
  female-centered, 206–207
  invisible loyalties in, 13, 52–
    66, 68, 72, 97, 184–210, 211,
    239, 256, 260
  needs originating in, 46–66, 83
  nonfamily members and, 191, 198
  objectivity in, 188–189
  setting limits in, 84–85, 205,
    207–208, 218
  sexual issues and, 239–242,
    244–245, 256
  sibling relations in, 214, 229–
    231
  support of, 72, 172, 219–220
  triangular relationships in,
    211–234
  see also children; parents of
    parents; parents, parenting
Father Center program, 150, 154
fathers:
  alone with child, 154, 156
  ambivalent feelings of, 138–
    142, 145, 148, 152–153, 170
  caregiving time of, 163–165,
    176–178
  depression of, 16–17

expectations of, 145–146, 151–
    153, 158–161
first parenting of, 18–23, 135–161
guilt felt by, 166
helplessness felt by, 142–144,
    148–151, 154–155
mother as supportive of, 154–
    161
motherhood issues as understood
    by, 162–183
mother's pregnancy and, 140–142
needs of, *see* needs
role models and, 13, 134, 135–
    136, 147–148
sexual issues of, 237, 243,
    249–250, 251–252, 253
unique parenting talents of,
    155–156
work life of, 144–147, 148,
    176–177
fatigue, parenting and, 19–22
fears, 21–22, 34, 94, 97, 109
  anger and, 114–115, 120, 126
  see also anxiety
fighting, marital, 110, 111–132
  avoidance of, 112–113, 114–116,
    125, 130
  breaking rules in, 131–132
  derisive tactics in, 118–122
  focusing in, 119, 120, 122–125,
    128–129
  follow-up to, 129–130, 131
  as learning experience, 127–129
  off-limits topics in, 125–126
  as positive element, 112, 116–
    118, 129–131
  timing of, 125, 131
Fogarty, Thomas, 33
forgiveness, 196
Friday, Nancy, 192
Friedan, Betty, 134, 163
Friedman, Edwin, 92

Galinsky, Ellen, 265
gender:
  behavior associated with, 34,
    135–137, 142, 144, 150–151,
    159, 173
  and expression of needs, 94–98
  identity issues and, 96, 135–
    136, 150, 178, 237
  sexual communication and, 249–
    250
  stereotypes and, 163–165, 170
  therapy and, 262
genetic endowment, fears about,
    21–22

Ginott, Haim, 138
Gottman, John, 129
Greenberg, Martin, 155–156
grief, *see* mourning
Guerin, Philip, 15, 73
guiding principles for change,
      257–266
   child rearing, 265–266
   patience, 260–261
   realism, 258–259
   self-help, 264
   therapy, 262–264
guilt, 134, 141, 166–169, 172,
      196, 250, 251, 253–254
   expression of needs and, 94,
      97, 100
   for growing up, 74–75

Haley, Jay, 221
Heine, Heinrich, 111
helplessness, parenting and, 18,
      20, 22, 142–144, 148–151,
      154–155
Hochschild, Arlie, 165
hyper- and hypoparent interac-
      tions, 31, 37–44, 91
   as cycle, 38–39
   invisible loyalties and, 52, 56
   see also reciprocal influences

in-laws, 212, 219, 221–233
   as second chance, 221
intimacy, 13, 23, 34
   differentiation and, 71
   invisible loyalties and, 52, 54

Jung, Carl, 266

Kuhn, Thomas, 190
Kunitz, Stanley, 89

Lamb, Michael, 138
Lerner, Harriet, 167, 264
Lewin, Kurt, 15
loyalties, invisible, 184–210,
      211, 239, 256, 260
   differentiation and, 68–75, 76–
      87, 184–188, 219, 229–234
   marriage and, 50–66, 68–87,
      119–120, 184–188, 219, 229–
      234
   parenting and, 13, 21, 23, 44,
      46–66, 97, 107, 134, 135–136,
      140–141, 147–148, 184–188,
      219 .

McGoldrick, Monica, 265
marriage:
   anxiety and, 30–31, 35, 77, 83,
      135, 212, 225–226
   blaming in, *see* blame
   communication in, 21, 91–110,
      114–118, 179–181, 226, 235,
      249
   differentiation and, 68–87,
      119–120, 184–188, 219, 229–
      234
   disrupted balance in, 25–44, 87
   egalitarian, 133, 163
   as experience of crisis, 266
   extended family and, *see*
      extended family; family
      systems; parents of parents
   fighting in, *see* fighting,
      marital
   idealization in, 51
   inherent tensions in, 15–16
   own childhood and, 50–66, 81–83
   parenting and, *see* parents,
      parenting
   pursuer-distancer cycle in, 31,
      33–37, 42–44, 52, 65, 91,
      206, 209, 226, 237–238
   satisfaction vs. communication
      in, 89–91
   Selfhood in, 76–88
   sexual issues in, 236–256
   traditionalization of, 163–165
   triangular relationships and,
      211–234
   trust in, 90, 102
masculinity issues, 96, 150, 178,
      237
maturity, independence vs., 72–
      73
Mead, Margaret, 15
money issues, 40–41
mothers:
   caregiving time of, 163–165
   child's identity with, 135–136
   depression in, 16, 25, 174, 175
   father as supportive of, 175–
      183
   fatherhood issues as understood
      by, 135–161
   first parenting of, 19–23, 25–
      27, 162–183
   guilt felt by, 134, 166–169,
      172
   instinct vs. learning of, 170–
      171, 178
   "invisible" caregiving by, 164
   isolation of, 171–174, 175

maternal identity of, 63, 97, 253–254
needs of, *see* needs
pregnancy issues of, 97, 140–142, 166
sexual issues of, 237–238, 249–250, 253–254
weaning and, 59–65
weight problems of, 174–175
working, 163–164, 165, 167–169, 171, 172
mourning, 82, 83, 196, 199–200, 260
mutuality, independence vs., 31, 34, 65, 72–73, 77–78

needs, 25, 26, 34, 38–39, 91, 93, 172, 180, 238
of children, 93, 97, 133–134, 135–136, 137
denial of, 94–95, 96–97, 100, 107, 142
dependence and, 69, 74–75, 105, 172–173
gender and expression of, 94–98
listening and, 101–102
originating in childhood, 46–66, 83
Self-focused communication of, 98–106
sexual, 34, 140, 174

orgasms, sexual abuse and, 247–248
Osherson, Samuel, 97

parental-leave policy, 147
parenthood:
as critical growth period, 265–266
transition to, 13, 14–23, 27–30, 47–50, 54, 83, 95, 134–135, 137–140, 183, 185, 214–215, 238, 242–243
parents, parenting, 13–23, 47–66, 162–183
advice given to, 20, 25–27, 96, 138–139, 168, 236, 238–239, 252, 257–258, 265
blaming and, *see* blame
communication between, 21, 25, 60, 98–106, 179–181
competence and strength of, 258
differentiation and, 13, 21, 23, 44, 46–66, 72, 97, 107, 134–136, 140–141, 184–188, 219
disappointments in, 20, 46

disruptive marital cycle in, 25–44
functioning levels in, 37–38
grandparents of, 189, 191, 206, 215
in "hyper and hypo" roles, 31, 37–44, 52, 56, 65–66, 91
irritability and, 19–23
need satisfaction and, *see* needs
neglect in, 19, 22, 26
pursuer-distancer interactions in, 31, 33–37, 42–44
sexual issues and, 236–256
shared responsibility in, 104–106, 120, 133–137, 154–157, 164–165, 170–171, 175–182
tolerance needed by, 158–161, 181–182
see also family systems; fathers; mothers
parents of parents, 190
competition with, 219
death of, 75, 196–202, 224
differentiation from, 68–75, 223–225, 229–234
increased involvement with, 217–218
as in-laws, 212, 219, 221–233
inner child of, 191–192
negativity of, 220
one-on-one relationship with, 202–205, 209, 224
significant role of, 215–216
triangular relationships with, 211–234
participative childbirth, 95
patience, change and, 260–261
Pederson, Frank, 16
Pruett, Kyle, 155
pursuer-distancer interactions, 31, 33–37, 205–206, 237–238
childhood influences and, 50–52, 65, 209, 226
dynamic aspects of, 33–35
graphic depiction of, 42, 43
personal contributions in, 42–44, 91
see also reciprocal influences

reactivity, *see* hyper- and hypoparent interactions; pursuer-distancer interactions
realism, expectations and, 20, 22, 30, 46, 104, 145–146, 151–153, 158–161, 258–259

reciprocal influences, 25–44,
    103–104
  improvements in, 42–44, 57–58,
    65, 84–87
  mutuality and, 31, 34, 65, 77–78
  negative, 26–31, 33–44, 56–57,
    80, 87, 109, 119–122, 128–
    129, 140
rejection, fear of, 94, 97
Reproduction of Motherhood, The
    (Chodorow), 135–136
requests, specific, 98–100, 108–
    109, 250
resignation, acceptance vs., 259
resistance, change and, 36, 84–
    85, 100, 109–110, 140, 146,
    147, 154, 260–261
responsibility:
  for own behavior, 28–29, 42–44,
    91–92, 99–100, 119
  sharing of, 104–106, 120, 133–
    137, 154–157, 164–165, 170–
    171, 175–182

Sartre, Jean-Paul, 217
Self-focused communication, 89–
    110, 250
  need satisfaction and, 93–110
  suggestions for, 98–106
self-help:
  change and, 264
  writings on, 96, 138–139, 168,
    236, 238–239, 252, 260, 265
Selfhood, 68–88
  characteristics of, 76–77, 91
  differentiation and, 68, 75–88,
    110, 188, 223–225, 229–234,
    239
  see also autonomy issues
self-sacrifice, 82, 86, 95, 97
sensate-focus exercises, 248
sequence-of-behavior charts, 42–
    43
sexual abuse, 192–196, 245–248
sexual issues, 34, 140, 174, 193,
    195, 235–236
  anxiety and, 235, 237–238, 248,
    251

communication and, 235, 249–
    250
  differentiation and, 239, 245,
    248
  family and, 239–242, 244–245,
    256
  guilt and, 250, 251, 253–254
  myths about, 235–236, 238
  physical aspects of, 251–252
  role models and, 240, 242, 243–
    244, 245, 249
  romance and, 236, 252–255
  techniques in, 245, 248–249
Silverstein, Louise, 167
space, relational, 28, 32–33
stress, 47, 66, 79, 125
  anxiety and, 30, 35, 135
support, 41, 105–106, 147–151,
    154–161, 175–183
  acknowledging needs and, 101–
    102
  of extended family, 72, 172,
    219–220
  see also triangular relation
    ships
systems thinking, 28–30
  benefits of, 43–44
  dynamics of, 33–41, 68

therapists, choice of, 263–264
therapy:
  change and, 262–264
  see also case histories
triangular relationships, 211–234
  and birth of child, 214–218,
    225
  escape from, 223–225, 229–234
  fears generated in, 219–220
  interlocking, 213
  power shifts in, 218–219, 220,
    233

weaning, 59–65
Whitaker, Carl, 32
Winnicott, D. W., 265–266
withdrawal, in disruptive cycles,
    25–26, 32–36, 38, 54, 59, 69,
    83, 96, 142